Praise for *Iraq after America*

"Joel Rayburn was a longtime adviser to General David Petraeus in Iraq, and it shows. His account of the political players of Iraq and the social forces that drive them—which have largely been ignored or misunderstood by most Western writers and analysts—is superlative. Rayburn is also a historian and he brings to *Iraq after America* the judicious judgments of that profession as well as the clarity and rigor of analysis of the professional intelligence analyst that he also is. The result is a book which will long be consulted by experts on Iraq and interested general readers alike."

—**Peter L. Bergen** is the author of
Manhunt: The Ten-Year Search for Bin Laden from 9/11 to Abbottabad

"*Iraq after America* provides the best description and the most incisive analysis I have seen of the political situation that has emerged in Iraq since 2003. Indeed, as both a historian and a practitioner, Joel Rayburn is admirably equipped for this task. With this book, he earns a position among the most perceptive observers of modern-day Iraq."

—**General David H. Petraeus**, US Army (retired),
Commander of the Multi-National Force-Iraq during the surge

"When most Americans of whatever persuasion talk about Iraq, they put the US role front and center. Joel Rayburn, one of the best and most incisive analysts of that troubled land, corrects the imbalance by putting the Iraqis at the center of their own story. His deeply researched analysis and history of Iraqi politics should be required reading for anyone trying to understand where Iraq has been or where it is going."

—**Max Boot**, Jeane J. Kirkpatrick Senior Fellow for National Security Studies, Council on Foreign Relations, and author of *Invisible Armies: An Epic History of Guerrilla Warfare from Ancient Times to the Present Day* and *The Savage Wars of Peace: Small Wars and the Rise of American Power*

"Joel Rayburn has written a masterful, insightful, and readable history of Iraqi politics that transcends the epoch of America's troop presence. This book identifies geopolitical trends within the Middle East that are likely to emerge as Iraq relapses into civil war alongside neighboring Syria."

—**Kimberly Kagan**, President, Institute for the Study of War, and author of *The Surge: A Military History*

With *Iraq after America*, Joel Rayburn has given us an absolute gem. It is hard to imagine a slim, lively volume so packed with insight and wisdom. Nothing is overlooked, but nothing is belabored. Rayburn deftly interweaves his deep academic knowledge of Iraq's history and society with his practical experience of Iraqi politics and security earned by his years there after the 2003 invasion. In its concision and erudition, *Iraq after America* offers an unparalleled understanding of the misery of Iraq today.

—**Kenneth M. Pollack**, Senior Fellow, Brookings Institution, and author of *Unthinkable: Iran, the Bomb, and American Strategy*

IRAQ AFTER AMERICA
Strongmen, Sectarians, Resistance

HERBERT AND JANE DWIGHT WORKING GROUP
ON ISLAMISM AND THE INTERNATIONAL ORDER

*Many of the writings associated with this
Working Group will be published by the Hoover Institution.
Materials published to date, or in production, are listed below.*

ESSAY SERIES:
THE GREAT UNRAVELING: THE REMAKING OF THE MIDDLE EAST

In Retreat: America's Withdrawal from the Middle East
Russell A. Berman

Israel and the Arab Turmoil
Itamar Rabinovich

Reflections on the Revolution in Egypt
Samuel Tadros

The Struggle for Mastery in the Fertile Crescent
Fouad Ajami

The Weaver's Lost Art
Charles Hill

The Consequences of Syria
Lee Smith

ESSAYS

Saudi Arabia and the New Strategic Landscape
Joshua Teitelbaum

Islamism and the Future of the Christians of the Middle East
Habib C. Malik

Syria through Jihadist Eyes: A Perfect Enemy
Nibras Kazimi

The Ideological Struggle for Pakistan
Ziad Haider

Syria, Iran, and Hezbollah: The Unholy Alliance and Its War on Lebanon
Marius Deeb

[For a list of books published under the auspices of the
WORKING GROUP ON ISLAMISM AND THE INTERNATIONAL ORDER,
please see page 289.]

IRAQ AFTER AMERICA
Strongmen, Sectarians, Resistance

Joel Rayburn

HOOVER INSTITUTION PRESS

STANFORD UNIVERSITY | STANFORD, CALIFORNIA

www.hoover.org

Hoover Institution Press Publication No. 643

Hoover Institution at Leland Stanford Junior University,
Stanford, California 94305-6010

First printing 2014
21 20 19 18 17 16 15 14   9 8 7 6 5 4 3

Manufactured in the United States of America

The paper used in this publication meets the minimum Requirements of the American National Standard for Information Sciences—Permanence of Paper for Printed Library Materials, ANSI/NISO Z39.48-1992. ⊛

Library of Congress Cataloging-in-Publication Data
Rayburn, Joel, 1969–   author.
Iraq after America : strongmen, sectarians, resistance /
Joel Rayburn.
     pages   cm — (Hoover Institution Press publication ; no. 643)
Includes index.
ISBN 978-0-8179-1694-7 (cloth : alk. paper)
ISBN 978-0-8179-1696-1 (epub)
ISBN 978-0-8179-1697-8 (mobipocket)
ISBN 978-0-8179-1698-5 (ePDF)
     1. Iraq—Politics and government—2003– . 2. Authoritarianism—
Iraq. 3. Iraq—Ethnic relations. I. Title. II. Series : Hoover Institution
Press publication ; 643.
DS79.769.R39   2014
956.7044'3—dc23   2014018175

HOOVER
INSTITUTION
STANFORD
UNIVERSITY

*The Hoover Institution gratefully acknowledges
the following individuals and foundations
for their significant support of the*

HERBERT AND JANE DWIGHT WORKING GROUP
ON ISLAMISM AND THE INTERNATIONAL ORDER:

Herbert and Jane Dwight

Donald and Joan Beall
Beall Family Foundation

S. D. Bechtel, Jr. Foundation

Lynde and Harry Bradley Foundation

Stephen and Susan Brown

Mr. and Mrs. Clayton W. Frye Jr.

Lakeside Foundation

CONTENTS

T HE CAUSE OF PEACE across the last half of the twentieth
century, and now well into the twenty-first, has been
severely set back by the failure to understand war.
Joel Rayburn's astonishingly knowledgeable and perceptive *Iraq
after America*, read in its global and historical context, marks a
turning point toward a desperately needed reeducation about the
strategic and moral realities of war and world order.

A parade of profound thinkers across the centuries have striven
to convey an awareness of "what needs to be realized about war,"
and what contemporary politics has turned it into. Altogether we
can count six points about war: First, war is always with us, part of
the burden of the human condition. Recurrent dreams that war is
an aberration, pronouncements that "there is no military solution," claims that all emerging conflicts can be headed off by well-
intentioned diplomacy, and acts aimed at achieving mutual
understanding without being backed by credible strength and the
shadow of force—these factors have had the opposite effect, making war-fighting more likely and longer lasting.

Second, all wars go wrong early on, as displayed by Pericles's
mistaken strategic steps at the outset of the Peloponnesian War, by
Abraham Lincoln's agonizing over the bungled opening campaigns
of the Civil War, and by the Allies' naïve misjudgments in both the
European and Asian theaters of the Second World War. Such
leadership flaws are a fact of life, and so are the vagaries of war
itself. "No plan survives contact with the enemy," Helmuth von
Moltke concluded; Carl von Clausewitz already had informed us

about "friction," or fog, as a physical principle of warfare. As a social-political category, noncombatant observers of war have evolved from picnicking sightseers on nearby hillsides, to patriotic war correspondents who unswervingly portrayed their side favorably, to media stars out to make their career by portraying every military error as a war crime.

Third has come the peculiarly distinctive characteristic of America's wars since the Korean "police action" of 1950: not fighting to win, but hoping that something will turn up to close out the conflict. That something for the past six-plus decades has been America's war-weariness and decision to depart conflicts even when the situation has stabilized and progress toward eventual success well under way. This self-obstructing approach has been the product not only of America's national character trait of preferring to distance itself from the miseries of the "Old World," but also from America's overwhelming military strength in modern times. Obviously, the United States could win the war, any war, but to do so could require using such devastating force that the result might be morally unbearable and materially debilitating. As a result, wars just go on and on, with more devastation over time than a lightning victory, however harsh, might inflict. American impatience is the equivalent of Samson's mane.

Fourth, a consequence of all the above is a popular assumption that there's no such thing as a good war, or no good thing to be said about any war. This in turn has produced a deleterious reinterpretation of Clausewitz's dictum that "war is the continuation of politics by other means." Clausewitz was right. But some politicians, officials, pundits, and segments of the media and public have hurried to demonize anyone involved in decisions to fight the war—and especially those who argued that it had been necessary. Wars, therefore, have become not so much the continuation of politics by other means but political weapons.

So, like a leper's bell in the medieval mist sounding the message "unclean!," the word "Iraq," like "Vietnam" before it, has been wielded as a stigma incorporating, in one word, all things anti-American. On the tenth anniversary of the U.S. decision to invade Iraq to overthrow Saddam Hussein and his dictatorship, some in the media summed up the war as "the worst mistake in U.S. history," predicting that America "will never recover."

This leads to the fifth principle about war, which has been ignored or discarded or forgotten in recent years. All major wars of the modern era have been fought to defend the established international world order against its most vicious enemies. World War II was this, fought to stop the Third Reich and Imperial Japan from achieving hegemonic spheres of influence upon which to impose their racist ideologies. The Cold War was a full-scale struggle for world order, fought by an American-led free world against international Communism that rejected every facet of the international state system accepted around the globe over many years.

Finally, a primary principle of war put forward by Immanuel Kant in his essay "Perpetual Peace" is that war is best avoided when democratic countries grow in number, because free peoples will curb the wanton behavior of their leaders and will be inclined to contain or shorten such wars as cannot be avoided. In recent decades, however, it has been the intelligentsia of America and Western Europe who have demonstrated little or no sense of the importance of either defending an open world order or seeing the international significance of democracy for peace.

On all of the above points, America's war in Iraq was more than justified, it was inevitable and necessary. Joel Rayburn's *Iraq after America* delivers exactly what its title indicates, so Rayburn wisely stays away from the decisions that led to the war and the fighting between 2003 and 2011. Nor is this the place to do it, other than to insist that it was thoroughly a war fought for the cause of world order, authorized under international law by UN Security Council resolutions dating back to the first international coalition war to stop Saddam Hussein's aggressions and that produced an international legal mechanism requiring compliance regarding Iraq's weapons of mass destruction. When Saddam Hussein in 1998 was declared in flagrant violation of those requirements, that mechanism authorized the war that began in 2003—which already had the legitimacy provided by a 2002 Joint Resolution of the U.S. Congress authorizing the use of U.S. armed forces against Iraq.

In the annals of "all wars go wrong early on" must be recorded America's unpreparedness for the upheaval that followed Saddam's downfall against the backdrop of the world's intelligence agencies failing to comprehend his successful years-long project to make the world believe he had active weapons of mass destruction even as he turned them into a "virtual" program, undetectable but easily reconstituted when desired.[1]

Iraq after America reveals that this modern war to defend world order produced an astonishing truth: that the regimes of the Middle East had been living a lie for most of the twentieth century, portraying themselves as a seamlessly united pan-Arab, pan-Islamic league of states whose only problem, in whatever field of governance, was the mere existence of Israel. As the Iraq War demonstrated, Saddam's rule, like that of other autocrats of the region, was in reality a lid of oppression, forcing down through pervasive fear of regime power a multitude of bitterly opposed factions organized around tribal, ethnic, religious, linguistic, or ideological demands. The revelation came swiftly after Saddam's fall and was taken to a regional level by ancient Shia-Sunni hatreds that emerged anew in 2006, a religious civil war about which the

---

1. For details, see the volume in this Hoover series by Charles Hill, *Trial of a Thousand Years: Islamism and World Order*, 89–114.

United States could do nothing. Thus came the horrible spectacle of a Hobbesian pre-civil society "war of all against all." The world had largely accepted the previous narrative of stable Arab-Islamic unity; now there appeared a complicated variety of narratives that Joel Rayburn here groups under "strongmen," "sectarians," and "resistance" headings, with a powerful under-theme of Sunni-versus-Shia animosity.

But also emerging from this maelstrom has come a spark of promise. The American operation to bring down Saddam Hussein is now visible as a point of ignition for a new Arab generation's urgings to transform the region into something approaching the outside modern world's better examples of free politics, open economies, and tolerant societies. The moment that Saddam's statue was toppled, a shock of recognition flashed across the minds of youth: we are not fated to live always under an odious dictatorship!

Iraq after America thus portrays Iraq, so central in many ways to the entire Middle East, as—however odd the image may be—a bellwether for the entirety. Rayburn concludes that the U.S. mission was to provide Iraq with at least a fair chance for stability upon which could be constructed a pluralistic parliamentary government representing all parties, serving as a model for its neighbors. But this prospect was darkened by America's wearied and politicized withdrawal before the military success of "the surge" and the institutional foundations of the occupation were solidified.

Rayburn's account of the post-Saddam Iraqi morass can be extrapolated into the plight of the region overall where in varying forms the old strongmen and militaries, the radical Islamists, ethnosectarian loyalists, and the not-to-be-extinguished hopes of the young Arab Spring generation all vie for power and leverage within an ever-more dangerous geostrategic balance of power between Shia Iran and Sunni Saudi Arabia. Should American leaders come to recognize the imperative of reengagement, what should be the basis for U.S. policy?

The answer is simple to state if not easy to implement: to support directly, or indirectly, whatever faction, party, sect, or regime that convincingly wishes to see the Middle East become what it promised decades ago but never delivered. That is, a region of legitimate states willing to conduct themselves in accordance with the minimal requirements of the international system—to be good international citizens able to adhere to the norms of diplomacy, comity, and mutual respect in a community of peoples around the world.

The reader should not feel daunted by the detailed narratives interwoven through this book. They depict the ways that Arab politics are carried out—or politics in most lands, for that matter. Like a great Russian novel, the confusion of the many characters with their unfamiliar names sort themselves out in the mind as the drama of the stories takes shape. No one can claim to comprehend Iraq, or the U.S. role in the world, or the international importance of the Middle East as a whole without spending time with *Iraq after America*.

CHARLES HILL
*Distinguished Fellow of the Brady-Johnson Program
in Grand Strategy at Yale University;
Senior Fellow, Hoover Institution—
Cochairman, Herbert and Jane Dwight Working Group
on Islamism and the International Order*
January 2014

ACKNOWLEDGMENTS

T HIS BOOK could not have been written without the input
of a great many Iraqis who patiently taught me most of
what I know about their country and helped me understand how they see the world and each other. Unfortunately, the
political climate in Baghdad is such that most of them cannot be
named. I hope a better day will come when I can acknowledge
them fully. Among those Iraqis that I can name, I owe special
thanks to Major General (Retired) Najim al-Jabouri, who spent
many hours with me explaining things that cannot be found in any
book, and to Mithal al-Alusi, who fears no one.

At the National Defense University, I owe a great deal to Dr.
Nicholas Rostow and Dr. Joseph Collins, who gave me wise coun-
sel as I wrote this book. Every author should be so lucky as to have
two such experienced scholars and strategists just down the hall.

I also owe much to the small community of "Iraq hands," those
analysts and officials mainly in Washington, D.C., and London
who made Iraq the focus of their careers and remained focused
upon it as others followed the crowd to the next big strategic thing.
They include Toby Dodge, Ken Pollack, Kim and Fred Kagan,
Derek Harvey, Marty Stanton, Emma Sky, Marisa Cochrane Sullivan, Mike Pregent, Michael Knights, Ali Kedery, Mike Gfoeller,
Ramzy Mardini, Reidar Visser, Rick Welch, Raad Alkadiri, Oubai
Shahbandar, Ahmed Ali, Michael Gordon, Brian Fishman, Roy
Alcala, Rick Brennan, Ned Parker, Judi Yaphe, Denise Natali, and
a few others I must leave unnamed. Many of them will recognize
in this book's main arguments the themes that ran through hun-

dreds of emails and roundtable discussions over the course of several years, and I thank them for what I learned from them and for helping me sharpen the arguments in these pages.

I owe special thanks to Major General H. R. McMaster, at whose side I spent most of my time in Iraq. Our country has rarely produced leaders of his talent and energy, and I have been fortunate to serve with him and learn from him on so many occasions.

I also wish to thank Professor Charles Hill for his encouragement of this manuscript and his insightful feedback to it. His brilliant foreword both honors and outshines this book, and I am honored that he should be associated with my work.

I especially wish to thank Professor Fouad Ajami, whose work and spirit inspired this book. He is my *ustaz* and my *marja*, a scholar without equal in a field he helped create.

Finally, I thank my wife, Clare, who never stopped encouraging me and never complained as I spent every waking moment for almost a year researching and writing this book.

LT. COL. JOEL RAYBURN
January 2014

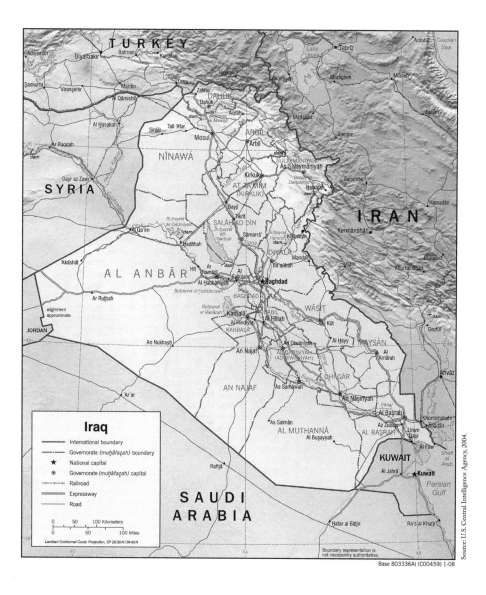

Iraq

──────── International boundary
------------ Governorate *(muḥāfaẓah)* boundary
★ National capital
◉ Governorate *(muḥāfaẓah)* capital
┼┼┼┼ Railroad
▨▨▨▨ Expressway
──────── Road

```
0        50       100 Kilometers
├────────┼─────────┤
0        50       100 Miles
```

Lambert Conformal Conic Projection, SP 29 30 N / 36 40 N

TURKEY
Adiyaman
Diyarbakır
Batman
Kurtalan
Şanlıurfa
Viranşehir
Mardin
Cizre
Al Qāmishlī
Zakho
DAHŪK
Dahūk
Aqrah
Buḥayrat al Mawşil
Maḥābād
Hakkari
Orūmīyeh
Marāgheh
Mīāneh
Ardabīl
Caspian Sea
Tabrīz
Zanjān
Al Ḩasakah
Sinjār
Tall 'Afar
Mosul
ARBĪL
Arbīl
Saqqez
Ar Raqqah
NĪNAWÁ
dam
AS SULAYMĀNĪYAH
As Sulaymānīyah
Kirkūk
Dayr az Zawr
SYRIA
AT TA'MĪM (KIRKŪK)
Buḥayrat Darbandīkhān
Ḩalabjah
dam
Sanandaj
Hamadān
Euphrates
Bayjī
Tikrīt
Buḥayrat al Qādisīyah
dam
SALĀH AD DĪN
Buḥayrat ath Tharthār
Sāmarrā'
Buḥayrat Ḩamrīn dam
Khāneqīn
Kermānshāh
IRAN
Al Qā'im
Hadīthah
Tigris
DIYĀLÁ
Mandalī
Borūjerd
Akāshāt
AL ANBĀR
Ḩīt
Ar Ramādī
dam
Al Fallūjah
Al Ḩabbānīyah
Ba'qūbah
Baghdad
Īlām
Khorramābād
Ar Rutbah
Buḥayrat al Ḩabbānīyah
BAGHDĀD
alignment approximate
Buḥayrat ar Razāzah
Karbalā'
BĀBIL
Al Hindīyah
Al Ḩillah
WĀSIŢ
Al Kūt
dam
JORDAN
KARBALĀ'
Dezfūl
An Nukhayb
An Najaf
Al Ḩayy
MAYSĀN
Al 'Amārah
Aḩvāz
'Ar'ar
AN NAJAF
AL QĀDISĪYAH (AD DIWĀNĪYAH)
Ad Dīwānīyah
As Samāwah
Euphrates
DHĪ QĀR
An Nāşirīyah
Al Başrah
Khorramshahr
Ābādān
As Salmān
AL MUTHANNÁ
Al Buşayyah
Az Zubayr
AL BAŞRAH
Umm Qaşr
Rafḩā
KUWAIT
Al Jahrā'
Kuwait
Al Faw
Shaṭṭ al 'Arab
Persian Gulf
SAUDI ARABIA
Hafar al Bāţin
Ra's al Khafjī

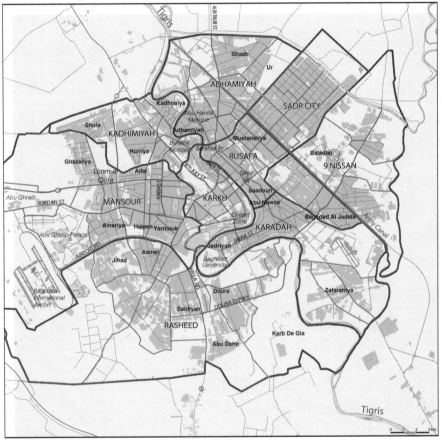

Source: Map courtesy of The Institute for the Study of War, Washington, DC; cartographer, Maggie Rackl; adapted by Ruth Engel.

Baghdad

INTRODUCTION

THE TEN-YEAR ANNIVERSARY of the invasion of Iraq
brought retrospectives aplenty. The vast majority of them
discussed the twin questions of whether the United States
should have entered Iraq in 2003 or whether it should have exited
as it did in 2011; however, with U.S. troops having departed the
country some three years ago, those questions are for historians.
For decisionmakers, it is more important to analyze in terms of
U.S. interests the new Iraq that is taking shape in the wake of
America's withdrawal—one with vast resources, a large and growing population, a significant regional role to play, and a civil war
that never really ended—than re-examine decade-old American
responses to the attacks of September 11, 2001.

This book examines the polity and political factions that have
emerged in Iraq since 2003. It is not meant to be a general history
of the Iraqi civil war period or of the many important activities the
United States undertook during that war. Instead, the book presents the various actors and groups in the Iraqi political landscape,
as well as their interrelations, with Americans factored out (except
where it is impossible to do so) so that the reader can judge the
Iraqis and their political battles on their own terms, as the Iraqis
themselves do in this post-America period.

Three trends dominate Iraq's post-America political order:
authoritarianism, sectarianism, and "resistance." This book traces
the origins of those trends in recent Iraqi history to explain the
political and social forces that produced them, particularly during
the intense period of civil war between 2003 and 2009. The book

examines some of the most significant players in the new Iraq, explaining how they have risen to prominence and what they aim to do.

The last eight years have seen an extensive consolidation of authoritarian power by Prime Minister Nuri al-Maliki and his cadre of Dawa Party loyalists. The first chapter of this book explains these new authoritarians' origins in the Iraqi Shia Islamist movement of the 1960s and '70s and the impact made upon them by a Baathist crackdown and the Iran-Iraq War. Chapters Two and Three analyze how these *Malikiyoun* managed after 2003 to grow from a weak junior partner in the Shia Islamist opposition into a powerful ruling network that controls virtually all the national-level institutions of government and dominates Iraqi political life. They also shed light on how Maliki himself grew during those years, from a weak premier who was elected because his rivals saw him as a harmless cipher to a strongman who has towered over the Iraqi political class, many of whom fear that he has led Iraq back into dictatorship. Finally, they describe the anatomy of the new regime Maliki and his allies created, including the leading personalities inside that regime, and describe the ways in which the *Malikiyoun* have been able to consolidate control of the pillars of the Iraqi state.

The middle chapters of this book trace the hardening of Iraq's sectarian and ethnic fractures into a rigid political order, so that Sunni-Shia and Arab-Kurd rivalries dominate every political question and enable ethnosectarian extremist groups and terror networks to thrive. Out of the Shia Islamist opposition to Saddam Hussein came militant factions, many of them associated with Iran, that sought to replace Iraq's Sunni political and social ascendancy with a Shia one. Chapter Four explains how these Shia supremacist factions took advantage of the collapse of Saddam's regime to gain control of state institutions and attempt to push Sunnis out of Iraq's mixed-sect provinces. Chapter Five examines the Sunni chauvinist factions that fought back against the new Shia ascendancy and used violence to try to derail the U.S.-led political process. The chapter traces the Sunni chauvinists' roots in the Sunni Islamist movement of the 1970s and '80s and Saddam's "Faith Campaign" of the 1990s. Chapter Six explores the roots of the Arab-Kurd struggle for power in northern Iraq, centering on the control of the oil-rich regions on which the viability of any future Kurdish state depends.

Chapter Seven discusses the Shia Islamist "resistance" movements that have come to play a large role in the life of the Iraqi Shia and in the sectarian conflicts raging beyond Iraq's borders. The chapter traces their origins in the grassroots Shia Islamist movement that grew in Iraq in the 1980s and '90s before evolving into a potent militant network after 2003.

Taken together, these trends of authoritarianism, sectarianism, and "resistance" have created a toxic political and social brew, preventing Iraq's political elite from resolving the fundamental roots of conflict that have wracked Iraq since 2003 and before. Chapter Eight examines how the political dynamics described in Chapters One through Seven combined in 2010 to produce the longest parliamentary stalemate in modern world history, followed by the Maliki government's brutal suppression of Iraq's own "Arab Spring" in 2011 and a crackdown against Sunni leaders that led to massive protests against Maliki's rule in 2012 and 2013. Chapter Eight continues by describing the spillover of the Syrian conflict into Iraqi politics and the resurgence of Al Qaeda in Iraq. Finally, Chapter Nine examines some aspects of the U.S. legacy in Iraq, while analyzing what it signifies that after more than a decade of conflict, Iraq's communities—and their political class in particular—have not yet found a way to live together in peace.

Americans have long since tired of Iraq, which they tend to consider, when they consider it at all, as little more than the site of an unpopular military expedition that Americans would prefer to forget. However, with the world's second-largest oil reserves and a strategic location, Iraq is too important to disregard, a country whose stability is not just an academic curiosity but a critical regional and global concern.

One of America's most accomplished diplomats, Ambassador Ryan Crocker, issued in 2008 a memorable prediction about the American legacy in Iraq: "In the end, how we leave and what we leave behind will be more important than how we came." Now that U.S. troops have gone, it is high time to take stock of the country they left behind, on its own merits, and to chart the post-American Iraq's trends and players so we can better judge what they mean for the United States and for the Middle East. Perhaps then we will see a clearer path for U.S. interests in the future. *Insh'Allah.*

THE STRONGMEN

CHAPTER ONE

The Roots of the Dawa State

T HE PERIOD AFTER December 2010 brought sweeping political changes in the Arab world, with popular movements toppling authoritarian regimes in Tunisia, Egypt, Libya, and Yemen and shaking another in Syria. Political developments in Iraq, however, went in the opposite direction. An ostensibly democratic system put in place after Saddam Hussein's fall began to revert to authoritarian form, as Prime Minister Nuri al-Maliki and his allies managed to marginalize their political rivals and consolidate substantial control over the Iraqi state.

The origins of this new Maliki regime lie in a nearly forgotten political struggle that took place more than five decades ago between Iraqi leftists and the Shia Islamists of Najaf and Karbala who mobilized to oppose them. Out of this battle grew Iraq's great Shia Islamist party, Dawa, the forerunner of every major Iraqi Shia party since. Modeled after Egypt's Muslim Brotherhood, Dawa built a huge grassroots following among the Iraqi Shia in the 1960s, only to be crushed by Saddam Hussein after a decade-long Dawa-Baathist struggle that ended on the eve of the Iran-Iraq War in 1980. Saddam's furious offensive against Dawa drove the party underground, where the formerly populist movement narrowed into an insular revolutionary vanguard in which young men like Maliki trained as militants.

THE DAWA MOVEMENT

Those who have become used to the scene of millions of Shia pilgrims making their way through crowded streets and squares to
Najaf and Karbala can be forgiven for not remembering that the
Dawa Party's origins lie in a time when the pilgrimage roads were
empty. Exactly one year after the July 1958 massacre of the Iraqi
royal family brought the leftist regime of General Abd al-Karim
Qasim to power in Baghdad, the clerics of Iraq's shrine cities were
dismayed to see only a few hundred pilgrims appear for the annual
procession celebrating the martyrdom of the Imam Hussein, the
lowest numbers ever registered. To the clerical establishment's
horror, Qasim's ascendancy brought a brief golden age for the
atheistic Communist Party in Iraq, the home of Shiism. Lacking
his own popular base, Qasim found the Communists useful allies,
and during his regime's early days the party's membership swelled
to more than twenty-five thousand, with particular appeal to the
Shia youth of Iraq's growing cities. In the holy city of Najaf,
Communist demonstrations drew larger crowds than the religious
festivals that had always been essential to the power and economic
livelihood of Iraq's shrine cities. An even harder blow, perhaps, was
that the Communists counted among their followers some sons of
Iraq's leading ayatollahs. For Iraq's Shia clerics, the message was
clear: Shia Islam was losing the Iraqi people, especially the youth,
to godless Marxism, and something had to be done.

The senior clerics of Iraq's holy cities were not well-equipped to
lead the kind of dramatic changes and outreach that would be
required to counter the Communist Party's growing strength.
During centuries of Sunni rule in Iraq, the Shia clerical establishment had adopted a mainly quietist approach to political matters.
Shia Islam's response to Marxism thus came not from its clerical
leaders, the small circle of spiritual guides known as the *marjaiyyah*,

but from a cadre of young Najafi clerics who embraced political activism as their elders were disinclined to do. In the months after Qasim's seizure of power, these young men founded a religious society, modeled on Egypt's Muslim Brotherhood, whose aim would be to restore the people to Islam by forming a network of laymen and propagating new ideas of political Islam. In 1960, this small movement named itself the Dawa Party.

The central concept of Dawa—which in Arabic means "the call"—was the pan-Islamic idea of returning laymen to Islamic traditions and reconciling Islamic jurisprudence with the needs of modern societies. As conceived by its founders, the Dawa Party was meant to be a cross-sectarian organization, working to transform society rather than seize political power. Dawa's founders, like those of the Muslim Brotherhood, believed that if society could be re-Islamicized, then eventually Islamic government would follow. Their goals and rhetoric were universal and pan-Islamic in nature, and in its early days Dawa sought to attract Sunni members as well as Shia ones.

THE ORIGINAL SADRISTS

Despite its pan-Islamic goals, the new Dawa movement drew upon some familiar Shia names for support. Family members of one of Iraq's grand ayatollahs, Muhsin al-Hakim, had led protests against Qasim's socialist land reforms in 1958 and were an important link between activists and the Najaf religious colleges known as the *hawza*. Dawa's founding members also included the Najaf-born Lebanese cleric Muhammad Hussein Fadlallah, who in later life became the spiritual father of Lebanese Hezbollah as well as the *marja* (spiritual guide) for the Dawa Party itself, illustrating Dawa's transnational links and regionwide aims.

But the core of the new movement's ideas and energy came
from a trio of great-grandsons of Ismail Sadr, one of the most
esteemed Shia *marjaiyyah* of the early twentieth century. Muhammad Baqir al-Sadr, not yet thirty at Dawa's founding in 1959 but
already among the most respected clerics in Najaf, wrote the trea-
tises that became Dawa's ideology, the party's intellectual center.
He eventually met an untimely end at the hands of Saddam Hussein in 1980, leaving behind a young son, Jafaar Baqir Sadr, who
later would be elected to the Iraqi parliament in 2010.

Muhammad Baqir's older first cousin and brother-in-law Musa
al-Sadr, meanwhile, did his work among the Shia of Lebanon,
founding the Amal Movement before being murdered by Colonel
Muammar Qaddafi during an ill-fated visit to Libya in 1978—a
crime that rankles Shia Arabs to this day. Added to these older
Sadrs was their younger first cousin Muhammad Sadiq Sadr, only
a teenager at Dawa's founding but destined to create a mass movement among Iraq's urban Shia poor that challenged the Baathist
regime before his murder in 1999. Sadiq Sadr's movement was
eventually commanded by his youngest son, Muqtada al-Sadr,
who himself married a daughter of Muhammad Baqir Sadr and
became a brother-in-law to Jafaar Baqir Sadr. The Sadiq and Baqir
Sadr families were even further intertwined: Muqtada Sadr's older
brothers Mustafa and Muammal had also married daughters of
Baqir Sadr, meaning that three sons of Sadiq Sadr married three
daughters of Baqr Sadr.

These three Sadr cousins, Muhammad Baqir, Musa, and
Muhammad Sadiq, worked their entire lives to coax Arab Shia
populations away from the leftist movements—first Communism
and then Baathism—that swept the Middle East during the Cold
War. Their method was to foster people conversant in Marxism
who could advocate for Islam as a competing worldview. Breaking
the tradition of Shia quietism and disinterest in politics, Muham-

mad Baqr al-Sadr in particular sought to reconcile Shia jurispru-dence with the matters that concerned a modern state, includ-ing economics (*Iqtisaduna*, 1961) and political philosophy. Baqir Sadr's "Our Philosophy" (*Falsafatuna*, 1959) employed the dialec-tic and discussed the merits of Hegel and Marx while presenting Islam as a viable alternative to both Marxism and capitalism. In his battle of ideas, Baqir Sadr was aided by the determination of Ayatollah Muhsin al-Hakim to use Shia traditions to repel Com-munism, such as Hakim's *fatwa* forbidding his followers from membership in the Iraqi Communist Party in 1960. Together, the three Sadrs and their activist associates in the broader Shia Islamist movement touched off a struggle for the soul of Shia Iraq that is still playing out, with Shia Islam on one side and Arab Socialism on the other.

Dawa and Muhammad Baqir Sadr against the Baath

From its small beginnings in Najaf, Dawa grew rapidly in the 1960s. Iraq's military regime became increasingly dominated by Sunnis, alienating many Shia from the regime, while large Shia populations that had migrated into the cities during Iraq's industrialization sank into poverty. Iraq's teeming Shia slums were fertile ground for a religious reawakening, and by the late 1960s Baqir Sadr in particular claimed a huge following among those Iraqis, so much so that the Dawa Party he had helped to found began to outrun him. By the time the Baathist regime seized power in 1968, its leader General Ahmed Hassan al-Bakr and his kinsman-deputy Saddam Hussein perceived Dawa and its fellow travelers as a threat to the regime's legitimacy. In 1969, the Baathist regime took steps to curtail the Shia religious establishment's power, beginning with the suppression of the *hawza* and the expulsion of thousands of

Shia students to forestall a supposed "Iranian threat." The *hawza* responded by confronting the regime head-on. The elderly grand *marja'* Muhsin Hakim denounced the regime's brutal tactics—including the imprisonment and torture of Hakim's own son Hujja—and forbade his followers from membership in the Baath, as he had forbidden Communist membership nine years before. The *hawza*'s faceoff with the Baath intensified in 1970, when the exiled Iranian Ayatollah Ruhollah Khomeini delivered in Najaf a widely distributed series of lectures calling for an end to secular regimes and the adoption of Islamic government under clerical oversight, a concept known in Arabic as *wilayat al-faqih*, or "rule of the jurisprudent."

To the secular Baath, the idea was anathema, as was the prospect of Shia religious resistance to Baathist rule. Eventually, the regime outlawed Dawa altogether, and the Baathist security apparatus waged a shadow war against the party. In 1974, this campaign reached a fever pitch when the Baath arrested and executed dozens of Dawa activists, driving the group underground. In subsequent years, the regime banned the annual Shia religious processions out of fear they could be used to organize opposition to the regime.

The Baath were right to worry. Support for Dawa spilled into the open in 1977, when tens of thousands of Dawa followers held the procession in defiance of the Baathist ban. What had traditionally been a peaceful festival became an armed uprising when regime security forces and armed Dawa members engaged in gun battles within the larger procession. The regime eventually used helicopter gunships to put the Dawa pilgrims to flight.

The confrontation with the regime was more than Dawa had bargained for. Despite their defiance of the Baath, Dawa's leaders had hoped for lower-profile, evolutionary political change of the sort advocated by the Muslim Brotherhood. Nor had they sought to inspire a mass movement that would include the lowest strata of Iraqi Shia society. Even in the late 1970s, Dawa drew its members mainly from the Shia middle classes rather than from the urban poor. Nevertheless, the onset of the Iranian revolution pushed the party into an all-out battle with the Baath for which many Dawa leaders were unprepared. The fall of the Shah in 1979 and installation of an Islamic government in Iran electrified the Iraqi Shia and caused a groundswell of Shia support for the extension of the revolution into Iraq.

Dawa leaders were split on the question of whether to embrace the revolution and sponsor an uprising against the Baath or treat the toppling of the Shah as an Iranian matter and wait for more peaceful political change. But Dawa's deliberations were soon overtaken by events. A number of prominent Shia leaders threw their support behind the newly empowered Ayatollah Khomeini, including Muhammad Baqir Sadr himself. Fearing the potential for a Shia Islamist revolt, Saddam's security officials arrested Baqir Sadr in June 1979 and caused other Dawa leaders, including Muhammad Baqir Hakim, to flee to Iran. The regime made Dawa membership punishable by death and carried out dozens of executions in early 1980, in response to which some Dawa members formed a militant wing and began to carry out attacks and assassinations against regime targets. On April 1 of that year, Dawa attempted to assassinate senior Baathist Tariq Aziz in apparent retaliation for the execution of Dawa members the month before. Eight days later, on April 9, 1980, Saddam's regime punished Dawa by brutally executing Muhammad Baqir Sadr and his sister, Bint al-Huda, reportedly killing Baqir Sadr by driving a spike through his forehead after forcing him to watch Baathist torturers rape his sister.

THE DISPERSAL AND FRACTURING OF DAWA

These events had a profound effect on the Dawa movement. In the space of a few months, Dawa's leadership inside Iraq had been decimated, its intellectual father murdered, and most surviving senior- and mid-level members forced to flee the country. The impact of the regime's crackdown was no less significant at the grassroots level. For a large number of young Dawa followers, Nuri Maliki among them, the battle with the regime in 1977–80 would have been a formative experience, alienating them from the Saddamists who had killed so many of their colleagues, friends, and brothers. Like Maliki, who fled Iraq in 1979, many young Dawa men went into exile as hard-core revolutionaries committed to the overthrow of the Baathist regime.

At the organizational level, the dispersal of its leaders and activists led to the fragmentation of the Iraqi Shia Islamic movement under the combined pressure of Saddam's regime and the new Iranian regime in Tehran. In Iran, Dawa established a political office eventually headed by future Minister of Education Ali Adeeb, but many Dawa members left the parent organization when their Iranian hosts pressed them to join the Islamic revolutionary cause and shift their loyalty to Ayatollah Khomeini and his doctrine of *wilayat al-faqih*. These changes in allegiance created serious tension among senior Dawa members, many of whom were troubled by the implications of adopting what they viewed as an Iranian doctrine. When one senior Dawa member in Tehran, the well-known cleric Ayatollah Kazim al-Haeri, called for Dawa to pledge allegiance to Khomeini in 1987, the party's Iraqi leaders decided to expel him. The expulsion was a significant loss for Dawa, since Haeri was a close ally of Muhammad Sadiq Sadr and would later become the spiritual mentor for Muqtada Sadr and the Sadrist movement.

The most notable Dawa "defection" to the Iranians came when senior Dawa member Muhammad Baqir Hakim worked with the Iranian regime to create the Supreme Council of the Islamic Revolution in Iraq (SCIRI)—later renamed the Islamic Supreme Council of Iraq, or ISCI—a new organization drawn from the tens of thousands of Shia who had fled into Iran. As the Iran-Iraq War dragged on, SCIRI's militant wing, the Badr Corps, drew from thousands of Iraqi prisoners of war to field paramilitary units that fought on the Iranian side. By the early 1990s, soon after the war's end, Badr had established an extensive network that enabled some of these Iraqi operatives to infiltrate back into Iraq and carry out sabotage and subversion, overseen by an enigmatic Badr Corps leader named Mustafa al-Sheibani.

Dawa, the source of all Iraqi Shia political parties, was breaking into several distinct branches.

DAWA IN EXILE: RADICAL REVOLUTIONARIES

Though most Dawa exiles made their way initially to Iran, many did not remain there. Despite the Iranian regime's recruitment efforts, Iraqi exiles were not necessarily well treated by Iranians, who tended to look upon the Arab refugees with condescension. Dawa exiles established an office in Damascus and accepted the support of Syrian ruler Hafez al-Assad, who by 1980 had become an archenemy to Saddam Hussein and the only Arab ally of Iran. Dawa members also ended up in Lebanon, where Muhammad Hussein Fadlallah had helped organize a sister Dawa organization of clerics who, like Fadlallah, had lived and studied in Najaf before settling in Lebanon. The twin Dawas, Iraqi and Lebanese, became a formidable militant alliance that developed close ties with, and in some cases merged into, Lebanese Hezbollah. In this incarnation, Dawa allegedly participated in some of the most significant terrorist acts of the 1980s, such as the bombing of the American and French embassies in Beirut and Kuwait and the assassination of the French ambassador to Lebanon. These Levant-based Iraqi Dawa members would have grown intimately familiar with Hezbollah operatives such as Imad Mughniyeh and senior Hezbollah clerics such as Muhammad Kawtharani, a former protégé of Muhammad Sadiq Sadr who later served as a liaison between Hezbollah and the Iraqi Shia religious movements. Dawa operatives also would have become familiar with the Iranian operatives, especially the Islamic Revolutionary Guards Corps, helping to direct Hezbollah, and Dawa militants probably participated in Iranian-led operations.

Further afield, some Dawa leaders wound up in the West, with London as a favored destination. The future Dawa prime minister Ibrahim al-Jaafari arrived in London in 1989 after nine years in Iran and became Dawa's leader in the west, though Jaafari notably did not develop an affinity with Western society or culture. In fourteen years in England, Jaafari did not learn English or earn a living, choosing instead to live on the dole and mainly keep the company of other Iraqi exiles. Unlike Jaafari, Dawa's Mowaffaq Rubaie, Iraq's future national security advisor, settled into British life, becoming a neurologist and serving his hospital residency in London alongside Bashar al-Assad.

From outside Iraq, Dawa briefly maintained a militant network inside the country that was active during the Iran-Iraq War and came close on multiple occasions to assassinating senior Baathist leaders. In 1982, Dawa operatives ambushed Saddam's motorcade in Dujail, north of Baghdad, but Saddam survived to wreak vengeance on the town, killing almost a hundred fifty men and boys who confessed knowledge of the Dawa operation—an act for which he would later be tried and executed by the Dawa-led Iraqi government in 2006. A later Dawa assassination attempt in Mosul in 1987 failed as well. Despite its occasional militant operations, Dawa by the late 1980s had lost almost all contact with the grass-roots base it had enjoyed in 1979. When the Shia of southern Iraq revolted against Saddam in the aftermath of the Gulf War in 1991, Dawa played virtually no role in the uprising.

* * *

With the end of the Iran-Iraq War and the quelling of the 1991 uprising, the Shia militancy of the 1980s began to subside. Dawa and the other Shia parties it had spawned settled into a pattern of exile politics so familiar in the Middle East, in which the Iraqi expatriate groups jockeyed to secure a notional share of the spoils in the unlikely event of Saddam's overthrow. Life as an exile party and underground militant network wrought changes in Dawa that probably would have disappointed its founders. Deprived of Muhammad Baqir Sadr's intellectual energy and of grassroots-level contact with the society it had once hoped to transform, Dawa became a party of political operatives little resembling the circle of brilliant Islamic philosophers who had begun the move-ment in Najaf. Like many other Iraqi opposition figures, Dawa leaders developed a near-paranoia about Baathist plots and coun-terplots, growing to distrust any but their closest circle of col-leagues lest Saddam's formidable intelligence services infiltrate and betray the movement. Cut off from a popular base inside Iraq, Dawa's leaders employed a closed, opaque decisionmaking process rather than drawing inspiration from the masses Dawa suppos-edly meant to liberate. After two decades of doing battle with the Baath from underground, Dawa had become the Baath's mirror image: an insular, vanguard party far removed from its original purpose of generating a mass Islamist movement. It was perhaps unsurprising, then, that once in power after 2003 this much-altered Dawa came to resemble the Baath in power.

CHAPTER TWO

Dawa's Road to Nuri Maliki

W HEN THE EXILED Iraqi opposition was unexpectedly called upon to form a government after Saddam's removal in 2003, Dawa became a junior partner to the larger Shia parties led by Abd al-Aziz Hakim and Muqtada Sadr. But once inside the government apparatus, Dawa managed to parlay its minority share of power into a majority one, eclipsing both Hakim and Sadr to become leaders of the Shia coalition. As this Dawa rise took place, Nuri Maliki rose as well, accumulating enough power to eclipse his Dawa rivals and become unquestioned master of both his party and the Shia political bloc.

MALIKI IN THE DAWA PARTY

Nuri al-Maliki was an unlikely figure to rise to command of the party. Unlike other Dawa leaders, he came from neither the clerical families of Najaf and Karbala nor the Shia notables of Baghdad. Born in 1950 in the small mid-Euphrates town of Twaireej, Maliki was the grandson of a local leader who had helped lead the 1920 revolt against the British. As a young man, Maliki fit the description of the middle-class laymen Muhammad Baqir al-Sadr had hoped to attract into Dawa's middle ranks. In the early 1970s, Maliki majored in Islamic studies at Baghdad's Usul ad-Din college, a school founded by Baqir Sadr himself. He had joined the Dawa Party while at the college, becoming politically active at precisely the time the Baathist regime was waging its shadow war on the party. Maliki went on to earn a master's degree in Arabic literature from Salah ad-Din University in Kurdistan and had a brief career in the Ministry of Education before fleeing to Syria in late 1979 during Saddam's massive crackdown on Dawa.

After about two years in Syria, Maliki spent the remainder of the Iran-Iraq War in Dawa offices in Iran, working under the nom de guerre "Jawad al-Maliki," a pseudonym he maintained until becoming prime minister a quarter century later. In 1990, Maliki moved back to Syria to head the Dawa branch in Damascus and edit the party's newspaper, jobs he held until 2003.

That Dawa was allowed to operate openly in Damascus was typical of the regional strategy of Syrian dictator Hafez al-Assad, who hosted the militant opposition to every neighboring government. Assad frequently used these groups to gain leverage in negotiations or conflicts in the region and beyond, an approach sustained by his son Bashar after 2000. Having Dawa in Damascus also may have lent some Shia religious legitimacy to the Alawite Assads that the regime had lacked until the 1970s, when Musa al-Sadr from his base in Lebanon issued a *fatwa* declaring the Alawites to be Shia Muslims rather than the non-Muslim heretics Sunni Islamists had long held them to be.

As the local leader of one of these Assad-sponsored opposition groups, Maliki would have developed close ties to the Syrian regime during his dozen years in Damascus, particularly with its intelligence branches. One of the main regime interlocutors (and perhaps paymaster) to the Iraqi opposition groups was reportedly security chief Muhammad Nasif Khayr-Bayk (known as "Abu Wa'el"), a senior adviser to both Hafez and Bashar al-Assad who plays an important role inside the embattled Syrian regime to this day. As a Shia political group, the Damascus branch of Dawa was probably also close to General Ali Mamluk, the highest-ranking Syrian Shiite in the Assad regime and the current head of Syria's General Intelligence Directorate. Whatever else he did or learned in Syria, Maliki is sure to have gained a deep understanding of the Syrian regime and its intelligence apparatus, and of their goals in Iraq.

Though an important figure in the Dawa Party, Maliki was not prominent outside it. Neither he nor his party sought close ties to the United States before 2002, and Dawa had been a reluctant participant in U.S.-sponsored opposition gatherings before the 2003 invasion. As a result, Maliki and many Dawa peers were unknown quantities to the Americans who helped arrange the new Iraqi government after Saddam's fall. Maliki himself was a second-tier functionary in the transitional governments from 2003 to early 2006, serving under Ahmad Chalabi on the de-Baathification Committee and as a member of Dawa's leadership council, subordinate to Ibrahim Jafaari. One American who interacted with Maliki during his tenure on the de-Baathification Committee recalled that "Maliki was the guy you went down the hall to chat with while you were waiting for an appointment with Ahmad Chalabi," who as Iraq's deputy prime minister had a much higher profile than Maliki before 2006.

Maliki was unexpectedly catapulted onto the world stage after the parliamentary elections of December 2005, when U.S. leaders decided to block the return of interim Prime Minister Ibrahim Jafaari, whom they deemed to be too closely aligned with the Iranian regime and the Iranian-sponsored militias inside Iraq, especially Muqtada Sadr's Jaysh al-Mahdi, or "Mahdi Army." In the ensuing scrum among Shia politicians, U.S. Ambassador Zalmay Khalilzad encouraged Maliki to put his name forward as a challenger to sitting Vice President Adel Abd al-Mahdi, the prime ministerial candidate of the SCIRI Party headed by Abd al-Aziz Hakim. By a vote of sixty-four to sixty-three, the Shia parliamentary bloc nominated Maliki rather than Abd al-Mahdi as premier, with the nomination hinging on the Sadrists, who threw their twenty-nine votes behind Maliki and thus comprised almost half of his parliamentary support. The new prime minister was therefore dependent on the very Shia militant group that Khalilzad and U.S. leaders had hoped to marginalize. Nevertheless, Khalilzad hailed Maliki as "independent of Iran" and as a key figure who could politically unify the country.

Maliki's elevation to premier stunned the post-Saddam Iraqi political class, which had been dominated by men from prominent Baghdad families whose fathers had been wealthy landowners or senior officials under the Iraqi monarchy. Many of these men had been schoolmates at Baghdad's finest prep schools, and their families had tended to intermarry, forming a complex web of familial relationships. As a scion of a modest family from Iraq's rural south, Maliki represented a departure from this traditional Iraqi ruling class. He also emboldened a host of ambitious would-be challengers: if a mid-level Dawa functionary could be prime minister, then perhaps anyone could. The idea that the prime minister's post might be ripe for the taking would lead to a string of challenges from every other major political bloc and a deepening of the Iraqi civil war.

THE NEW PREMIER IN THE CRUCIBLE

The new prime minister faced an unenviable situation. When Maliki formed his cabinet on May 20, 2006, more than five months had elapsed since the parliamentary elections, and during that interregnum Iraq's sectarian civil war had kicked into high gear.

The conflict intensified after the Al Qaeda[1] bombing of the Askari Mosque in Samarra, burial site of two Shia imams and one of the four most important shrines in Shiism. By mid-summer, the death toll for Iraqis had shot to over a hundred a day, with U.S. and government forces unable to control the situation, even after the killing of Al Qaeda leader Abu Musab al-Zarqawi in early June.

The cabinet that Maliki headed had been billed at its formation as a national unity government, with ministers from each of Iraq's major sects and political blocs, but the coalition was in reality a division of ministries among parties that were effectively at war with one another outside the Green Zone, the fortress-like enclave of government buildings and embassies on the west bank of the Tigris River. The political conundrum for all involved was that the crisis called for strong, decisive Iraqi leadership, but Maliki had been acceptable to other parties precisely because he was a lowest common denominator—a prime minister whose relative weakness would ensure he could not curtail his rivals' power inside the government. His problematic dependence upon Sadrist support also meant he could do little to rein in the Sadrist militias that were wreaking havoc upon the Sunni population of greater Baghdad, for fear of losing his parliamentary base. U.S. National Security Advisor Stephen Hadley encapsulated these concerns in a November 2006 memorandum that, in marked contrast to Khalizad's earlier pronouncements, expressed doubts about whether Maliki was

---

1. Some Western observers have taken great care to distinguish between Al Qaeda—meaning the original core organization of Osama bin Laden—and Al Qaeda in Iraq, or, as one newspaper has anachronistically termed it, in an admixture of Arabic and Greek terms, Al Qaeda in Mesopotamia. Iraqis and others in the region have made little such distinction, usually referring to this terrorist organization as simply "Al Qaeda" and considering it an outgrowth of the extremist movement founded by bin Laden. The author therefore uses "Al Qaeda" and "Al Qaeda in Iraq" interchangeably in this book.

either willing, or strong enough, to halt the consolidation of Shia
sectarian power in Baghdad.

CHALLENGES IN PARLIAMENT

In December 2006, the month after Hadley's memorandum,
Muqtada Sadr announced his party's provisional withdrawal from
the government in protest against its cooperation with U.S. military
operations against Sadrist fighters. As U.S. troop reinforcements
began to arrive in early 2007—the now-famous "surge" ordered by
President George W. Bush—Sadr predictably de-nounced the
government's cooperation with the U.S. counteroffensive and pulled
his six ministers from the cabinet for good, thereby withdrawing the
Shia parliamentary bloc's swing vote that had secured the premiership for Maliki the previous spring. Most likely to the Sadrists'
surprise, Maliki then gained the backing of the rival parties that
had favored Adel Abd al-Mahdi just months before, and the government remained intact without Sadrist participation. With the
Sadrists no longer in the cabinet, the new Maliki-led coalition
began weeding out some Sadrists who had infiltrated the government's security forces, and Iraqi government troops began undertaking limited operations against the Sadrist militias.

     As Sadr withdrew his ministers, the Sunni Tawafuq ("Accord")
bloc led by Vice President Tariq al-Hashemi and the elderly parliamentarian Adnan al-Dulaimi did the same, for the opposite
reason. Tawafuq and other Sunni groups claimed Maliki's government was complicit with Shia sectarian killings of Sunnis and
with U.S. military operations against the Sunni community writ
large, and they particularly objected to the Baghdad Security Plan
as directed against Sunnis.

Tawafuq's withdrawal rendered Maliki's government a coalition of Shia and Kurdish parties only, and the prime minister next had to counter a serious challenge from within that Shia-Kurdish bloc. By the fall of 2007, Shia leaders from outside Maliki's Dawa Party had grown resentful of the prime minister's practice of making government decisions in consultation with only a small circle of Dawa allies, not all of whom held senior government positions. The leaders of SCIRI and Badr in particular began to rethink their support of Maliki's premiership and consider a parliamentary challenge to his rule. In December 2007, SCIRI leader Adel Abd al-Mahdi teamed with Kurdistan Prime Minister Nechirvan Barzani—nephew of Kurdish President Massoud Barzani—to attempt to gather the parliamentary majority of 138 votes needed to withdraw confidence from Maliki as prime minister.

Mathematically, Abd al-Mahdi and Barzani could probably garner enough votes, but in political terms no major Iraqi party would move against Maliki without a "green light" from either the United States or Iran. Accordingly, during U.S. Secretary of State Condoleezza Rice's visit to Baghdad in mid-December 2007, Abd al-Mahdi and his allies asked for Rice's support for a no-confidence vote. Wary of repeating the destabilizing five-month interregnum of early 2006, Rice declined to support a no-confidence measure unless the challengers could agree on a full governing coalition that would succeed Maliki's. Frustrated by the Americans, Abd al-Mahdi traveled to Tehran just days later in early January 2008 to seek support for a no-confidence vote from Iranian Supreme Leader Ali Khamenei. Perhaps perceiving Abd al-Mahdi as too closely allied with the United States, Khamenei, like Rice, declined to support the measure, and the Abd al-Mahdi-Barzani initiative fizzled out, despite the fact that a majority of the Iraqi parliament had effectively withdrawn its support for Maliki's continued leadership.

THE SHIA CIVIL WAR

Sadrist public support had been dealt a blow in August 2007 when
the nation was shocked by footage of Sadrist militiamen provoking gun battles with Iraqi troops guarding the shrine of Imam
Hussain in Karbala. The sight of militia members killing pilgrims
in their crossfire was deeply discrediting for a Jaysh al-Mahdi
militia that had been formed expressly to defend them. Maliki's
response to the fiasco was decisive and popular. The prime minister
gained widespread approval when he led a police force from Baghdad to Karbala and arrested hundreds of Sadrist officials and militiamen. The incident was embarrassing enough to compel Muqtada
Sadr to announce a six-month "freeze" of Jaysh al-Mahdi operations and a retooling of the entire Jaysh al-Mahdi into a less militant social services organization. If Sadr had hoped his actions
would bring an end to government and U.S. military operations
against his militia, however, he was soon disappointed. In the
months following the Karbala incident, the Maliki government
became increasingly cooperative with U.S. actions against the
Sadrists, leading Muqtada and his top advisers to begin planning
another political challenge against Maliki. This, the fourth and
final challenge to Maliki's premiership, boiled over into direct war
in 2008, with Maliki's forces ranged against a faction of his own
Dawa Party and the Sadrist bloc that had elected him.

   In truth, the pact between the Sadrists and the prime minister's
government was already strained past the breaking point. Across
Iraq's southern provinces, the rivalry between the Sadrists and
other Shia parties had turned to violence in the summer and fall of
2007, especially between Sadrist militiamen on one side and government officials loyal to SCIRI and Badr on the other. Maliki
and Dawa had originally stood neutral in this Sadr-Hakim battle,
but since the Sadrists' attacks against Hakim loyalists were often a

matter of militiamen fighting against local government officials, Maliki was increasingly drawn into the fray as the leader of the government the Sadrists were attacking.

The prime minister's roundup of Sadrists in Karbala in late August had come only days after Sadrist assassins killed the SCIRI governors of the southern provinces of Qadisiyah and Muthanna. The Iranian regime hastily convened a meeting in Tehran in September to broker a reconciliation between Sadr and the Hakims, but the pact had quickly broken down. Intermittent clashes between the two sides continued in Iraq's southern cities, with the Iraqi Army an active participant, and weeks after the Sadr-Hakim pact, a large-scale Iraqi Army offensive supported by American and Polish troops evicted Sadrist militants from Diwaniyah, an important Sadr stronghold near Najaf.

These clashes in southern Iraq heralded a change in Maliki's military strategy. Throughout 2007, the shared top priority of the Maliki government and the U.S. military had been to defeat Al Qaeda in central and northern Iraq, but by the beginning of 2008 Maliki's goals and those of his U.S. partners were diverging. When U.S. commanders proposed in March shifting operations to Mosul to finish off Al Qaeda in the north, Maliki and his allies responded by traveling instead to southern Iraq to launch an offensive against the militias, including Sadrists, that had long run free in the Shia city of Basra.

From Maliki's point of view, the need in Basra was greater than in Mosul, and as Iraq's second-largest population center and the hub of the oil sector on which roughly 90 percent of government revenues depended, Basra had a greater bearing on the government's power base. British troops had withdrawn from the city center in the late summer of 2007 as part of a nonaggression agreement with Sadrist militia leaders in the city, after which Basrawis had complained that militias and organized crime factions had carried out a wave of murders to consolidate control of the city. Militant groups even controlled the country's only major port at nearby Umm Qasr. To Maliki and his allies, militia control of Basra's streets was a challenge to the government's legitimacy even more serious than the Sadrists' attacks on the government in other southern provinces in late 2007. An Iraqi government that could not control Basra would be a government in name only.

The situation was further complicated by a bitter power struggle between the central government in Baghdad and the local government in Basra. For centuries Basra had been an important Persian Gulf port, unused to being under Baghdad's control, and when the British had formed modern Iraq in 1921 Basrawi notables had petitioned unsuccessfully to remain outside the new country under British protection. Under the post-2003 Iraqi constitution, Basrawi parties such as Fadhila, a Sadrist offshoot, sensed their moment had come again. They pressed for a separate Basra "region" like the Kurdistan Regional Government to the north, in control of its own oil and troops, an idea that was anathema to Maliki and his project of centralization.

Anxious to verify reports of Basra's chaos, and distrustful of Basra's Fadhila governor, Maliki dispatched a fact-finding team from Baghdad led by General Nasier Abadi, the Iraqi military's highest-ranking Shia officer, and Adnan al-Zurfi, a Dawa Party ally who had led the fight against the Sadrist uprising in Najaf in 2004 before becoming deputy director of intelligence in the Interior Ministry. After traveling to the front lines in Basra, Zurfi and Abadi returned to Baghdad in January 2008 with a grim report of a city out of government control, ruled by marauding gangs who committed dozens of murders each week. Sadrist militants had been so brazen as to surround a government outpost and take dozens of policemen hostage, while the Iraqi military commander in the city had responded ineffectually.

The Sadrists had grown brazen in Baghdad as well. Three weeks after Abadi and Zurfi's fact-finding mission, hundreds of Sadrist gunmen descended on an Ashura service in the Shula neighborhood to abduct or perhaps assassinate Mowaffaq al-Rubaie, Maliki's national security adviser and a longtime Dawa leader. The swarm of militiamen surrounding the mosque included both loyalists to Muqtada Sadr and militants from the Iranian-trained "Special Groups," and these competing Sadrist factions came close to blows over which side had rights to the prey-besieged inside. Rubaie and his entourage were narrowly rescued by an armored convoy led by Interior Minister Jawad al-Bolani, but the Sadrists had made the government look impotent in its capital.

THE "CHARGE OF THE KNIGHTS" AND THE
JAAFARI-SADR REBELLION

Just weeks after the Sadrists' Ashura assault on Maliki's cabinet members, Maliki launched his now-famous "Charge of the Knights" offensive in Basra on March 24. The operational details have been ably recounted elsewhere, but the political details are somewhat more obscure. The prime minister's strike at militia power in Basra was a serious threat to the Sadr movement and its offshoots, and the Sadrists responded by launching an intense weeks-long bombardment against the U.S. Embassy and the absent prime minister's seat of government in Baghdad's Green Zone.

The Sadrist political strategy could soon be discerned. The pro-Sadrist Ibrahim Jaafari and Ahmad Chalabi, Maliki's greatest Shia rivals, stepped forward to propose that a parliamentary committee headed by Jaafari himself should broker a ceasefire and "peace process" between Maliki and Sadr. The initiative was meant to reduce the leader of the government into merely one party in a negotiation between warring political gangs, with the expectation that the prime minister's apparent weakness would lead the parliament to dismiss him. Maliki's sacking would enable the Sadrists to lead the way in appointing a new premier who would then cease all operations against them. Sadrist leaders signaled a willingness to accept "anybody but Maliki" as prime minister—including Adel Abd al-Mahdi, whose premiership they had blocked two years before—as long as the Sadrists were seen to regain their role as kingmakers.

Undeniably, however, the Sadrists' preference was for Jaafari himself, with Chalabi returned to the cabinet as well for good measure. The Sadrists had only reluctantly switched their support from Jaafari to Maliki in the contest for Prime Minister in early 2006. The Sadrist vote had enabled Jaafari to win the Shia bloc's nomination for premier, beating out Adel Abd al-Mahdi by one vote just as Maliki would later do. When Jaafari subsequently was unable to form a government, the Sadrists warned other Shia parties from deserting him, saying, in the words of one Mahdi Army commander, "If Ibrahim Jaafari leaves the government, the Mahdi Army will leave the government."

For his part, Jaafari had long had genuine sympathy for the Sadrists, having joined Muhammad Baqir Sadr's movement in its infancy in 1966. In Jaafari's eyes, the Sadrists were the same downtrodden people the opposition had worked so hard to liberate from Saddam. When U.S. troops closed in on the Jaysh al-Mahdi in the Najaf uprising in August 2004, Jaafari had loudly objected, demanding that Americans withdraw from the city. It later emerged that as prime minister in 2005, Jaafari had allowed thousands of Sadrist militiamen to infiltrate the Ministry of Interior and other government security offices. Jaafari had not taken being supplanted by Maliki well, and the Sadrist challenge offered him a chance to regain the leadership of Dawa, if not the premiership itself.

In its early days the Jaafari-Sadr rebellion's prospects looked quite good. Having gambled by taking personal command in Basra, Maliki looked weak when his disorganized and undermanned government units made little headway against the city's militiamen. Shortly after Maliki arrived in the city, Sadrist mortar crews bombarded Maliki's headquarters with impunity, killing his head bodyguard and coming close to hitting the prime minister himself. Over a thousand of Maliki's troops deserted during the first day of Sadrist counterattacks.

The Jaafari-Sadrist gambit soon fell flat, however. Forced to choose between Maliki and the Sadrists, the leaders of Iraq's other parties shocked the Sadrists by unanimously choosing Maliki during a pivotal April 5 meeting of Iraq's major political blocs that made the Sadrists' isolation clear. Bolstered by this political victory, the prime minister next won a military victory as well after the arrival of reinforcing U.S. air power and several thousand predominantly Sunni Iraqi troops from Anbar. The militants of Basra, unused to the kind of hard fighting their Baghdad counterparts had endured for four years, wilted under the attack of U.S. and British aircraft and melted away to Iran by the hundreds. In mid-April, two Iraqi Army brigades fortified by American and British advisers swept through the Sadrist strongholds of Basra with little resistance.

DEFEAT OF THE SADRISTS AND SETBACK
FOR THE QUDS FORCE

With unified political backing, Maliki followed up the Basra campaign by authorizing joint U.S.-Iraqi operations against all remaining Sadrist strongholds in Baghdad and the south. In April, the prime minister approved a U.S.-Iraqi assault on Sadr City itself, the first major operation against the Sadrist enclave since 2004. Repeating the formula that had worked in Basra, U.S. gunships decimated the Sadrists from the air while U.S. and Iraqi troops seized ground, partitioning Sadr City and ending the weeks-long Sadrist bombardment of the Green Zone. On May 20, Sadrist leaders capitulated to the Iraqi Army's occupation of Sadr City, and more than ten thousand Iraqi soldiers walked into the remaining Sadrist neighborhoods with no resistance as they had done in Basra a few weeks before, leaving the Sadrists to lodge a weak complaint that the prime minister was sending more troops into Sadr City than he had agreed to do.

The story was much the same in the Tigris River cities of the south that had long been Sadrist domains. After arresting hundreds of Sadrists with little resistance in Kut in March and April, Maliki's forces seized control of Amara in June, putting the central government in complete charge of the Tigris valley for the first time since Saddam's fall.

Maliki's defeat of the Sadrists was a serious setback for the Iranian regime, and the prime minister's experience in Basra had influenced his attitude toward the Shia militias' Iranian patrons. Amidst the fighting, Maliki became convinced the Iranian consulate in Basra was helping to lead the battle against him, and angrily phoned Iranian President Mahmoud Ahmadinejad to demand that it stop. Ahmedinejad reportedly implied that the consulate was not under his control, and gave the prime minister permission to assault the building if it were used as a base against the Iraqi leader. Since the Quds Force of the Islamic Revolutionary Guards Corps controlled Iran's diplomatic facilities in Iraq, Ahmedinejad seemed to be authorizing Maliki to attack operatives working for Quds Force commander Qassem Soleimani.

Maliki's anger was not misplaced. Soleimani had been heavily involved in the fracas from its start. While the Iraqi political blocs

met in Baghdad, Soleimani had been involved in an entirely separate political track to settle the conflict on the Quds Force's terms.
On March 31, Soleimani had reportedly met Jalal Talabani and
Adel Abd al-Mahdi on the Iraqi-Iranian frontier to discuss a cease-
fire between Iraqi government forces and the Sadrist militias that
were Soleimani's clients. The spectacle of the president and vice
president of Iraq driving to a remote clandestine meeting place to
make entreaties with the Iranian supreme leader's head of militant
operations was a revealing indication of the nature of the relationship between the Iranian regime and the Iraqi state.

In the years since the intra-Shia faceoff of 2008, some observers have credited Soleimani with brokering a peace between
Maliki and the Sadrists and have taken Soleimani's role as a
sign that the Iranian regime was committed to stability in Iraq.
In actuality, the sweeping military defeat of the Sadrists was a
severe blow to the Iranian regime's strategy of arming Iraqi
proxies to force the U.S. military out of Iraq and to establish
an Iranian-allied "state within a state" on the model of Lebanese
Hezbollah.

* * *

The withering of Sadrist resistance in Baghdad and the south
shocked the Iraqi political class and many outside observers as
well. Maliki's forces had easily seized Sadrist neighborhoods that
many western and Iraqi officials presumed the Sadrists would
defend into rubble, like Stalingrad. The campaign exposed that the
Sadrists could not match the growing power of the Iraqi military,
which had swelled by over a hundred thousand troops and policemen in 2007 and was capable of fielding units in places the militias
had previously held uncontested.

As the country realized the relative weakness of the Sadrists'
armed wing, the political balance of power would shift as well.

Maliki and his Dawa allies had traveled from the obscurity of exiled opposition to a share of power in Baghdad. Once there, they had used the power of the U.S.-led Coalition and the Iraqi military to gain an advantage over their major Shia political rivals. In the next phase, they would seek to steal the other Shia parties' local bases of support and gain control of the state outright.

CHAPTER THREE

The New Authoritarian
Regime of Nuri Maliki

T HE MALIKI GOVERNMENT'S VICTORY in the Shia civil
war demonstrated in a stroke that Maliki and his loyalists
were the strongest of the Iraqi Shia factions. Maliki sought
to capitalize on this change by turning his battlefield victory into
a political and electoral victory as well. He also sought to take full
control of the Dawa Party, marginalizing other candidates for
party leadership and making it his personal political organization.
Once in complete control of Dawa, he would seek to make himself
the only plausible choice for leadership of the Shia community as
a whole. As Maliki took these steps, the core of the Dawa Party
would travel with him, eventually melting into the state apparatus
Maliki was attempting to appropriate, becoming an alliance of
political operatives far removed from the idealistic Islamist movement they had once been.

CAPITALIZING ON THE VICTORY

Their defeat at the hands of Maliki's forces stunned the Sadrists.
As thousands of the militants fled across the border to be sheltered
by the Iranian regime, the movement's grassroots base in Baghdad
and the south was left leaderless, and Maliki and his allies were
determined to draw as much of that base as possible into Maliki's

camp of supporters. Even as the fighting raged in the south, the prime minister showed that he intended to follow up his military action by creating an alternative to the militia-backed powers that had effectively controlled Basra and some other southern cities since 2004.

The "Awakening," or *sahawa*, was a largely Sunni tribal movement against Al Qaeda and other Salafi terrorist groups that began in Anbar province in late 2006 with U.S. military support and eventually spread in 2007 to comprise more than eighty thousand Sunni auxiliaries to U.S. and Iraqi troops throughout central Iraq. Maliki had adamantly opposed the extension of the Awakening into the Shia tribal areas of the south, but as he confronted Sadrist power in mid-2008 he took a page from the Awakening playbook by organizing tribal support councils in key Shia areas. As government forces pushed militants out of Basra, for example, Maliki organized a council of Basra's major tribal leaders, including cousins Mansour and Muzahem al-Tamimi of the Beni Tamim tribe. Unlike the Awakening, the tribal support councils would answer to, and be paid by, the government in Baghdad rather than the U.S. military or even the Basra provincial government.

As the fighting receded, Maliki also moved quickly to reestablish government control through reconstruction initiatives for the territories that had been won. The prime minister allocated hundreds of millions of dollars for Basra, Sadr City, and the mid-Tigris region and dispatched close Dawa Party allies to administer the enormous funds. To Basra he sent a Basrawi demagogue whom the U.S. Embassy and military had judged to be among the worst-performing ministers in Maliki's cabinet. A similar situation played out in Sadr City, where Maliki's own chief of staff, Tariq Najim Abdullah, was appointed to oversee the $100 million reconstruction of the vast slum. Unsurprisingly, none of these reconstruction efforts had a material impact on the newly conquered cities:

within months the money had largely evaporated with little construction done. The "reconstruction" of Basra did not even result in the clearing of trash from the canals that once had given the city the nickname "the Venice of the Gulf." The vast funds had apparently gone not to restore government services, but to dole out largess and cement the loyalty of new clients of the prime minister's party ahead of the provincial elections scheduled for the end of 2008.

For Maliki, the military campaign had not just been a victory over the Sadrists; it had also been a victory over his rivals within Dawa. As a triumphant commander in chief, Maliki enjoyed a new stature exceeding that of other Dawa leaders who had once outranked him. Ibrahim Jaafari in particular had been politically damaged by his apparent sympathy with the defeated Sadrist militants. Along with Jaafari, senior Dawa leaders Ali al-Adeeb, Haider al-Abadi, and Mowaffaq al-Rubaie would henceforth be supporting characters in a Maliki-dominated party rather than his peer rivals. These were men, all several years older than Maliki, who had joined Dawa when the prime minister was only a teenager and were old enough to have known Muhammad Baqir Sadr well. They had all been more prominent in the party than Maliki until 2006: Jaafari and Abadi had been on Dawa's leadership council for almost a quarter of a century when Maliki joined it in 2003, while Adeeb had headed Dawa's Iran branch from the start of the Iran-Iraq War and Rubaie had been a prominent Dawa leader in London. Joining them in Maliki's shadow was Hussein al-Shahristani, a powerful Shia independent who had been close to the Dawa movement for decades. Shahristani, once an important scientist in Saddam Hussein's nuclear program, had held senior posts in the Allawi and Jaafari governments and had been considered a potential candidate for both the premiership and the leadership of the Dawa bloc. But with Maliki's ascendancy, Shahristani was relegated to the second rank along with the others.

One factor that both signified and enhanced Maliki's sole leadership of the party—and, increasingly, of the government—was his control of Iraq's diplomatic and legal relationships with the United States. In particular, Maliki and his close advisers controlled negotiations over the legal authorization for the U.S. military's continued presence in Iraq, the most basic element of the U.S.-Iraq relationship. Until 2007, Iraq's annual requests to extend the UN Security Council Resolution authorizing the U.S. military presence had been a routine matter, but in late 2007 U.S. officials found themselves negotiating not with the Iraqi foreign minister, but with a team composed of Maliki's legal adviser Dr. Fadhel Muhammad, Maliki's parliamentary ally Sami al-Askari, and Maliki's longtime political adviser Sadiq al-Rikabi. For U.S. officials who were negotiating the U.S. military's authorities inside Iraq, the trio proved maddeningly hardheaded. They sometimes displayed an unfamiliarity with diplomatic procedures and an unwarranted distrust of standard legal language, leading some frustrated U.S. officials to vow not to deal with the Maliki advisers in the longer-term security negotiations slated for the following year. Maliki's control of his government's U.S. portfolio made him an indispensible partner for the United States, far more important for U.S. interests than any other Iraqi politician.

FROM JUNIOR TO SENIOR PARTNERS

The Shia civil war of 2007–08 had begun as a struggle for supremacy between the two strongest Shia parties, the Islamic Supreme Council of Iraq (ISCI, formerly SCIRI) and the Sadrists, both of whom were clients of the Iranian regime. At the outset of the conflict, each of these parties had enjoyed greater political power than Maliki and Dawa, controlling, between the two of them, eight of Iraq's nine southern governorates and ten ministerial portfolios in the cabinet. Each party also had a large armed wing that could operate independently of the government, while Dawa had none. It might be said that Maliki was elected prime minister in 2006 because neither the Hakims nor the Sadrists trusted the other to have the premiership, and were willing to give the top office to their nonthreatening Dawa junior partners rather than see it in the hands of their chief rivals.

The course of the Shia civil war turned this power relationship on its head. By their incessant fighting in 2007, ISCI and the Sadrists weakened one another both materially and in popular support. Maliki and Dawa had no independent armed wing, but they had grown stronger throughout 2007 by quietly emplacing loyalists throughout the state security institutions, including the army and counterterrorism forces, or by co-opting key officials. The prime minister and Dawa also garnered a great deal of popular support by appearing to bring order and security to the chaos that ISCI and the Sadrists had created. Meanwhile, Maliki's campaign against the Sadrists won him, albeit temporarily, the support of both the Sunni and Kurdish blocs in the parliament, meaning he was no longer in danger of losing the premiership by means of a simple vote within the Shia bloc. The prime minister also benefited from the weakening of his most senior ISCI opponent: Abd al-Aziz Hakim, who had led ISCI since 2003 and whom the United States had once declared a "strategic partner," was by mid-2008 showing signs of the lung cancer that would eventually kill him the following year. The other Iraqi parties were beginning to estimate how much clout ISCI might lose when leadership of the party passed to Hakim's untested thirty-seven-year-old son Ammar.

As a result, when the dust settled at the end of the Shia infighting in the summer of 2008, Maliki was undisputedly the most
powerful Shia political leader, with a new reputation as a nationalist willing to enforce order against any group, regardless of sect. The
prime minister and his allies capitalized on this new reputation by
announcing a new political coalition, the State of Law (*dawlat al-
qanoon*). Formed around a core of the Dawa Party and Shia independents who were Maliki supporters, the State of Law aimed to
break ISCI and the Sadrists' hold on the southern provinces in the
provincial elections of 2009.

THE 2009 PROVINCIAL ELECTIONS AND SHIA POLITICS

The elections for provincial government councils in January 2009
brought a stunning turnaround in Iraqi politics, resulting in a
sweeping defeat of the incumbents whom many war-weary Iraqis
blamed for leading the country into sectarian civil war after the
elections of 2005. In both Sunni- and Shia-majority areas, the
election turned the political arrangement of January 2005 upside
down as incumbent parties lost the governor's seat in every province that held an election, with the exception of sparsely populated
Muthanna. The elections of January 2005 had injected a number
of destabilizing dynamics into the country's local and national
politics, most significantly a widespread boycott by Sunni voters,
and the 2005 polling had also taken place amid extensive violence as terrorist and insurgent groups had attempted to block
voters from the polls. By contrast, the 2009 elections were conducted with virtually no violence and were observed by international monitors for the first time in Iraqi history, giving the polls
credibility.

The 2005 elections, during which Maliki's State of Law had not been in existence, had been dominated in the south by Abd al-Aziz Hakim's Supreme Council, which had won six of the nine southern governorships. Two of the remaining three, Wasit and Maysan, had gone to the Sadrists, with the great prize of Basra going to the Sadrist breakaway Fadhila Party. Until late 2008, it had not been clear the Sadrists would even contest the 2009 elections, owing to the defeat of their militias earlier in the year and the fact that parliament had passed a law at the height of the crisis in April banning parties with illegal militias from holding office. But having won his clear victory over Muqtada Sadr's fighters in the spring, Maliki shrewdly negotiated in the fall to bring his defeated foes back into the political process in order to accomplish his next political objective: the breaking of the Supreme Council's hold on the south. Maliki and his slate were the principal Shia beneficiaries of the 2009 electorate's rejection of incumbents. They were easily the most popular party in the elections, winning just under 20 percent of the aggregate national vote while no other party polled above 7 percent.

State of Law's dominant share in the local governments of the south put Maliki and his allies in an advantageous position for the parliamentary elections scheduled to follow in 2010. For a full year before the national parliamentary polling, Maliki's allies would be able to cement a base of support by doling out jobs in the government and local security forces. The win also validated Maliki's decision to break from the rest of the Shia parties and contest the elections on a platform emphasizing law and order rather than religious duty. In 2005, the Shia Islamists had enjoyed the endorsement of Grand Ayatollah Ali al-Sistani, who had ruled it a religious obligation for Shia Muslims to vote for Shia Islamist parties. But in later elections Sistani was no longer willing to stake his reputation on the parties that had helped lead the country into chaos, and without his backing the Shia Islamist parties fell flat.

Meanwhile, in a sign of things to come, the secular Iraqi National List of Ayad Allawi won more than four hundred thousand votes nationwide, a surprising eighty thousand of them coming in the Shia south. Allawi's strong showing indicated that despite the religious parties' six-year dominance of the south, there might still exist a southern constituency for a secular nationalist platform.

On the whole, Iraqis appeared after six years of war to be rejecting militancy and embracing nationalism, and the free and fair nature of the 2009 elections indicated that a democratic political culture was beginning to take root in Iraqi society as well. This political development coincided with the country's sharp drop in violence from almost a thousand violent attacks per week in mid-2007 to fewer than two hundred per week in January 2009, allowing a semblance of normal life to return to major cities.

As long as these new trends in Iraqi provincial politics and society continued, there was every hope for a similar outcome in the national parliamentary elections slated for the following year. Unfortunately for the forces of secular democracy in Iraq, 2009 would bring a backlash from two directions, one authoritarian and the other sectarian.

THE "EVACUATION" FROM THE CITIES

The Sadrists had appeared to many to represent both the worst of Shia sectarianism and the malign influence of Iran, and in defeating them in 2008 Maliki was widely credited as a nonsectarian nationalist. But this aura did not last long. Well before the elections, Maliki had alienated the other parties in his governing coalition by his noninclusive decisionmaking process and his increasing reliance on a small circle of Dawa Party advisers rather than the Council of Ministers. The negotiations over the U.S. military presence in 2007 and 2008 had shown that Maliki was increasingly acting virtually as head of state rather than head of government, usurping prerogatives of the Iraqi presidency and the cabinet. This trend continued in summer 2009, when Maliki's exclusive control of the Iraqi government's relationship with the United States intersected with his aim of casting himself and his party as a nationalist force that deserved credit for restoring order to the country. The U.S.-Iraqi agreement of December 2008 that Maliki's advisers had negotiated included the proviso that in June 2009 U.S. forces should hand over to Iraqi troops the responsibility for securing Iraq's cities. The details of the handover had been left mainly unspecified in 2008, but by mid-2009 Maliki sought to make the U.S. withdrawal from urban areas as comprehensive and visible as possible. By drawing attention to the withdrawal, Maliki might deflect accusations that he and his government were propped up by American power, the same charge many government opponents had levied against the Allawi and Jaafari governments.

In truth, U.S. forces had already left most cities in 2008, but Maliki's rhetoric grew strident nonetheless as the symbolic withdrawal date approached. He declared the withdrawal day of June 30, 2009, a national holiday, and in a nationally televised address labeled the departure of U.S. forces with the same negatively charged word, *jela'a*, that Gamal Abdel Nasser had used to describe the "evacuation" of the British from the Suez Canal zone in 1956. Maliki also declared the occasion a moment of "great victory" and a "repulsion of foreign occupiers" comparable in Iraqi history to the 1920 revolt against the post–World War I British army of occupation. His Dawa Party colleague Ali al-Adeeb declared that U.S. troops would become virtually invisible in the country, essentially "turn[ing] into genies." Maliki seemed to imply that the departure from cities represented the Iraqi people's defeat of an army of American occupiers rather than the culmination of a joint U.S.-Iraq campaign against common terrorist enemies, while Adeeb seemed to depict U.S. troops as evil spirits, or *djinni*—ungenerous statements for allies of the United States to make. Nor did Maliki apparently wish to acknowledge to Iraqis that it had been Coalition military support that had enabled him to survive the Sadrist offensive the year before.

THE AUTUMN BOMBINGS

Maliki's emphasis on his government's full responsibility for securing Iraqi cities was a political gamble. The prime minister had staked his reputation on his perceived ability to protect Iraqis from terrorism and crime, but he had just celebrated the marginalization of the U.S. troops that had been by far the most effective counterterrorism force in the country.

Maliki's gamble backfired on a large scale in the autumn of 2009. On August 19, seven weeks after Maliki had hailed the *jela'a* of American troops, Al Qaeda operatives conducted one of the war's largest terrorist attacks, penetrating the perimeter of the Finance and Foreign Ministries in Baghdad with massive truck bombs that killed and wounded more than 560 people. Maliki and his allies responded by accusing former Iraqi Baathist leaders in Damascus of masterminding the attacks with the Assad regime's complicity, going so far as to demand a United Nations special tribunal to investigate Syria's role in Iraqi terrorism, similar to the tribunal investigating Syria's role in the assassination of Lebanese leader Rafiq Hariri. Maliki's credibility took another blow just weeks later, on October 26, 2009, when terrorists conducted an even larger attack against ministry buildings inside the Green Zone itself, this time killing and wounding almost nine hundred Iraqis.

Breaking the Shia front

The autumn bombings came at a bad time for Maliki and his coalition. By the fall of 2009, Maliki's Shia rivals had begun to rebound from their provincial election defeat and were busily realigning for the national elections just months away. ISCI, the Sadrists, Jaafari, and other Shia parties made it clear they intended to recreate the unified Shia bloc that had won the 2005 elections, and they aimed to bring Maliki and his branch of Dawa into their electoral alliance, on their terms.

For Maliki's rivals, there were compelling reasons for incorporating the prime minister into the Shia alliance. The Iraqi constitution specified that the largest bloc in the election would have the first chance to nominate a prime minister and form a government under him. Bringing all the major Shia parties into one electoral bloc would therefore ensure that the Shia would lead the formation of a new government, as they had done in 2005–06. But it would also mean that the next premier would be elected by a vote among all the Shia bloc's members, raising the real possibility that Maliki's numerous Shia rivals could band together to block his reelection. It was also clear that the Iranian regime wanted the Iraqi Shia to contest the election in a unified sectarian bloc to ensure that Iraq's next government would be friendly to Iran and Shia-led, and to prevent Sunnis or former Baathists from gaining a meaningful share of power.

For Maliki, conversely, there were compelling reasons for staying out of the Shia alliance if possible. Maliki's patronage network was extensive, but immature, and if he were forced to surrender control of the premier's office, the network would probably collapse. To put it simply, Maliki and his "politburo" could not be confident they would be safe once out of power. For these reasons, when Maliki and the other Shia parties entered into talks about reforming the Shia alliance in the fall of 2009, Maliki drove a hard bargain, insisting that his price for rejoining the Shia bloc would be his rivals' preselection of him as their prime minister nominee. For the other Shia parties, this demand was unacceptable, since their main electoral aim was the unseating of Maliki. It was not surprising, then, when the non-Maliki Shia parties announced the formation of the National Iraqi Alliance on August 24, 2009. Thereafter, Maliki could still join the alliance, but only on his rivals' terms.

The break between Maliki and his former partners in the Shia alliance set the stage for intense intra-Shia competition throughout the winter before the elections of March 2010. The competition was not about ideology, but about power. By late 2009, the original Dawa core around which State of Law had been built was barely recognizable, no longer the ideologically driven party of Muhammad Baqir al-Sadr, but rather a collection of politicians united by loyalty to the personal leadership of Nuri Maliki. Reflecting on this shift, one longtime Dawa member lamented, "There is no Dawa any longer. It has been totally absorbed into the government machine." The original Dawa had held a distinct ideology that envisioned Iraq's gradual transformation into an Islamic society, from which an Islamic state would naturally spring in a long-term, bottom-up political process. The Maliki coalition, by contrast, seemed to operate without any clear long-term vision for Iraqi society, certainly none that promised to resolve the fundamental open question of how Sunnis, Shiites, Kurds, and other minorities could finally live and thrive together in one state. The heirs of the Dawa Party had let go of their founders' legacy completely.

THE MALIKIYOUN

While grassroots movements in other Arab countries dismantled or shook half a dozen authoritarian regimes after 2010, a new one was under construction in Baghdad, where it became increasingly appropriate to speak not of the Iraqi government, or of a Shia-dominated government, but rather of a Maliki regime. The "Malikists"—or, in Arabic, the *Malikiyoun*, an analogue to the *Saddamiyoun* that Iraqis once knew—had become the newly dominant force in Iraqi politics.

On an individual level, the Malikiyoun did not really represent Maliki's Dawa party. The innermost circle of Malikiyoun was instead composed of Maliki's family and personal advisers. Those Malikiyoun who hail from Dawa have tended to be "orphans": Dawa members with no independent base of their own in the party or in the larger movement that spawned it. The Malikiyoun have also included a sizeable contingent of former Baathists, some of whom once worked for Saddam or other senior leaders in the old regime. These Baathists-turned-Malikiyoun have been common in the intelligence services and among top generals, who were almost all formerly high-ranking officers in Saddam's army.

In sectarian terms, the Malikiyoun are majority Shia, and exhibit clear favoritism toward their sect along with extreme distrust, sometimes crossing into paranoia, toward Sunnis and the Baath. But they are not driven foremost by Shia sectarian interests. In fact, they include Sunnis, Kurds, and a few other minorities among their ranks. Though the Malikiyoun use Shia sectarianism when it serves their political purposes, they suppress Shia opponents almost as readily as Sunni ones. Nor are the Malikiyoun Iranian puppets, though they are aligned with the Iranian regime's foreign policy in the region. As a result, the Maliki regime has sometimes behaved as a Shia sectarian power in the broader region to a greater extent than they have done inside Iraq. At the same time, the Malikiyoun are distrustful of Iranian intentions, and this has led them to try to preserve a relationship with the United States to balance what would otherwise be dominant Iranian influence.

In social terms, the most powerful of the Malikiyoun have backgrounds that resemble Maliki's. They are from middle-class—or lower-middle-class—Shia families of the south, and they seem to bear some resentment against the old social elite of Baghdad, members of which the Malikiyoun do not often admit into their circle. The Malikiyoun have been bitter opponents of politicians from the eminent families of Baghdad, such as Adel Abd al-Mahdi, Ahmad Chalabi, Adnan al-Pachachi, and Tariq al-Hashemi, all men whose fathers and grandfathers were powerful ministers and businessmen going back to Ottoman times. The ascendancy of the Malikiyoun thus represents, to some extent, the decline of the old Iraqi aristocracy.

On the level of ideas, the Malikiyoun are not motivated by a shared ideology, but by the acquisition and holding of power, and are deeply committed to keeping their patron, Prime Minister Maliki, in power. The common characteristic among all Malikiyoun is that their power derives almost entirely from their association with Maliki.

THE MALIKI "POLITBURO"

From an early stage in his tenure as prime minister, Maliki relied far more on the advisers he had gathered into his own office than on the ministers in his cabinet, making decisions with the input of a narrow "politburo"-like clique of handpicked Dawa allies. Most of these men are, like Maliki, mid-level Dawa officials in their fifties who came of age as young Dawa operatives in the 1970s and '80s. Collectively, they are, with the exception of Maliki, the most powerful men in the Iraqi government.

Tariq Najim Abdullah, Maliki's chief of staff, is a sober man who has tried to impose puritanical standards on his office colleagues, warning them, for example, of the frivolity of soccer (Iraq's national pastime), and once scolding a guest of the prime minister for not grooming his eyebrows. (The guest is said to have gamely replied that his unruly eyebrows were emulating those of the Imam Khomeini.) Tariq exercised far more power than his position as office manager implied, administering all government actions that required Maliki's approval and sometimes asserting the authority to overrule government ministers himself. Politicians and diplomats dealing with Maliki were often frustrated to receive Maliki's approval for government actions, only to have them held indefinitely by Tariq afterwards. ("It's Maliki's way of turning down requests without seeming to say no," explained one Iraqi official.) Almost as influential as Tariq was Sadiq al-Rikabi, a chain-smoking longtime Maliki friend and political adviser who led the prime minister's negotiating team and worked in Maliki's office as Tariq did. Both Tariq and Sadiq spoke English and had lived in London.

Also an English-speaker, Sami al-Askari was a longtime Dawa member active in the expatriate Iraqi opposition before 2003. Elected to parliament in 2005, he played an unusual role for a parliamentarian, acting as an unofficial adviser and occasional spokesman for the head of Iraq's executive arm of government, the prime minister. Meanwhile, handling Maliki's interests in the cabinet was Ali al-Allaq, the chief of the secretariat of the Council of

Ministers who administered government actions requiring the full cabinet's approval. He also controlled the administration of the Green Zone, including the all-important issuing of access badges, assignment of security details, and doling out of government housing and office space.

Much less prominent than these four "politburo" members, but almost as influential, were several functionaries within Maliki's office. First was Maliki's chief of protocol, Gata Njeiman al-Rikabi, known as Abu Mujahid, a Dawa member from the town of Rifai on the waterway connecting Nasiriyah and Kut who, like Maliki, had lived in Syria before 2003. Abu Mujahid seems to have played some role in Dawa's militant phase of the 1980s, and told an international Islamist gathering in 1987 that Dawa was in the process of organizing Hezbollah cells inside Iraq, implying that Hezbollah was a subordinate militant arm of Dawa itself.

In Maliki's inner circle, Abu Mujahid's responsibilities went far beyond protocol, often including political matters and the handling of Maliki's financial interests. After more than half a dozen years in power, Maliki's financial holdings are allegedly quite substantial but held by intermediaries such as the controversial Iraqi businessman Assam al-Asadi, who one senior Iraqi politician believed could be holding up to hundreds of millions of dollars in assets on Maliki's behalf.

Next were Maliki's spokesmen, the men who interacted with the Iraqi and international media. Official spokesman Ali al-Dabbagh was not a Dawa member, but served as a close Maliki adviser and as a minister of state in Maliki's cabinet beginning in 2010. Dabbagh cultivated close ties with the Recep Tayyip Erdogan government and sometimes acted as Maliki's unofficial liaison to Turkey. Coming from a different background altogether was Yassin Majid, a Dawa member from Amara whose family was of Persian origin.

Majid had been among the fifteen thousand Arabized Persians deported by Saddam to Iran in 1980, and among Maliki's advisers he had perhaps the closest ties to the Iranian regime. Though not an official spokesman, Majid often wrote Maliki's speeches.

Probably Maliki's most trusted adviser was his own brother-in-law, Ali Musawi, who was married to Maliki's sister and hailed from Maliki's hometown of Twaireej. Musawi displayed an understanding of western media and public-opinion trends that was rare among the prime minister's corps of advisers and sometimes conducted outreach to Washington-based think tanks on Maliki's behalf. Also influential in Maliki's inner circle was Abd al-Halim Zuhairi, a Dawa cleric sometimes referred to as Maliki's "spiritual adviser," who also sometimes served as a liaison to the Iranians.

Through these trusted advisers Maliki gradually gathered control of a number of important government activities, including some discussed elsewhere in this study: the diplomatic relationship with the United States, intermittent initiatives to reconcile with the Iranian-armed "Special Groups" militias, and the reconstruction of the southern cities that had been reconquered from militias in 2008. The prime minister's "politburo" also controlled many of the mundane matters that were nonetheless essential to the everyday functioning of the government and of senior government officials, turning them into tools of patronage. This was especially the case in the highly secured Green Zone where parliament and several key ministries were located, as well as much of the foreign diplomatic corps. The Iraqi government owned the vast majority of the land and buildings in the Green Zone, and since the prime minister's confidantes controlled access to highly sought government housing and office space, they could trade it for political favors and other perquisites on Maliki's behalf, and could do the same with the provision of access badges, security details, and armored cars. This control gave Maliki and his inner circle leverage over the behavior of the hundreds of senior Iraqi officials and parliamentarians who required access to the Green Zone and extensive security arrangements to guard against the threat of assassination or attack.

Control of the prime minister's office and the Council of Ministers secretariat also enabled Maliki's "politburo" to dole out jobs and benefits to a vast network of relatives, friends, and other clients. "Maliki's Dawa is the new Baath," observed one Iraqi official in late 2008. "Anyone who wants a government job, scholarship, or house is finding it best to join them."

PROBLEMS AND LIMITS OF THE "POLITBURO"

Life in the "politburo" was not always harmonious. As Maliki's inner circle gained greater control over the state's largess, the stakes grew greater as well, leading inevitably to internecine struggles as those below Maliki jockeyed for proximity to the seat of power. This was court politics par excellence, a contest for power among the principal advisers eventually settled in favor of the ruler's son, Ahmed Maliki, and his brother-in-law, Ali al-Musawi. The losers tended to be banished from government and Baghdad altogether, such as Tariq Najim and Sadiq Rikabi, both of whom by 2010 were living in London, still drawing salaries as Maliki advisers but frozen out of his inner circle, though Tariq returned to Maliki's side by 2013. Joining them in disfavor was Ali Dabbagh, forced to resign his post in 2012 for his alleged part in a bribery-ridden arms deal with Russia.

The power struggles and quiet doling out of favors in the Maliki "politburo" represented the drawbacks of the governing of a large state by former underground oppositionists. Maliki and his inner circle were finding it difficult to break out of the conspiratorial, insular mode that had protected them during their long, dangerous experience as a hunted vanguard in exile.

Fortified by his "politburo" and its tightening control over routine government actions, Maliki allowed his insular governing style to become even more pronounced after his political victory over his principal Shia rivals—the Sadrists and ISCI—in the 2009 provincial elections. By mid-2009, Maliki began to argue that Iraq's parliamentary system was too inefficient, and that the proper governance of the country might require a return to the presidential system that had existed before 2003. Maliki's implication was clear: that he, elected as one of 275 parliamentarians, should rightfully exercise the power of both head of government and head of state, as Saddam had done. As events would show, Maliki would become intent on creating a virtual "presidential prime ministry," with practically all state power consolidated in his hands, unbound by a cabinet responsible to the parliament.

MALIKIYOUN CONTROL OF THE IRAQI MILITARY

Maliki's efforts to take control of the government went far beyond the making of policy decisions. From 2009 onward, he and his loyalists sought ever-tighter control of the key institutions of the state, gradually bringing them under the direct purview of the prime minister's office. Modern Iraqi governments have seized and retained power by holding the two main pillars of the state: the security apparatus and the substantial revenues of the Iraqi oil sector. The Malikiyoun systematically took control of both of these. In the Iraqi security sector, they consolidated control of the national security institutions, beginning with key units of the Iraqi Army. The prime minister's Office of the Commander-in-Chief was created in 2006 as a body to advise Maliki on military policy, but over time it became essentially an operational headquarters, using the authority of the prime minister to take operational control of key military units. By 2011, the prime minister's office had established an independent network of officers embedded in several Iraqi Army commands known as the Office of Security and Information, considered by some local officers to be "commissars" meant to gather information on the army rather than on enemy threats. This system of control was familiar to Iraqi officers, since it resembled the working of the Presidential Diwan under Saddam Hussein.

The prime minister's office also came to exercise operational command of Iraq's highly proficient Special Operating Forces (ISOF), American-trained green-beret-type forces that were perhaps the most effective and experienced counterterrorism force in any Middle Eastern country. The several thousand ISOF troops technically fell under the Iraqi military chain of command, but over time Maliki used the Counterterrorism Bureau—another office that had, like the Office of the Commander in Chief, been created as a coordinating and advisory body only—to assign the ISOF to missions and other tasks. Under the direction of General Talib al-Kenani, the Counterterrorism Bureau proved itself willing to unleash the ISOF not just against legitimate terrorist targets, but also against Maliki's political enemies. The use of the ISOF against political targets led the Iraqi parliament to deny the Counterterrorism Bureau funding in the Iraqi budget, but the bureau was kept alive with discretionary funds directly from Maliki's Council of Ministers, which bypassed the parliament to expand the bureau to more than ten thousand employees by mid-2009.

Other special units joined the ISOF under the effective command of the prime minister's office. The Baghdad Brigade, a unit
nominally under the Iraqi Army's 6th Division, took control of
Green Zone security in 2009 and became a sort of praetorian
guard for the Malikiyoun, answering directly to Maliki's son
Ahmed, who oversaw his father's personal security. As the troops
of the Baghdad Brigade became more visible in the Green Zone
and around Baghdad, Iraqis took to calling them the "Fedayeen
Maliki," drawing a parallel to the Fedayeen Saddam that had been
under the command of Saddam's son Udai before the fall of the
Baathist regime. At the same time, Ahmed Maliki used the
authority of the prime minister's office to control the operation of
the many contractors who had lived and worked in the Green
Zone since 2003, expelling many of them from their offices and
homes, which could then be doled back out to Malikiyoun allies,
and forcing the reregistration of those who stayed. Ahmed also
took effective control of the private security guards that had helped
secure Green Zone facilities in the post-Saddam era.

Ahmed Maliki's role in the control of the Baghdad Brigade and
other security forces in the Green Zone indicated that these units
were Maliki's "coup-proofing" forces, similar to Saddam's Special
Republican Guard, intended to protect the Malikiyoun from the
many coup plots they assumed were constantly in train.

As the U.S. military presence in Iraq diminished in 2010–11,
the Malikiyoun gradually sought to weed out some senior officers
who were not Maliki loyalists, or who had been notably pro-
American, and to replace them with Shia officers whom the Malikiyoun trusted. A few notable cases illustrated this trend. When
the Maliki government signed an agreement in the fall of 2011 to
receive U.S. F-16 aircraft, Maliki summarily ordered the retirement of General Nasier Abadi, the pro-American vice chief of

staff who had been the highest-ranking Shia officer in the Iraqi military, even though Nasier was the most experienced Iraqi air force officer and had overseen the country's F-16 program for several years. Some Iraqi politicians believed the Malikiyoun feared General Nasier because his distinguished family pedigree and his professional reputation could make him the most credible leader of a military junta.

THE CORPORATE IDENTITY OF THE IRAQI ARMY

The Malikiyoun's efforts to shape the upper ranks of the Iraqi military probably reflect, at least partially, Iraqis' recognition that the Iraqi Army has a history of violent interference in Iraqi politics. The Arab world's first military coup took place in Iraq in 1936, and Iraqi military officers subsequently led every successful coup in the country's history (in 1941, 1958, 1963, and 1968) as well as numerous failed coups. Throughout Iraq's modern history, the army has asserted the right to play a political role in times of perceived crisis, somewhat akin to the historical role of the Turkish military, and the Iraqi officer corps has managed to maintain an integral identity even after periods of deep purges. In one notable example, army leaders confronted Saddam in 1986 to demand that he give up operational control in the battle for the Fao Peninsula, where Iraqi commanders believed his inexpert interference was leading them to defeat. That army officers handpicked by Saddam for their loyalty would challenge him in this way illustrates the durability of their corporate identity.

The same corporate identity has occasionally manifested itself in the post-Saddam army. Coalition officers who spent extensive time with senior Iraqi Army counterparts could attest to hearing Iraqi officers in unguarded moments show disdain toward the

Iraqi political class and imply that the army might do a better job of running the country. Similarly, one Iraqi politician was surprised to hear a late-night delegation of senior generals in 2009 express concern over Maliki's consolidation of power and ask for the politician's advice about whether the officer corps should actively prevent Maliki from becoming a dictator. Even more surprising was that some in the delegation were officers thought to be close Dawa loyalists. For their part, Maliki and the Malikiyoun were reportedly angered by the perception that the Iraqi officer corps had supported Ayad Allawi in the election of 2010.

These factors mean the Malikiyoun never may be fully confident in the Iraqi military's loyalty, and may explain why Maliki and his inner circle have worked so hard to create coup-proofing forces under their direct control. In the meantime, though, the Malikiyoun seem to have seeded enough Maliki loyalists in the general officer ranks to neutralize the Iraqi military as a threat to the prime minister's rule. While some pro-American officers were apparently being purged in 2011, pro-Maliki Shia officers had come to dominate the senior military ranks, a trend that alarmed General Babakir Zebari, the Kurdish officer who was the Iraqi military's chief of staff. General Babakir had been a senior Peshmerga commander for Massoud Barzani and the Kurdistan Democratic Party (KDP) before his appointment to the chief of staff post in 2004, but since 2007 he had been progressively marginalized by Maliki's Office of the Commander in Chief. In the fall of 2011, the frustrated General Babakir sent a report to President Jalal Talabani outlining the ways in which Maliki and his loyalists had gained control of the Iraqi military, and he reported that nineteen of the top generals in the Iraqi Army were Shia Maliki loyalists who owed their appointments to the prime minister. Babakir reported that Kurdish and Sunni officers were being systematically purged from the senior ranks at the same time.

MALIKIYOUN CONTROL OF IRAQI INTELLIGENCE

The purge and staffing of the Iraqi general officer ranks showed
that the Malikiyoun place heavy emphasis on the coercive arms of
the state. Malikiyoun loyalists can now be found in the highest
levels of the Ministry of Defense, Ministry of Interior, and Iraqi
intelligence. When reorganizing Iraqi intelligence after Saddam's
fall, the International Coalition intended to separate the intelligence services from the executive authority of the prime minister
and presidency to avoid a replication of Saddam's secret police,
and they also ensured the separation of the civilian and military
intelligence agencies. But when Maliki took office in 2006, the
Iraqi intelligence community itself was a battlefield, with the U.S.-
sponsored Iraqi National Intelligence Service (INIS)—meant to
be Iraq's version of the CIA—virtually under assault from the
extraconstitutional Ministry of State for National Security Affairs
(MSNSA), another of the many organizations that were intended
in 2003–04 to be mere coordinating bodies but developed an
operational role over time. Under Dawa member (and former
Baathist) Shirwan Al-Waeli, the MSNSA grew into a shadow version of the INIS, with thousands of operatives of its own, but
unlike the INIS cultivating close ties to the Iranian regime and
Qassem Soleimani. In 2009, Maliki took control of the MSNSA
by giving its directorship to his own dual-hatted national security
adviser, Falah Fayadh, a Dawa party functionary whom a Spanish
court indicted in ab-sentia on eighty-seven counts of murder in
December 2013 for his alleged role in attacks against the Iranian
dissident group Mujahideen-e Khalq.

    With Iraqi intelligence under his purview, Maliki did not shy
from using intelligence resources in his political battles with rival
politicians. Though Iraqi intelligence has traditionally been dominated by the collection and processing of human intelligence sources,

the prime minister, according to some Iraqi observers, eventually acquired the capability to monitor communications, so that by 2011 he was able to confront some of his political rivals with recordings of incriminating phone conversations. The reconsolidation of an Iraqi intelligence apparatus that was purposely subdivided to prevent its politicization has been an important factor in the prime minister's growing political power.

"Shadow Ministries," Independent Institutions, and the End of Checks and Balances

The Iraqi military and intelligence apparatus that the Malikiyoun came to control constituted one key to the power of the Iraqi state. Control over Iraq's vast oil revenues was the other. In the post-Saddam era, the Coalition and the framers of the Iraqi constitution had intended that the spending of oil revenues would be determined in a budget set by the Iraqi parliament, executed by the various Iraqi ministries. Since leadership of the ministries was divided among Iraq's major political blocs, this arrangement was meant to ensure a balance of power and division of oil revenues. But during Maliki's tenure, the authorities of both the ministries and the parliament have gradually been usurped by the prime minister's office. The secretariat of the Council of Ministers, meant to be a small staff that coordinates meetings of Maliki's cabinet, has grown in the past several years into a virtual "shadow government" that replicates some of the key functions of the Iraqi ministries. Under the direction of Maliki's Dawa ally Ali al-Allaq, the Council of Ministers secretariat now has committees that exercise executive authority—in the council's name—in the areas of defense, finance, and other major state functions. These committees have asserted the authority to reallocate funds from ministerial budgets into projects that the council secretariat generates, which effectively makes the committees mini-ministries in their own right.

The migration of ministerial power to the Council of Ministers and the prime minister's office was precisely the kind of consolidation of state power that the new Iraqi constitution was meant to preclude. One way the constitution aimed to prevent the prime minister or presidency from accumulating Saddam-type power was in the creation or empowerment of independent institutions answerable either to the parliament or to no other arm of government at all. Some of these entities were powerful indeed, such as the Committee for Public Integrity and the Board of Supreme Audit, which investigated corruption cases; the Martyrs' Commission, which oversaw the payout of pensions to the families of slain Iraqi soldiers; the Iraqi Central Bank and the Iraqi Trade Bank, which oversaw monetary and trade policy, respectively; and the High Electoral Commission, which oversaw the conduct of elections nationwide.

Steadily, after 2008, the Malikiyoun brought these ostensibly independent bodies under the direct control of the prime minister's office, first by pressuring them and later by receiving a favorable Supreme Court ruling that placed them under Maliki's supervision. The Malikiyoun at one point or another jailed or investigated the heads of three of the independent bodies. After Maliki made the unfounded complaint that the head of the High Electoral Commission, Faraj al-Haidari, had participated in a plot to fix the parliamentary election against Maliki in 2010 (see chapter seven), the Malikiyoun briefly jailed Haidari and one of his deputies in April 2012 on the specious charge of paying $87 "bribes" to their own electoral commission employees. Upon his release, Haidari fled to Iraqi Kurdistan, leaving the Electoral Commission without a director and leaving Iraqis with the message that the Malkiyoun would not tolerate election officials who did not produce the election results Maliki wanted.

Maliki had for several years clashed with the head of the Iraqi Central Bank, the respected economist Sinan al-Shabibi, over Shabibi's policy of maintaining large reserves in order to guard the stability of the Iraqi dinar, but the prime minister decisively won the dispute in October 2012 when a parliamentary committee led by Maliki allies charged that the bank governor had committed financial improprieties, though they did not disclose what those were. Maliki's political opponents believed the prime minister had sought to sideline Shabibi so he could access the bank's reserves to help fund the government budget. They also believed Maliki had been pressured by the Iranian regime to get Shabibi out of the way, since the bank governor had been alarmed when it appeared that the bank's large sales of U.S. dollars, sometimes $300 million–$400 million per week in 2011–12, might be going to Iranian regime currency traders who were using Iraq to gain foreign currency in contravention of international sanctions.

The Malikiyoun could not have managed this takeover of the independent entities without the agreement of the Iraqi judiciary, especially the supreme court—known formally as the Higher Juridical Council—headed by Judge Medhat al-Mahmoud. In Iraq's system, Medhat served as both top judge and the arbiter of constitutional disputes. A former senior judiciary official of Saddam's regime, Judge Medhat issued between 2010 and 2012 a series of rulings granting the prime minister far more power than the framers of the constitution had envisioned. Three rulings were most significant in this regard. The first came in 2010, when Medhat reinterpreted the constitution to allow Maliki to have first chance at forming a government despite the fact that his slate did not win the parliamentary elections. The second, in early 2011, gave the prime minister control of the independent entities (as discussed above). The third came in 2012, when Medhat ruled that only the prime minister and his cabinet, and not parliament, could initiate legislation, in effect deciding that in Iraq's parliamentary democracy the legislature did not have the power to legislate. Asked by a Shia associate why he appeared to be complicit in greatly expanding Maliki's authority, Medhat reportedly replied that he had no other choice given Maliki's power over him. Whatever the case, Medhat's seeming complicity with the Malkiyoun has neutralized the Iraqi judiciary as an independent check on executive power. This fact did not escape Maliki's parliamentary opponents, who made a failed attempt to sack Medhat on grounds of de-Baathification in February 2013.

THOUGHTS ON IRAQI POLITICAL CULTURE

By 2012, with the Iraqi military, intelligence community, independent entities, and judiciary under their virtual control, the Malikiyoun had succeeded spectacularly in sweeping away the numerous checks and balances written into the Iraqi constitution only seven years before. It is a curious fact that the Maliki regime's drive to power has been abetted, directly or indirectly, by the prime minister's own rivals. Maliki had little difficulty in playing his opponents against one another, so that the Malikiyoun have been able to coerce, intimidate, and even terrorize one isolated opposition group after another while the rest have looked on, having been coopted or bribed, rather than defend the democratic system. The same applies to the international community, which has done little to check—and has sometimes assisted—Maliki's rise in power.

All of these actors, Iraqi and international, could have done otherwise had they wished; after all, Maliki's consolidation of power has taken place in full view. Among the Iraqi political groups, none of Maliki's rivals has seriously demanded the overhauling of the overcentralized structures of the Saddamist state and the vast administrative and financial powers that have come to reside in the prime minister's office, or the blocking of the prime minister's practice of seeding personal allies in key posts throughout the government. It seems clear that most rival political leaders did not resist these matters because they hoped to benefit from them themselves. It is likely for the same reason that few political groups have pressed for a crackdown on the economic corruption that has become the norm among senior government officials and their cronies, and hardly any senior officials have been tried for corruption.

These factors lead to the question of whether Iraq has an irretrievably antidemocratic, winner-take-all political culture. In the post-Saddam era, those who believe Iraq's political culture created Saddam rather than the other way around tend to attribute Nuri Maliki's rise and the nature of the regime he has built to that same Iraqi political culture, drawing the conclusion that Iraqi society naturally tends toward an authoritarian model of government. It is true that Maliki and his loyalists are behaving largely as previous Iraqi regimes have done, especially those that have taken power after regime change, as happened five times in modern Iraqi history before 2003. In 1941, the Iraqi monarchy was reestablished after being overthrown by a pro-Axis junta the year before. In 1958, a military coterie wiped out the monarchy and established a dictatorship under the leftist general Abd al-Karim Qasim. In 1963, another military faction replaced Qasim's dictatorship with an Arab nationalist republic after killing the dictator and dumping his body in the Tigris. In 1968, the Baath overthrew the republicans and established a socialist state. Finally, in 1979, Saddam Hussein purged the Baath from within and established a totalitarian state.

Despite these regimes' dissimilar political philosophies, each tended to consolidate power in the same way. They began by removing the old regime's remnants, since in none of the major regime changes in Iraqi history did the new rulers come to a power-sharing agreement with significant elements of the old regime, choosing instead to purge the core of the old regime from Iraqi government institutions, and to imprison, exile, or kill those they considered the most threatening of the old regime's members. After these purges, the new Iraqi regimes found themselves, like the regimes they replaced, in command of a vast system of patronage, able to fill tens of thousands of government and military positions with their own relations, friends, and would-be clients. The institutions of the state continued largely as they had done before, but with different officials in charge. To create breathing space for this turnover of the patronage system to take place, most new Iraqi regimes also attempted immediately to pacify the Kurds by offering them some measure of autonomy and, often, some representation in the newly formed government, as well as some share of Iraq's oil revenues. These agreements were essential in that they defused the Kurdish question long enough for the new regime to consolidate its power in the rest of Iraq. This consolidation was usually a messy affair, since the new regimes contained disparate factions whose main unifying characteristic was their common opposition to the old regime. With the old regime swept away and the patronage of the state up for grabs, these factions became rivals engaged in a winner-take-all struggle for control within the new regime, carrying out political maneuvers and, sometimes, street warfare that lasted until one faction emerged as the clear winner. The winning faction usually then attempted to co-opt the remnants of the others. In the regime changes of 1958 and later, these winners valued the appearance of popular support, and used large-scale street demonstrations rather than elections to give their regimes an air of popular legitimacy. As they consolidated power, new regimes built mass organizations—such as youth clubs—that would enable them to deploy large crowds whenever useful.

This common pattern of behavior among Iraqi regimes has diverged to some degree after those regimes have consolidated power, simply because Iraqi monarchists, republicans, socialists, and Saddamists have had different conceptions of how Iraq should be ruled. Even so, through all of these different systems of government, a common pattern of behavior has emerged once new regimes have consolidated power in Baghdad. First, once safely in control, each Iraqi regime has moved to quell the Kurds. Without exception, new Iraqi regimes wound up abrogating their agreements with the Kurds and going to full-scale war in Kurdistan, usually at about the time they had consolidated power in Baghdad and the rest of non-Kurdish Iraq. These wars between Baghdad and the Kurds usually resulted in the Iraqi Army brutally taking control of the accessible portions of Iraqi Kurdistan, but leaving the more mountainous areas in the hands of the peshmerga.

After quashing the Kurdish question in this way, Iraqi regimes tended to revisit Iraq's enduring foreign policy problems. Despite the differences in their political philosophies, Iraqi regimes from the monarchy to Saddam held similar conceptions of Iraq's foreign grievances. Once firmly established in Baghdad, each new Iraqi regime challenged Iran on the issue of border delineation, especially in the Shatt al-Arab. They also challenged Kuwaiti control of oilfields near the Iraqi border, and invaded or threatened to invade

Kuwait over this issue in the 1930s, 1960s, and 1990. New Iraqi regimes also attempted to solve Iraq's long-running rivalry with Syria by striking an alliance, threatening war, or both. Finally, each Iraqi regime eventually sought leadership of the Arab world on matters most important to the Arab street, especially the issue of Palestine. From the Iraqi monarchy to Saddam, each Iraqi regime jockeyed with other Arab states for the privilege of being perceived as the strongest protector of the Palestinians. Even before Saddam took power, Iraqi governments sent forces to fight in the Arab-Israeli wars of 1948, 1967, and 1973.

* * *

Not all of these characteristics apply to the process of regime change taking place in Iraq today under Maliki and the Malikiy-oun. The previous cases all involved transfers of power between Sunni-dominated groups, and the new Shia-dominated regime of today has found it more difficult to subdue the externally supported Iraqi Sunnis than previous Iraqi regimes found it to subdue the isolated Iraqi Shia. It is also true that no previous Iraqi regime had to contend with as heavy a level of sectarian violence as the present government faces or as potent a terror group as Al Qaeda.

But despite these differences, the major regime changes in modern Iraqi history serve as reference points for Iraq's present leaders, most of whom were of age when the regime changes of 1968 and 1979 took place, or even participants in the changes. Iraqi Arabs aware of their own political history probably see a clear path to security and stability by following precedent: pursue and wipe out the old regime, accommodate the Kurds, and purge internal rivals, after which attention can be paid to settling scores in the surrounding region. Along the way, Iraq's political class has always seemed willing to sacrifice the effectiveness of the state in favor of control, a tradeoff inherent in any regime's choice to appoint bureaucrats on the basis of political loyalty rather than technical competence, but one that can run the risk of angering the neglected population to the point of revolt. These are the exact patterns Nuri Maliki and his regime would follow during the historic Arab Spring events of 2010–12.

THE SECTARIANS

CHAPTER FOUR

The Shia Supremacists

M ANY OBSERVERS of the Iraq conflict have concluded that the regime change of 2003 inevitably led to sectarian violence and politics by opening up preexisting sectarian fractures. Saddam and the Baath had indeed cultivated ethnic and sectarian differences to shore up their rule, as other Iraqi regimes had done before them, but the deep sectarianism of the last decade was neither foreordained to follow Saddam's fall nor completely natural in Iraqi society. That sectarianism was instead the calculated objective of powerful factions that emerged after Saddam's disappearance in 2003 with explicitly sectarian agendas in mind. Shia supremacists, Sunni chauvinists, and Kurdish maximalists all aimed to exploit the post-Saddam political vacuum to advance their narrowly defined communal interests.

Among Iraq's Shia groups, Iranian-allied exiles returned to Iraq in 2003 with the intention of cementing a permanent Shia ascendancy in Iraqi politics and society. Some of these Shia supremacists also were determined to wreak vengeance on the Baath in particular and the Iraqi Sunnis in general for the damage done to Iraqi Shia parties from the 1970s to the '90s. In pursuit of these goals, the Shia supremacists meant to form a united Shia political front and use the weight of numbers to win control of the government in Iraq's new democratic system. From their posts in government, they would then use the arms of the Iraqi state to remake greater Baghdad, a city Sunni Arabs had long considered part of their birthright, into a Shia domain.

Homecoming of the Supreme Council and Badr

As Nuri Maliki and his fellow Dawa expatriates returned from their long exile in Syria and the West in 2003, another group of Shia expatriates was returning from the East. The Badr Corps and the Supreme Council for the Islamic Revolution in Iraq (SCIRI) were also coming home, no longer the indoctrinated young prisoners of war and defectors who had joined the fight against Saddam's army, but hardened middle-aged men ready to punish those responsible for three decades of anti-Shia persecution.

They sowed in fertile ground. Iraqi Shia communal grievances ran deep after the repression of the 1980s and the terribly costly Shia uprising of 1991, which Saddam's regime had ended by killing as many as a quarter of a million Shiites, though no one really knows the death toll. Whatever the number, the horrors of 1991 left few Shiites untouched: across Baghdad and the south, virtually every Shia family had lost its martyrs or knew those who had. Tens of thousands of Shia homes had walls on which pictures of the family martyrs were displayed, and each family knew exactly whom should be held to account, if ever the chance arose.

In form, the Badr Corps was a subordinate armed wing of SCIRI, a sort of Provisional IRA to SCIRI's Sinn Fein. Both organizations had been founded in 1982 by Muhammad Baqir Hakim, who had later passed command of Badr to his cleric brother, Abd al-Aziz Hakim. In practice, however, the Badr Corps and its leaders were under the operational control of Iran's Islamic Revolutionary Guards Corps (IRGC), meaning that senior Badr commanders would have functioned essentially as senior IRGC officers, just as Lebanese Hezbollah's notorious operative Imad Mughniyah did.

Perhaps it is not surprising, then, that some of the Badr Corps' actions in the early post-invasion days seemed to be driven by Iranian interests. Badr operatives continued to conduct operations against the Iranian regime's bête noire, the Mujahideen-e Khalq (MeK), after Saddam's fall, when the MeK posed virtually no threat to SCIRI and Badr from the small bases on which the U.S. military had interned the group. Beyond the MeK, Iraqi pilots had also been the objects of intense Iranian hatred since Iranian cities had suffered terrible damage from Saddam's air force during the Iran-Iraq War. The Badr Corps reportedly began, upon its return to Baghdad, to track down Iraqi air force pilots and assassinate them in a spate of murders that later prompted Iraqi President Jalal Talabani publicly to offer former Iraqi pilots asylum in Kurdistan.

SCIRI and Badr leaders sought retribution for the Iran-Iraq War on a policy level as well. In December 2003, Abd al-Aziz Hakim, outright leader of SCIRI after his brother Muhammad Baqir's assassination in August 2003, raised Iraqis' ire by arguing that since Saddam's Iraq had caused the Iran-Iraq War, Iraq should pay reparations for war damage, up to $100 billion. The notion that a country in the midst of its own postwar reconstruction effort should pay such an enormous sum to a distrusted neighbor gained Hakim little favor with the Iraqi public.

Beyond the idea of punishing their native country for the Iran-Iraq War, the SCIRI and Badr returnees aimed to change the character of Iraq's public institutions, giving them a Shia Islamist face. Under the Baath, most Iraqi mosques had effectively been Sunni ones, especially those overseen by the state-run religious endowment, or *waqf*. In the aftermath of the regime's fall, SCIRI and other Shia parties took control of key mosques in Baghdad and other mixed-sect areas, replacing their clergy with Shia imams.

This changeover to Shia control was the case in every Baghdad-area mosque that fell under SCIRI control, since SCIRI had had no presence in Baghdad at all before April 2003.

SHIA ASCENDANCY AND THE NATURE OF SCIRI

To cement a Shia political ascendancy, SCIRI leaders put two political initiatives in motion. The first was the gathering of all Shia Islamist parties into the United Iraqi Alliance (under Abd al-Aziz Hakim's overall leadership), whose candidates received the implied endorsement of Grand Ayatollah Ali Sistani and the Najaf-based *marjaiyyah* in the 2005 elections. The second was SCIRI's proposal that Iraq's nine southern provinces should form a federal region. SCIRI had played a pivotal role in ensuring that the constitution of 2005 allowed for the formation of such regions, with one of SCIRI's senior officials, Sheikh Humam Hammoudi, a worldly cleric of Baghdadi background, leading the campaign for southern federalism on the constitutional drafting committee. SCIRI's leaders judged that the Shia south's fundamental problem had been that too much power had been concentrated in the central government in Baghdad, and that Shia interests would therefore be best served by a deep decentralization of state power. Their proposed southern region—which western observers dubbed "Shiastan"—would function as the Kurdistan Regional Government did, with its own regional parliament, regional security forces, and control over natural resources. Once formed, Shiastan would have a population of more than thirteen million, as well as effective control over the southern oilfields that provided most of Iraq's gross domestic product. The state in Baghdad would be reduced to a shell of its former self, supplanted for the first time in Iraq's history by a new seat of power in SCIRI's base of Najaf: a Shia Islamist government guided by a super-empowered *hawza*.

The idea that the south should enjoy a far greater share of Iraq's wealth and power resonated deeply with the more than ten million Shia southerners, who saw themselves as a distinct, traditionally neglected Iraqi community whose time to rule had finally come. But the SCIRI plan for a separate region was unpopular with many Arab Iraqis, for whom federalism was an unfamiliar concept that they perceived as the partition of a unitary state. Many Iraqi critics of the plan also feared that a southern region would quickly become a satellite of Iran, a fear that was exacerbated by SCIRI's awkward policy stance toward *wilayet al-faqih*, the Khomeinist doctrine that required Shia Muslims to follow the guidance of Iran's supreme leader. Since its founding, SCIRI's raison d'être had been the extension of Iran's Islamic revolution to Iraq, as the party's very name indicated, and while based in Iran the party had explicitly espoused *wilayet al-faqih* and pledged allegiance to Supreme Leader Ali Khamenei. If SCIRI were able to form and govern a southern region, Iraqis wondered, would their government take instruction from the ruler of Iran?

The question of SCIRI's adherence to *wilayet al-faqih* was significant enough to prompt the party to change its name and declared objectives in 2007. Abd al-Aziz Hakim announced in May 2007 that since Saddam's regime had been toppled, the revolution in Iraq was already complete, and SCIRI therefore no longer needed to cast itself as a revolutionary party—omitting to mention that SCIRI's original mission had been to bring to Iraq an Islamic revolution, not a democratic one. The step seemed to indicate that the newly named Islamic Supreme Council of Iraq (ISCI) was distancing itself politically from the Iranian regime, as the Supreme Council's deepening relationship with the

United States in 2006–07 already appeared to show. In early December 2006, Abd al-Aziz Hakim had made a prominent trip to Washington to announce jointly with President Bush that the United States and the Supreme Council had formed a "strategic partnership," a distinction no other Iraqi political party enjoyed.

On an operational level, however, ISCI's ties to Iran were as strong as ever. Just two weeks after Hakim appeared with Bush in the White House, American troops captured several Iranian intelligence operatives on a late-night raid inside Hakim's own compound in Baghdad, including a senior Quds Force officer with close ties to Lebanese Hezbollah. That Iraq's most senior Shia politician should personally host a Quds Force commander made clear that ISCI did not consider the Iranian regime's terrorist arm an enemy of the Iraqi government, even as the Quds Force conducted a proxy war against ISCI's American "strategic partners."

The tension between ISCI's strategic partnership with the United States and its client-patron relationship with the Iranian regime grew stronger the farther one traveled from the Green Zone. In Baghdad, ISCI leaders enjoyed good relations with senior U.S. officials, owing partly to the fact that some prominent ISCI leaders were cultured English speakers who could communicate easily with western diplomats and commanders. Adel Abd al-Mahdi, the Iraqi vice president who had twice narrowly missed being prime minister, was the most notable of these. Originally from Nasiriyah and the son of a former education minister for the Iraqi monarchy, Abd al-Mahdi had started his career as a socialist and had studied and lived in France before joining the Hakims in opposition to Saddam. Once back in Baghdad, he surrounded himself with astute western-educated Iraqi advisers, and in his discussions with western counterparts he expressed a liberal democratic political philosophy. Like Abd al-Mahdi, ISCI's Bayan Jabr Solagh cultivated close relationships with western officials, especially those involved in security or finance. A genteel, English-speaking Shia Turcoman, Jabr played an important role in the Iraqi government as minister of interior and minister of finance, successively, between 2005 and 2010. In the provinces beyond Baghdad, however, ISCI and Badr representatives tended to be devout religious hardliners who viewed the world through sectarian lenses and regarded westerners with thinly disguised contempt or distrust. Some had put down roots in Iran during their decades of exile, marrying Iranian women and raising Persian-speaking children.

State Capture

Other Badr veterans played a pivotal role in another sectarian development after 2003: the takeover of select government institutions for the purpose of using them to purge Baghdad and the Iraqi ministries of Sunnis who had served in Saddam's regime. Among the most significant security decisions taken by Ibrahim Jaafari and his government allies in 2005 had been the induction of hundreds of Badr officers into Iraq's security sector, especially the Ministry of Interior. The period of 2005–06 was a window of opportunity to shape the Interior Ministry and its police forces, which were expanding from a prewar level of about sixty thousand to almost half a million. Once appointed to senior and mid-level Interior Ministry positions, Badr officers absorbed thousands of Shia militants into the ministry to serve as rank-and-file soldiers in the sectarian cleansing campaign Badr intended to carry out.

Supervising this process was the Supreme Council's Bayan Jabr, interior minister in Jaafari's cabinet. The most prominent case of the Interior Ministry's sectarian initiative was that of Bayan Jabr's Badr Corps ally, Bashir Nasser al-Wandi (known commonly as

"Engineer Ahmed"), deputy director of the Interior Ministry's intelligence directorate in 2005–06. Though he nominally worked for intelligence director Hussein Ali Kamal, a Kurdish official who was an ally of Massoud Barzani, in reality Engineer Ahmed ran an extensive secret police operation beyond Kamal's control, composed of units that did not appear on the ministry's rosters and that ran their own secret prisons and interrogation centers. From 2005 to 2007, these secret police units abducted, tortured, and sometimes killed an unknown number of Iraqis: some who may have been involved in insurgent activities, but many who seemed merely to have been associated with the old regime. The shadowy operation was uncovered in late 2005 when American officials stumbled across more than one hundred prisoners in secret cells at Ahmed's command bunker in the Baghdad neighborhood of Jadriyah. American advisers to the ministry were puzzled to find that some of the detainees seemed to have been seized because they were relatives of Iraqi pilots, a factor perhaps linked to the alleged Badr Corps targeting of air force officers.

Elsewhere, the ministry's police forces were playing a leading role in the large-scale sectarian cleansing of Baghdad. The National Police, a gendarmerie of more than thirty thousand created for antiterrorism operations, became infamous during Jabr's tenure for their close links to Shia militant groups and for their commanders' tendency to arrest large numbers of Sunnis. In one high-profile case, National Police general Mehdi al-Gharrawi was placed on trial for his brigade's systematic torture of Sunni prisoners, fourteen hundred of whom had been discovered in holding cells in Gharrawi's base in east Baghdad. The case against the general collapsed, however, when one witness after another recanted their testimony, leaving Gharrawi free to eventually be promoted to command of a police division in Mosul.

The induction of Badr officers and Shia miltiants into the Interior Ministry's ranks for the purpose of prosecuting a sectarian war produced deep fissures in the ministry's officer corps. Before Badr's infiltration of the ministry, the officer corps had consisted largely of former Iraqi Army officers whose formative experience had been the Iran-Iraq War. Though many of these officers were Shia, their service alongside Sunnis, Kurds, Christians, and Turcomans in the trenches in the 1980s had resulted in cross-sectarian relationships that often trumped the new sectarian divisions emerging after 2003. For these men of the war generation, the Badr Corps officers who began to arrive in 2004 and 2005 had been enemies rather than comrades, traitors who had betrayed their nation by fighting on the Iranian side. The distinction created an underlying tension between many mid-level officers and the senior Badr officials that had been appointed over them. Late at night, when the ministry's Iraqi veterans might gather to reminisce about their war experiences, the Badr Corps men would not be welcome.

THE SECTARIAN CLEANSING OF BAGHDAD

The Badr officers who took command of much of the Ministry of Interior in 2005 unleashed the police machinery on the population of greater Baghdad in 2005–06. The gradual displacement of the city's population into sectarian enclaves had been taking place practically since the fall of the regime in 2003, often with police complicity, but this process accelerated after the Samarra mosque bombing in February 2006. From that point onward, police units in the city had a direct role in pushing hundreds of thousands of Sunnis out of mixed-sect neighborhoods, especially on the west side of the city.

The sectarian cleansing of Baghdad played out on a geography of mosques, bridges, police outposts, slums, and posh neighborhoods. For its entire modern history, Baghdad had been a city on the two banks of the Tigris River, with important bridges connecting the two and the river serving as a "high road" much as the Thames served London. Every Baghdadi, when asked where they were from, could be expected to answer either Rusafa, the sub-city on the east bank, or Karkh, the sub-city on the west bank; and a number of social assumptions could be drawn from that answer.

On the east bank, Rusafa was a bustling commercial center populated by small merchants and working classes. On the outer edges of Rusafa's haphazardly arranged older quarter were vast planned housing developments, filled with state-built apartment blocks laid out on grids. The largest of these, Sadr City—formerly "Saddam City," and before that the "Revolution" district—had been built by Abd al-Karim Qasim's regime to accommodate the many "proletarians" who were leaving southern farms to seek jobs or state welfare in the city. Subsequent governments had built similar neighborhoods on either side of Sadr City. These migrations from the south gave Rusafa a decidedly Shia majority, but the sub-city was also home to sizable Christian and Kurdish neighborhoods. On Rusafa's northern end was the overwhelmingly Sunni Adhamiyah, a district of three hundred thousand that had grown up around the famous Abu Hanifa mosque, an eleventh-century shrine housing the remains of the founder of one of Islam's four great schools of jurisprudence. Adhamiyah had once been its own city before modern Baghdad had expanded to join and absorb it. In recent times, it had become home to a large number of military officers and other Baathist officials. On Rusafa's southern end, the Karrada peninsula jutted west, surrounded by the winding Tigris on three sides. Karrada and its sub-neighborhood of Jadriyah were mixed-sect, filled with expensive homes, upscale shopping, and the University of Baghdad, a well-to-do area with a lifestyle far different from that of Sadr City.

West across the Tigris, in Karkh, the restricted Green Zone hugged the river, housing the Iraqi government and many diplomatic missions. Two miles northwest of the Green Zone lay the ancient Buratha mosque, originally a pre-Islamic Aramaic church, situated near Baghdad's oldest quarter and the busy Haifa Street. Two miles further northwest lay the ancient Shia shrine city of Kadhimiyah, home of the remains of two Shia imams, joined to its twin city of Adhamiyah by a bridge, and like Adhamiyah formerly an independent city now surrounded by modern Baghdad. Just west of Kadhimiyah were the planned neighborhoods of Hurriyah and Sh'ula, built like Sadr City to accommodate an influx from the countryside. South of Hurriyah and west of the Green Zone lay Mansour, Adel, and other middle-class neighborhoods crossed by two east-west highways, one leading to Baghdad airport and the other to Abu Ghraib and Anbar. South of Mansour lay the planned industrial areas of Jihad, Rashid, Saidiyah, and Doura, mixed-sect working-class neighborhoods joined to Rusafa by a cross-Tigris expressway and dominated on the skyline by the huge, smoking Doura refinery that produced one-third of Iraq's gasoline. Most of these districts were filled with far more spacious homes and streets than were typical in Rusafa, as well as a larger population of Sunnis. Indeed, Baghdadis had a traditional sense that the eastern half of Baghdad was a Shia sub-city and the western half a Sunni one.

The civil war of 2005–08 changed that sectarian balance. By 2006, Sunnis were largely driven out of Rusafa, except for Adhamiyah, where Sunnis clung to a toehold on the east bank of the river, and the Abu Hanifa mosque and its environs became a Sunni insurgent base at war with Sadr City. Adhamiyah was the likely origin of many of the car bombs and suicide bombers that caused such destruction in markets and mosques around Sadr City, and the militants of Sadr City responded by conducting raids and assassinations of their own against Adhamiyah's people. Raids and assassinations also emanated from the neighborhood across the Tigris from Adhamiyah, where ISCI parliamentarian Jalaluddin al-Saghir, a former Badr commander, had taken control of the Buratha mosque and was suspected by many Baghdadis of using it as a Badr Corps base and death squad headquarters. This certainly appeared to be the conclusion of Baghdad's Sunni militants on April 7, 2006, when three suicide bombers penetrated the mosque to cause almost two hundred fifty casualties, with one bomber reaching al-Saghir's office and narrowly missing killing the cleric himself.

ISCI and Badr also established strongholds on the southern end of Rusafa in Karrada and Jadriyah. Abd al-Aziz Hakim and ISCI had their headquarters complex on the peninsula, not far from the secret prisons and torture chambers run by Badr officer "Engineer Ahmed" and his rogue Interior Ministry units. From Karrada, Engineer Ahmed's men had easy access across the Tigris to the government in the Green Zone. They were also within easy striking distance of the Sunni neighborhoods of Doura, which in late 2006 and early 2007 were virtually besieged by National Police under the command of officers tied to Badr and other Shia militant groups. Doura and nearby Saidiyah had not always been heavily Sunni, but had become increasingly so since 2003 as Sunni insurgents chased away the neighborhoods' Shiites.

SECTARIAN CLEANSING: THE GRASSROOTS DIMENSION

Bayan Jabr, Engineer Ahmed, Jalaluddin al-Saghir, and many hundreds of senior Shia officials and politicians played important roles in driving Sunnis out of Baghdad. Yet the most powerful force in the sectarian cleansing of the city was probably not the Shia leaders at the top, but the Shia masses at the bottom, particularly those living in Shia slums such as Sadr City. The reshaping of Baghdad's population between 2004 and 2008 cannot be understood without appreciating the condition of Sadr City in 2003, when the neighborhood's 28 square kilometers were packed with as many as 2.5 million people, a population density of well over eighty thousand per square kilometer, roughly double or triple that of the world's most densely populated cities, including Manila, Mumbai, and New York. Strangely to western eyes accustomed to urban sprawl, beyond Sadr City and other large housing developments lay not suburbs, but empty state-owned wasteland on which the ineffective and often corrupt state bureaucracy was slow to authorize anyone to build. This constraint meant that the great city ended abruptly, with sharply defined edges beyond which its teeming population could not spill.

The result was a bloody competition for the neighborhoods and housing that already existed. Above all, the sectarian cleansing of the city was a matter of the Shia lower classes breaking out from their slums in Rusafa to colonize the roomier Sunni-majority neighborhoods of west Baghdad. Early on in this process, the shrine district of Kadhimiyah had become a Sadrist stronghold, dominated by Jaysh al-Mahdi groups under the command of Sadrist cleric Hazim al-Araji and his brother Baha al-Araji, who headed the Sadrist bloc in parliament. From Kadhimiyah, Sadrist militants—from both Jaysh al-Mahdi and its eventual rival Asa'ib Ahl al-Haqq—branched west into Hurriyah and Sh'ula, gradually chasing Sunnis from their homes and then resettling Shia families from Rusafa into them. In these neighborhoods, the Jaysh al-Mahdi and Asa'ib Ahl al-Haqq became virtual apartment brokers, doling out homes to their supporters and to those willing to pay commissions or rent. On the southern edge of those neighborhoods, new Shia police outposts sprang up to protect the territorial gains and push the Shia colonization line further south. In Adel, just south of Hurriyah, Sunni militants attempted to hold back this Shia tide by launching terrorist attacks from the Umm al-Qura mosque, built by Saddam in the late 1990s but becoming by 2004 the headquarters of the radical Sunni cleric Harith al-Dhari and his Association of Muslim Scholars. Dhari's organization had seized the complex after Saddam's fall, and the minarets the dictator had designed to look like AK-47 barrels and SCUD rocket launchers made it a fitting symbol of Sunni defiance, until the government-run Sunni Endowment expelled the association in mid-2007.

On the southern side of Karkh, meanwhile, the industrial area of Abu Dshir south of Doura became another Shia militant stronghold, from which fighters could threaten the Sunnis to their north. The Jihad neighborhood southwest of Mansour similarly became a base from which Jaysh al-Mahdi and "Special Groups" fighters could raid Sunni neighborhoods and also launch rocket and mortar attacks against the U.S. base at the Baghdad airport. But the most potent Shia militant forces were the death squads that nightly sallied forth from Sadrist strongholds in Rusafa to cross the Tigris bridges and conduct killing raids in west Baghdad, often dumping dozens of mutilated bodies in the vacant lots of Doura and Rashid. This cross-Tigris threat grew severe enough in early 2007 to prompt Sunni militants to try to isolate Karkh from Rusafa by destroying the bridges connecting the two. In the space of three weeks in March–April 2007, militants bombed three Tigris bridges, moderately damaging two but succeeding in completely dropping the Sarafiyah bridge and rendering it unusable for a year and a half.

These Sunni militant countermeasures were to little avail. By 2007, U.S. officials perceived that Shia militant groups, with government complicity, had clamped the Sunni neighborhoods of west Baghdad in a pincer, pressing southward from Sh'ula, Hurriyah, and Kadhimiyah and northward from Jihad, Rashid, and Abu Dshir. U.S. officers believed that between these pincer arms, the Iraqi government was waging a campaign of exhaustion against the population, cutting off municipal and state services such as sanitation, banks, and health care to compel Sunnis to migrate west to Anbar.

THE "MEJHOOL" AND THE HORRORS OF DAILY LIFE

The signs of the large-scale sectarian cleansing of Baghdad were unmistakeable long before the Samarra mosque bombing of February 2006. The small town of Salman Pak, fifteen miles south of Baghdad, was a picturesque spot on the Tigris River known for the huge ancient Arch of Ctesiphon, the one-time capital of the Persian Empire and the site of an Ottoman victory over a British army in 1915. But by early 2005, it had become a morgue, with the inhabitants of Salman Pak and the nearby town of Suwayrah regularly doing the grisly work of pulling dead bodies out of the Tigris. Iraqis had a name for the dead: *al-mejhool*, "the unidentified": Baghdadi victims of Sunni and Shia death squads whose corpses were dumped in the Tigris and left to float downstream. On one day in April 2005, fifty-seven bodies washed up near the two towns, Shia victims of Sunni militants who had taken them hostage just south of Baghdad and killed them as government troops approached. Later, in mid-2006, Iraqi officials in Suwayrah reported that they had collected 339 dead bodies of men, women, and children from the town's irrigation barriers since January 2005, but even that figure must have represented a small fraction of the dead. "We used to fetch [the bodies] out," one fisherman told reporters, "but now there are so many we leave them. Otherwise, there would be no time for fishing."

Back in Baghdad, daily life held an increasing number of shibboleths. With Sunni and Shia death squads operating throughout Baghdad, each trying to cleanse neighborhoods of the opposite sect, ordinary Baghdadis who simply needed to move through neighborhoods other than their own began carrying two sets of identity cards, one with Shia names and one with Sunni names, to enable them to get through the militant checkpoints they were sure to encounter on their way. Parents began teaching their children to carry two different identities, complete with backstories, to be able to give to the Sunni or Shia police or militants who might stop them on the way to or from school. Baghdadis who commuted across the city by car even learned to have radios blaring Sunni or Shia music, or to have Sunni or Shia symbols hanging from the car mirror, as they passed through various neighborhoods.

These terrors of everyday life left Baghdadis governed by fear more than anything else, and this fact directly caused the most deadly incident of the war. On August 31, 2005, thousands of Shia pilgrims crossing the Tigris bridge from Adhamiyah to the shrine neighborhood of Kadhimiyah stampeded when rumors spread that a suicide bomber was in their midst. In the ensuing panic, almost a thousand Iraqis were either crushed to death by the massive crowd or forced to jump to their deaths in the river below. There had been no suicide bomber, but the terrorized masses had nonetheless done more damage to themselves than any suicide bombing in the entire war.

The Government Cleansers

The denial of services in Sunni areas of Baghdad highlighted that the cleansing of the city was not merely a matter of unofficial militias and their fellow travelers in the police forces. The Iraqi government was playing a direct role. In the most egregious example, the Health Ministry had come under the control of the Sadrists in Maliki's new cabinet of May 2006, enabling Sadrist militants to use government ambulances to move fighters and weapons around the city. The Sadrist deputy health minister, Hakim al-Zamili, was arrested and tried for using Health Ministry guards as death squads, but he was freed when fearful witnesses changed their stories.

The prime minister's own office was not uninvolved in the sectarian campaign itself. In the Office of the Commander in Chief (OCINC), Maliki's staffers began to involve themselves in the deployment of army and police units against Sunni targets. Tactical commanders were ordered to target Sunnis suspected of militant associations, often based on flimsy evidence. At one point in the spring of 2007, six different military intelligence officers from west Baghdad units were sacked because they had targeted Shia militants in the city, indicating that for the prime minister's office, action against the Shia militias was tantamount to support for Sunni terrorism.

The prime minister himself was also occasionally involved in the sectarian campaign. He and his close advisers paid inordinate attention to a few Baghdad neighborhoods, such as Saidiyah, where they seemed determined to restore a Shia majority and were hypersensitive to reports of anti-Shia violence phoned in directly to Maliki from a network of associates on the spot, similar to the reporting network that would later inform him of the deteriorating situation in Basra. Maliki also over time came to use his prime ministerial authority to direct Iraqi forces against Sunni political rivals, as in an August 2008 incident in which Maliki ordered the elite Iraqi Special Operations Forces to raid the Diyala provincial government office. Maliki's troops killed the Sunni governor's secretary in the process of arresting a Sunni provincial council member and the Sunni president of Diyala University.

THE "X FACTOR" AND THE BACKLASH AGAINST SECTARIANISM

Nevertheless, long before Maliki ordered the foray into Diyala, the steam had begun to leak out of the sectarian cleansing campaign, for a handful of reasons. Most visibly, the surge of U.S. and Iraqi forces in 2007 had enabled the stationing of troops directly on central Iraq's sectarian fault lines, including in the mixed-sect Baghdad neighborhoods that had been the sectarian battlegrounds of 2006. For more than two years, Shia and Sunni death squads had roamed the Baghdad region with near impunity, but the deployment of more than a hundred seventy thousand additional Iraqi and American troops in 2007 was gradually filling the security vacuum, making it more difficult for death squads to move freely, particularly between the two sides of the city.

At the same time, senior Interior Ministry officials had begun to rein in the Badr-Sadrist elements that had wreaked havoc in 2005–06. After ISCI's Bayan Jabr had been reassigned from the Interior Ministry to the Finance Ministry in November 2006, his successor, the independent Shia politician Jawad Bolani, had set out to sideline quietly those officials most closely associated with the sectarian killing. Problematic officers, including Engineer Ahmed, were marginalized by a process Iraqis call "freezing": promoting or reassigning troublesome officials into positions with imposing names but no real authority.

Along with these changes in the security posture, Iraqis in 2007 were experiencing a deeper undercurrent of popular discontent with the sectarian cleansing, an emotional trend harder to discern than the security presence on the street but just as important—a mood change that one former American official visiting Iraq in late 2007 dubbed the "X factor."

Three iconic events in mid-2007 captured the mood of an Iraqi populace that was seemingly ready to embrace a cross-sectarian agenda wherever one could be found. At the end of March, a young Iraqi woman named Shada Hassoun won by a landslide the Beirut-based singing competition "Star Academy," a wildly popular Arabic version of "Pop Idol" that drew a huge viewing audience across the Arab world. Hassoun received millions of phone-in votes from across Iraq after a final performance of the traditional song "Baghdad" during which she had draped herself with an Iraqi flag. The effect on the war-ravaged Iraqis was astonishing, with street celebrations and nonstop television coverage throughout the country (including Kurdistan), all parts of which claimed her as their own "Daughter of Mesopotamia" since she had refused throughout the singing contest to reveal her family's sect or ethnicity.

The popular euphoria that had greeted Hassoun rose even higher in July, when the Iraqi national soccer team—a club whose practice schedule had often been disrupted by car bombs—shocked the region by winning Iraq's first-ever Asian Cup with a dramatic 1–0 victory over Saudi Arabia viewed by a TV audience of half a billion. In every Iraqi city, jubilant crowds poured into the streets to dance and fire celebratory gunfire, with hundreds of thousands celebrating in Baghdad alone. Iraqi media were quick to note that the team's winning goal had been a three-man play involving a Kurd, a Sunni, and a Shiite. In the popular Iraqi imagination, the victory was taken as a metaphor for the Iraqi war, with a cross-sectarian Iraqi team turning back a challenge from the "Wahhabi" footballers from Saudi Arabia.

Unexpected as it was for western troops and officials, the Iraqi soccer victory created a significant enough popular response to produce a political effect and demonstrate that the seemingly ascendant sectarian militant groups were out of step with the popular mood. It was against this backdrop that Muqtada Sadr's Jaysh al-Mahdi prompted a nationwide backlash less than a month later when they provoked a gunfight outside the Imam Hussein mosque in Karbala, the holiest shrine in Shia Islam. Horrified Iraqis watched footage of a shootout in which Sadr's men exchanged fire with the mosque's uniformed, ISCI-affiliated police force, resulting in the deaths of at least fifty people, including dozens of pilgrims who had been caught in the crossfire. The fighting spilled over later in the day as Sadrists and ISCI followers faced off in Baghdad, and the crisis threatened to escalate into a full-blown intra-Shia turf war. Prime Minister Maliki was quick to respond, personally leading a convoy of security personnel the following morning from Baghdad to Karbala, where he imposed a curfew, arrested more than a hundred Sadrists, and sent home the hundreds of thousands of pilgrims who had come to celebrate the birthday of the twelfth imam.

The Jaysh al-Mahdi shootout fiasco gave Iraqis the impression that a militia whose original raison d'être was to protect pilgrims had degenerated into a rabble that was actually murdering them, and the danger to the Sadrists' reputation and political position was acute. Two days after the fighting in Karbala, Sadr attempted damage control by blaming rogue elements within the militia for the killings and announcing that he would freeze the Jaysh al-Mahdi's activities for six months in order to bring it back under control.

THE CLEANSING OF BAGHDAD: A COORDINATED STRATEGY?

The Shia civil war of early 2008, the concurrent Sunni Awakening, the vast expansion of Iraqi and U.S. security forces in Iraqi neighborhoods, the sidelining of the worst sectarians in the security ministries, and the popular revulsion against sectarian militias all signaled the dramatic slowdown of the sectarian cleansing in greater Baghdad in mid-2008. These developments halted the advance of the "cleansing line" in west Baghdad and froze the sectarian arrangement of the city in place. Some outside observers have since claimed that the sectarian cleansing ended because there were no further mixed-sect neighborhoods to cleanse—that the sectarian fire had burned itself out. But this argument is belied by the city map, where sectarian fault lines abounded even after the killing largely stopped in 2008. The Shia sectarians who had attempted to purge west Baghdad of Sunnis stopped short not because there were no Sunnis left to displace, but because they could no longer roam freely through the city killing and threatening the populace with police assistance. The same applies to the Sunni sectarian cleansers, whose attacks against Shia Baghdadis largely ceased not because they were satisfied with the progress of sectarian cleansing, but because massive security operations forced them to move their bases of operation far outside the city and its surrounding belts.

Still, though the sectarian cleansing had been halted, it would prove extremely difficult to reverse, especially in those districts in Karkh where sectarian militias had resettled Rusafa families. One incident illustrated the difficulty. In the summer of 2008, the independent parliamentarian Mithal al-Alusi created a sensation by assembling more than a thousand Iraqis who had been displaced and threatening to lead them in convoys to reoccupy their Baghdad homes if the government did not restore them first. Al-Alusi's demonstration prompted an outpouring of public support, but was criticized by the prime minister and other government offiicials who claimed the convoys could create a security threat in the city. Within days of Alusi's demonstration, his own home in Mansour was blown up by assailants who were able to pack it with explosives despite the Iraqi military checkpoint just yards from the house. The west Baghdad home of a female parliamentarian who had joined Alusi in the resettlement initiative was attacked in a similar fashion. Alusi claimed the Iraqi government had staged the attacks to prevent the reversal of the sectarian colonization of Karkh. Whether Maliki and his lieutenants were responsible for the attacks or not, it was certainly true that the Iraqi government ultimately restored few families who had been chased from either Karkh or Rusafa to their original homes, indicating that as Alusi had claimed, the government had little interest in restoring the city's precleansing sectarian balance.

It is difficult to judge how many Sunni Baghdadis were forced from their homes during the worst of the violence between 2005 and 2007. The UN High Commission for Refugees estimated that between February 2006 and October 2007, approximately one million Baghdadis—roughly one-sixth of the city's population—became internally displaced persons, with an additional three hundred thousand displaced persons in the adjacent Diyala province. Clearly these were not all Sunnis; a great many Iraqi Shia, Christians, and Kurds fled their Baghdad homes during the same period, many of them forced to move by Sunni insurgents who were just as eager to cleanse mixed neighborhoods as their Shia counterparts were. But it seems equally clear that the brunt of the displacement was born by Sunni-majority Karkh, where U.S. troops in 2007 estimated Mansour and other Sunni-majority neighborhoods had a vacancy rate of between 40 and 60 percent.

It is also clear that the Shia sectarians of Baghdad enjoyed government assistance in ways Sunni sectarians did not. The dramatic acceleration in forced displacement in Baghdad and its surroundings after the Samarra bombing in February 2006 strongly indicates the existence of a coordinated campaign. A substantial number of Shia politicians, officials, and security force members took part in pushing Sunnis out of west Baghdad—a campaign so vast that it defies belief to label it something other than a deliberately planned strategy by Iraq's most senior Shia political leaders. Asked about the Iraqi political class' responsibility for the cleansing, a Dawa Party ally perhaps summed it up best when he sadly conceded to U.S. officers, "It is our great shame."

Between 2003 and 2007, the Iraqi Shia supremacists succeeded in their aim of rendering Baghdad, for the first time, a Shia city—a transformation the Iraqi Sunnis would neither accept nor forgive.

CHAPTER FIVE

The Sunni Chauvinists

T HE SHIA SUPREMACISTS' calculated campaign to install a permanent Shia ascendancy in Baghdad was not the only sectarian project launched after Saddam's fall in 2003. Shia supremacism was matched by a harsh Sunni chauvinism that had grown out of the Sunni Islamic movement and its interaction with the Baathist regime. As the Iraqi Shia parties gained ground in the post-Saddam political order, Sunni chauvinists began to wage war on the new Iraqi government and on the Iraqi Shia population, hoping to terrorize the Shia back into subservience and to awaken the Sunni Arab world to the cosmic war against Shiism.

The story of how the Iraqi Sunni community that had overwhelmingly embraced secular nationalism from the 1950s to '80s came to be dominated by militant Islamists after 2003 is a study in strange bedfellowship. Initially, Sunni Islamists and Saddamists fought one another fiercely, with the Baathist regime repressing the Sunni Islamist movement in the 1970s and '80s just as harshly as it repressed Dawa. But in the early 1990s, Saddam performed an about-face, embracing the Sunni Islamists as part of a campaign to shore up his flagging state. The result was a strain of state-sponsored Salafism that would eventually underpin the brutal Sunni insurgency of 2003–11, bring about the infusion of Al Qaeda in Iraq, and ignite a devastating sectarian civil war.

ROOTS OF THE SUNNI ISLAMIC MOVEMENT

Like their Shia counterparts, Iraq's Sunni clerics were alarmed by
the spread of atheistic communism in the 1950s. Founded in 1959,
the Iraqi Islamic Party was the Iraqi Muslim Brotherhood's political response to the Iraqi Communist Party and the leftist regime
of Abd al-Karim Qasim. The Islamic Party was initially cross-
sectarian, with Shia members among its political officers. In its first
foray into politics, the party was highly critical of the Qasim regime,
and Qasim quickly proscribed it. For the duration of Qasim's rule,
Islamic Party members continued their work in secret, focusing
mainly on education on moral values rather than political activism.

After Qasim's assassination in 1963, the new Arab nationalist
regime of the Arif brothers lifted the constraints Qasim had placed
on the Islamic movement, enabling Islamist parties to flourish
briefly by operating as NGOs, such as the Muslim Brotherhood
Association. The lifting of restrictions allowed Islamist parties to
build a large following among Iraq's secondary school and university students. Among Sunni Islamists, the overall leader of the
movement in this period was Dr. Abdul Karim Zaidan, the chair of
Islamic Law (Sharia) at Baghdad University and the academic
mentor of most of the clerics who would later lead the movement.

This moment of Islamist activism did not last long. When the
Baath seized power in 1968, they cracked down as Qasim had
done, imprisoning the Islamic movement's leaders for several
months and forcing them to agree to conduct no political activities, nor to adopt the Muslim Brotherhood or Iraqi Islamic Party
labels. The curtailing of the movement in 1968 left thousands of
students and young activists leaderless, as Zaidan was restricted
to giving lectures at his college. The movement went into dor-
mancy, with only scattered groups holding secret meetings from
1969 to 1979.

THE SUNNI ISLAMISTS AND THE IRAN-IRAQ WAR

The instability brought on by the Iranian Revolution and the Iran-Iraq War prompted the former Iraqi Islamic Party cadre to renew their political work in 1979–80. These Islamic Party members believed Saddam's war against fellow Muslims in Iran was an immoral project that Iraqi Muslims had a duty to oppose. But conscientious objection was not an option, since the Baathist regime executed deserters and anyone else who evaded military service, sometimes hanging them in front of their homes as their families watched. Nevertheless, the Islamic Party cadre decided to oppose the compulsory military service Saddam had instituted.

As a first step, the Islamic Party cadre held secret leadership elections, convinced that if the Sunni community remained devoid of leadership outside the Baath, it would be destroyed in Saddam's war. The effort was led not by the movement's original leaders, such as Zaidan, but by a second generation of activists who had grown frustrated with the original leaders' passivity. Deciding to bypass Zaidan and other senior clerical leaders, the young activists sent an envoy directly to the Muslim Brotherhood's general secretary Umar al-Tilmisani in Cairo. Arguing that Saddam was sending the Iraqi Muslim community to be crushed in the war, the Islamic Party asked for authorization to form a secret Iraqi Muslim Brotherhood branch to work against Saddam. Tilmisani gave the Iraqis a green light to proceed and promised support from Cairo.

Back in Iraq, the leaders of the secret new Iraqi Muslim Brotherhood began to organize in political and operational cells to work toward the stoppage of the war and a diplomatic solution to the enduring Iraq-Iran dispute. In short order, the party had spread throughout wartime Iraq, with thriving branches not just in the north, but also in the southern regions of Basra, Amara, Kut, Nasiriyah, Babil, and Diwaniyah. The party quietly worked with other opposition groups, including the Dawa Party, but report-edly declined Dawa's offer to conduct joint militant operations against the Baath, because Brotherhood leaders considered them-selves committed to evolutionary social change rather than politi-cal revolution.

Instead, the Brotherhood formed an underground network to evacuate deserters and draft evaders to safe havens in Kurdistan, taking care to give each cell only a limited knowledge of the net-work's full extent. Nevertheless, many of the Brotherhood's mem-bers were caught while engaged in these activities and executed, though because of the network's secrecy it is impossible to know how many. The Brotherhood generally eluded detection until 1986–87, when the regime's intelligence services uncovered and rolled up the entire network, imprisoning most of the party's oper-atives in Abu Ghraib and executing dozens, if not hundreds, of them, by one senior Muslim Brotherhood leader's estimate. Sad-dam was reportedly shocked to discover that several thousand Muslim Brotherhood members had been working underground against the regime for years.

Though most Brotherhood operatives had been sentenced to death, many in Abu Ghraib had their sentences commuted to twenty years, and were eventually released after only three years when Saddam granted a general amnesty on the eve of war with the United States in 1990–91. (The presidential amnesty granted by Saddam ironically excluded "the criminal Jalal Talabani.") After the release, senior Muslim Brotherhood leader Adnan al-Dulaimi worked to reassemble the remnants of the movement. Between 1988 and 1991, Saddam had announced that he would allow the formation of other political parties than the Baath, but the Islamic movement members sensed a trap and did not take up Saddam's offer. Dulaimi and his colleagues instead formed a secret Iraqi Islamic Party organization in Baghdad in 1991–92, but Dulaimi's movements were tracked constantly by Iraqi intelligence, and he eventually fled to Jordan in 1992. His departure left Iraq's Muslim Brotherhood leaderless again, at precisely the moment Saddam was deciding to take over leadership of the Islamic movement himself.

SADDAM'S FAITH CAMPAIGN AND THE PROMOTION OF SALAFISM

In the wake of his war with the United States over Kuwait and the large-scale uprisings that followed, Saddam sought means to shore up his regime against the pressure of external sanctions and internal threats. Accordingly, he initiated an "Islamic Faith Campaign" designed to gain support for the regime from influential mosques and religious leaders. Though Saddam did not formally kick off the campaign until June 1993, there were earlier signs that he was adopting an Islamic veneer to his secular regime. Immediately following the Iraqis' expulsion from Kuwait in 1991, Saddam had added the phrase "God is Great" to the Iraqi flag and had even made attempts to portray the decidedly secular Baathist movement as having always been grounded in Islam—such as his dubious claim that the original founder of the Baath, the Syrian Christian Michel Aflaq, had converted to Islam on his deathbed.

To lead this Faith Campaign, Saddam appointed his second-in-command, Izzat Ibrahim al-Douri. With Saddam's blessing, al-Douri began to organize tribal and religious groups and sponsor their pilgrims on the *hajj*. He also sponsored select Iraqi imams, giving them money, cars, and property and building mosques for them, while exempting from taxes any businessmen who agreed to build mosques of their own. This proliferation of mosques allowed the Islamic movement to flourish, as did the regime's lifting of security observation of the Islamic movement's leaders. As one religious leader later observed, "Our movement worked mainly in mosques, and without them we would have suffocated."

In his Faith Campaign, Saddam chose to mainly promote Salafi Islam in order to develop Salafism as an alternative to the Muslim Brotherhood, whom Saddam considered a threat to his rule. Saddam sent Baathist intelligence officers and political officers to pray and study in the new mosques and take lectures from Islamic scholars such as Muhsin Abdul Hamid, even though these officers were theoretically trained in Baathist ideology. Saddam believed he was sending into the Islamic schools committed Baathists who would remain loyal as they established a foothold in the mosques from which the regime could then monitor or manipulate the Islamist movement. In actuality, the reverse happened. Most of the officers who were sent to the mosques were not deeply committed to Baathism by that point, and as they encountered Salafi teachings many became more loyal to Salafism than to Saddam. Baathist officers who had been involved in the regime's human rights abuses were particularly attracted to the Islamic teaching of *yetoob*, the idea of confessing one's crimes to God and receiving absolution for them.

Not everyone in Saddam's inner circle believed the regime's embrace of Islamists was wise. Saddam's half-brother Barzan al-Tikriti, perhaps the third-most-powerful man in the regime, worried that Saddam's strategy might backfire. In a private journal entry in 2000, al-Tikriti recorded that he had met with Saddam to warn him—presciently, as it turned out—that an embrace of the Sunni Islamists would polarize the country on sectarian lines by raising Shia fears, while alienating other Arab regimes in the region. "The alliance with the religious trends . . . is a true mistake because the Ba'th texture and modern thinking cannot be married to the religious thinking," Barzan wrote, adding, "I told the president of the danger of alliance with the religious trend." He also warned Saddam that the Salafis the Baath were sponsoring would eventually turn against them and attempt to topple the regime.

There were signs that Barzan's concerns were well founded. By the late 1990s, the proliferation of Salafism had empowered not just Salafi regime loyalists, but also "pure" Salafis who had long opposed the Baath. By the late 1990s, some of these anti-Baathist Salafis were conducting a low-level terrorist campaign against the regime that included car bombings and assassinations similar to those that became so common in Iraq after 2003. The "pure" Salafis' resort to violence highlighted a key ideological difference between the Salafis and the Muslim Brothers whom Saddam had viewed as the more threatening. The Egyptian Muslim Brotherhood had formally dissolved its armed wing after the revolution of 1952, declaring itself a nonviolent organization thereafter. Many Salafis, by contrast, had never disavowed violence, and the Baathists who became Salafis would see no religious grounds against political violence when war came to Iraq in 2003. As one senior Iraqi Muslim Brotherhood member observed, "When the Salafis entered politics, they entered with guns."

In the short term, this Salafi proclivity for violence seemed to serve the Baathist state's ends. Iraqi Muslim Brotherhood members believed Saddam and Izzat al-Douri had focused on forming Baathist-Salafi organizations to prepare for Islamist resistance in the eventuality that the regime should fall to either an internal uprising or an external attack from the United States or Iran. Members of these regime-sponsored militant groups could observe Baathist ideology and Salafi ideology at the same time, making cross-membership easy.

The Muslim Brotherhood's ideology, by contrast, was mutually exclusive with that of the Baath Party, meaning that there was little cross-membership between the two. One prominent case illustrated this divide. Perhaps the most notable Muslim Brotherhood leader to keep his distance from Izzat al-Douri and the new Baathist Islamists was Harith al-Dhari, a former doctoral student of Abdul Karim Zaidan who by the 1990s had become the chair of Hadith studies in Baghdad University's Islamic Law college, where Zaidan was chair of Islamic Law. Dhari was nationally known because his grandfather had helped spark the famous 1920 Iraqi revolt against British rule by murdering the well-known British political officer Colonel Gerard Leachman near Fallujah. Considered to be from a family of national heroes, Dhari did not deign to accept al-Douri's largess. As a result, Saddam's intelligence services shadowed him constantly, eventually forcing him to move to the Gulf countries, from which he did not return until 2004.

The Muslim Brotherhood was not alone in finding itself at odds with Salafi ideology during Saddam's Faith Campaign. Though he had been tasked to lead the campaign that promoted Salafism, Izzat al-Douri himself was a Sufi, a member of the sect known in western paralance as dervishes and in Ottoman parlance as Naqshbandis. Located mainly in Iraq's northern regions (and with a sizable contingent in Anbar), the Sufis had a centuries-long tradition of peaceful Islamic mysticism, but under al-Douri's leadership during the Faith Campaign, the groundwork was laid for them to join Salafis in future regime-sponsored resistance. Al-Douri fostered a fraternity of Sufi military and intelligence officers inside the Baathist regime, a parallel network to the Baathist Salafis the regime had created. The Sufis' unorthodox practices made them and Izzat al-Douri himself objects of hatred among the new Baathist Salafis. In the Salafi mosques to which the regime had sent them, many Baathist officers were being taught that Douri's Sufism amounted to an abhorrent paganism.

After Saddam's Fall: The Baathist Salafi Resistance

When Saddam's regime fell in April 2003, Iraqi Sunnis did not immediately take up arms against the invading Coalition armies. "We were in shock, and Baghdad was in chaos," one Sunni explained, "so everyone returned to his tribe for security." Across the north, including Saddam's home territory, Sunni leaders waited to see what the Americans intended for them. "At first no one fought the Americans; not the Baath, not the army officers, and not the tribes," a northern Sunni related. "But when the Americans formed the Governing Council [in July 2003] with thirteen Shia and only a few Sunnis, people began to say, 'The Americans mean to give the country to the Shia,' and then they began to fight, and the tribes began to let Al Qaeda in."

As the Sunnis began to take up arms, many Baathist Salafi officers whom Saddam had sent to the mosques quickly formed Islamic resistance groups. In doing so, these officers acted consistently with a Baath Party directive Saddam had issued in January 2003 instructing Baathist networks throughout the country to prepare for the chance that a limited U.S.-led attack against the regime would spark internal uprisings across Iraq, as had been the case in 1991. Labeled an "emergency plan," the directive held that if "God forbid[,] the Iraqi Command falls to the coalition forces: American, British and Zionist," then local Baath Party branches should destroy their offices, disperse, and conduct sabotage against public infrastructure. The plan delegated authority to the local branches to conduct security operations, instructing them to "recuit dependable sources" inside the Najaf *hawza*, to infiltrate Islamist parties, and to "make friendly relations" with returning expatriates, after which the Baathists should "buy stolen weapons from the streets" and "assassinate clergies in the Mosques." In the directive, the regime seemed to anticipate the important role the *marjaiyyah* and expatriate ayatollahs such as SCIRI's Muhammad Baqir Hakim could play in the aftermath of regime change, and the regime's simple prescription was to assassinate the clerics before they could wield their influence.

Saddam and his inner circle probably did not intend to organize for insurgency against a U.S.-led occupation force, because even on the eve of the invasion Saddam miscalculated that the United States would not actually invade. Throughout the pre-invasion crisis, the Iraqi leader assured his lieutenants that the UN Security Council would be able to block the United States from a ground invasion. Instead, the January 2003 directive was most likely meant to lay the groundwork for a counterinsurgency campaign to secure the regime against other Iraqis in a 1991-style uprising. Yet by decentralizing authority, instructing local Baathists to procure weapons, and ordering sabotage operations and assassinations, Saddam was inadvertently equipping his followers to conduct a large-scale insurgency. Within months of Saddam's fall, militant Baathist-Salafi groups began an insurgency against U.S. troops and the new Iraqi government. These groups were formed around a core of Salafi-educated former regime officials, with strong ties to the senior regime officials who fled to Syria after regime change. As a result, the Iraqi Salafi insurgent movement received financial and material support from the Syrian Baathist regime of Bashar al-Assad.

THE BAATHIST INSURGENCY AND SYRIA'S ASSAD REGIME

From its beginning in 2003, the Baathist-Salafi insurgency in Iraq was bolstered by support from Syria, both from the remnants of Saddam's regime in exile and from the decidedly non-Salafi Alawite regime. The top surviving leaders in Saddam's regime, headed by Izzat al-Douri, sought refuge with the Assad regime in the weeks following the fall of Baghdad. That they should do so was a supreme irony. Though the Iraqi and Syrian Baath had grown from the same movement founded by pan-Arab socialists, the two parties had by the 1970s become mortal enemies, both pressing counter-claims to regional Baathist leadership. In Damascus, Hafez al-Assad had labeled his regime the rightful government of both Syria and Iraq, and his Syrian Baath Party structure included an Iraqi wing comprised of Iraqi Baathists who opposed Saddam. In Baghdad, Saddam had returned the favor by maintaining a Syrian branch of his own Iraqi Baath Party and by sheltering the actual founder of the Syrian Baath, Michel Aflaq, as well as by constantly hatching unrealistic schemes to topple Assad and replace him with Syrian Saddamists. In 1982, a few months after Assad's famous crackdown against the Muslim Brotherhood in Hama, Saddam's senior lieutenant Tariq Aziz even suggested that the Iraqi regime should support a Muslim Brotherhood-led government in Damascus if it meant getting rid of the Assad regime. (That Tariq Aziz himself was Christian demonstrates the utter cynicism of the protagonists caught up in this political play.)

Against this backdrop, the Syrian Baath must have discerned a golden opportunity when al-Douri and the defeated Saddamists arrived in Damascus as supplicants in 2003. According to a former Syrian regime senior official, Douri arrived with a fantastic proposal that the two Baathist regimes should merge into one, with himself and Bashar in co-command, and should fight together to expel the U.S. military from Iraq. The offer amounted to a suggestion that Bashar should share his state power with former enemies who had lost their own. Unsurprisingly, Bashar had something else in mind: that the weakened Iraqi Baath should be absorbed into the Syrian Baath Party's existing structure, subordinated to the previously irrelevant Iraqi wing his father had created around obscure Iraqi Baathists. In doing so, Bashar could realize his father's dream of establishing Syrian supremacy over the regional Baath.

Within Syria, the Assad regime closely monitored and sometimes directed or curtailed the activities of the Iraqi Salafi insurgent groups, often through the Syrian military intelligence apparatus headed by Bashar al-Assad's brother-in-law Assef Shawkat. The Assads' position toward all Iraqi insurgent groups based in Syria was that operations directed into Iraq were permissible, but only if the Syrian regime were kept fully informed. As one former regime official put it, "For the regime to be aware of the militants' activities was the norm, and the regime only cracked down on those who tried to conduct operations without the regime's knowledge." Throughout the course of the Iraq war, the Syrian regime's strategic and operational decisions regarding support for the Iraqi insurgency were made by Bashar al-Assad himself. "Anyone who thinks otherwise," said a former Syrian official in 2012, "does not understand how our regime worked."

Nonetheless, for seven years after Saddam's fall, the Assad regime repeatedly and disingenuously claimed that any support flowing to the Iraqi insurgency from Syria was an inadvertent matter of porous borders rather than a formal Syrian regime policy.

THE SALAFI-SUFI MARRIAGE OF CONVENIENCE

Though spurned by Bashar al-Assad, Izzat al-Douri was not without means and an insurgent network of his own. For some time after Saddam's fall, Douri and his loyalists in Syria and elsewhere in the Arab world had a large quantity of the former regime's hidden cash reserves at their disposal, some of which likely went to support the newly organized insurgent groups drawn from Douri's prewar Sufi network. From the earliest days of the Salafi insurgency, Sufi militants also fought against U.S. troops and the new Iraqi government, especially in the upper Tigris valley from which Douri hailed and in Fallujah. The most prominent Sufi insurgent group was the Jaysh al-Rijal al-Tariq al-Naqshbandi (JRTN), or "Naqshbandi army," a highly effective collection of Baathist Sufis who retained close ties to Douri throughout the war. Former Iraqi insurgents have described the Naqshbandi army as the militant arm of Douri's wing of the Baath party, and have also attributed whatever political strength Douri enjoys to the Naqshbandis' militant power.

In doctrinal terms, the Salafi insurgents and Al Qaeda considered Sufis to be just as heretical as the Shia. But in the post-Saddam insurgency, this doctrinal schism was papered over by the fact that the Salafi and Sufi insurgents had both adopted a rejectionist stance toward the U.S.-sponsored political process, and this shared objective enabled the two otherwise hostile sects to enter a marriage of convenience and cooperate in militant activities.

THE INSURGENCY AND THE 2005 ELECTIONS

In 2004, Harith al-Dhari returned to Iraq from the Persian Gulf, where he had been in exile since running afoul of the Baathist regime in the mid-1990s. He arrived at a key point for the Iraqi Muslim Brotherhood, which was split by the question of whether to join the more extreme Salafis who had gone into insurgency or to work within the political process the U.S.-led coalition had set in motion. Dhari and other non-Salafi Sunni clerics had already formed a political Islamic front, the Association of Muslim Scholars (AMS), against the international occupation in April 2003, and upon his return to Iraq, Dhari and the association became increasingly vocal critics of the U.S. military presence. In early 2004, Dhari and his association colleagues opted to covertly join the insurgency, despite the Brotherhood's previous distaste for violence. From their compounds in Anbar or Jordan, Dhari's own son and nephew became key leaders in this Muslim Brotherhood–associated insurgency, helping to provision militant groups and plan attacks.

With the Baathist Salafis, "pure Salafis," Baathist Sufis, and a portion of the Muslim Brotherhood lined up in the insurgency against the U.S.-sponsored political process, the elections slated for January 2005 became a critical test of the competing sides' strength. The prelude to the elections had been marked by large-scale battles in Fallujah and Mosul, where U.S. and Iraqi troops had aimed to break the insurgent hold on Anbar and Ninewa to allow voting to proceed in Iraq's two largest Sunni provinces. In the second week of November, U.S. troops had begun to drive the insurgents out of Fallujah, only to see them appear in Mosul at almost exactly the same time and overrun virtually all the city's security forces in the space of twenty-four hours. Though a combined U.S. and Iraqi force retook Mosul within weeks, the rejectionist insurgents had demonstrated their power, and the vast majority of Sunni voters in Anbar and Ninewa followed the insurgents' instructions to boycott the voting of January 2005. The turnout in Sunni-majority Ninewa was less than 15 percent, while in Anbar it was below 1 percent.

The boycott proved to be a major blunder by the Sunni rejectionists, who had calculated that the political process would collapse without their participation. They soon realized that ceding provincial government and parliamentary representation was a mistake. As the new parliament and an Iraqi government formed under the premiership of Ibrahim al-Jaafari in the spring of 2005, the rejectionists were dismayed to find themselves unable to halt the drafting of a new federal constitution, which, if activated, would mean the end of the unitary state the rejectionists had aimed to preserve. Under these conditions, all but the most extreme Sunni insurgent groups decided to attempt in the political arena what had failed on the battlefield, and to allow the constitutional referendum of October 2005 and the parliamentary voting of December 2005 to go forward with full Sunni participation. Western observers hailed the high Sunni turnout of December 2005 as a sign that the Sunni community had made an about-face since January and had accepted the legitimacy of the political process. In fact, the opposite was about to take place. In joining the voting, the Sunni rejectionist groups had actually presumed that they would win the elections, since they operated on a badly mistaken assumption that Sunnis were a majority or plurality of the population. When the outcome of the December election went decisively against them and a Shia Islamist bloc gained almost half the parliament, the Sunni rejectionists apparently decided to return to violence, concluding that the political process was not a viable route to securing what they considered their rightful share of power, well before the iconic bombing of the al-Askari shrine in Samarra that has often been credited with sparking Iraq's sectarian civil war.

THE SUNNI INSURGENCY AND AL QAEDA IN IRAQ

The Sunni insurgents' decision to resume their war against the new Iraqi government eventually led to Al Qaeda's dominance of the insurgency. Al Qaeda's role in the Sunni insurgency was a secondary one before 2005. Hard-pressed in the battles of Fallujah and Mosul in 2004, the native Sunni insurgent groups had initially welcomed Al Qaeda's assistance, viewing the foreign mujahideen coming into the country as timely reinforcements.

Several formidable allies came to the Sunni insurgency with Al Qaeda, including the non-Baathist Salafi militant groups Ansar al-Islam and Ansar al-Sunna, both of which had operated in northern Iraq before 2003. Ansar al-Islam had been built around a core of Kurdish Salafi militants who had fought alongside the Taliban in Afghanistan before relocating to the mountains of Iraqi Kurdistan in 2001–02. Abu Musab al-Zarqawi had brought his own group of Salafi mujahideen, called *Tawhid wa al-Jihad* ("Monotheism and Holy War"), from Afghanistan to Ansar al-Islam's Kurdish enclave at the same time. Not until October 2004 did Zarqawi rename his group Al Qaeda in Iraq and pledge allegiance to Osama bin Laden.

Zarqawi and his allies considered themselves to be fighting a global war to reestablish the universal caliphate rather than a limited campaign to liberate Iraq. In this important respect they were far different from the vast majority of Iraqi Salafi insurgents, who were nationalists who viewed Al Qaeda and its cosmic aims with some distrust. Many Iraqi Islamists, especially the Muslim Brotherhood, were also uncomfortable with Zarqawi's indiscriminate attacks against the Iraqi Shia, by which he meant to incite a sectarian civil war that the Sunni Islamists did not necessarily want. Zarqawi's aims to start a broad regional war against the Shia had been obvious from an early stage; his own father-in-law, in fact, had been the suicide bomber who killed Muhammad Baqir al-Hakim and more than one hundred others in Najaf in August 2003. In a letter intercepted in February 2004, Zarqawi indicated his desire to draw the Shia into civil war as a means of mobilizing the Sunnis:

> The solution that we see, and God the Exalted knows better, is for us to drag the Shi'a into the battle because this is the only way to prolong the fighting between us and the infidels.

... [T]he Shia have declared a secret war against the people of Islam. They are the proximate, dangerous enemy of the Sunnis, even if the Americans are also an archenemy.... Our fighting against the Shia is a way to drag the [Islamic] nation into battle.

Nevertheless, the native Iraqi insurgents found it expedient to work with Zarqawi in a marriage of convenience in 2004–05.

One Foot in Government, One Foot in the Insurgency

As the Sunni rejectionists returned to the battlefield in December 2005, a number of Sunnis who had joined the political process worked to subvert it from within, essentially serving the new government by day and the insurgency by night. These subversives included three of the four most senior Sunni politicians in the country, Khalaf Ulayan, Mahmoud al-Mashhadani, and Adnan al-Dulaimi.

Khalaf Ulayan, a member of the Dulaim tribe from Anbar, had served as a senior officer in Saddam's army. In 2005, he became one of three leaders, along with Adnan Dulaimi and Vice President Tariq al-Hashemi, of Tawafuq, the parliamentary coalition of Sunni Islamist parties considered to represent most of the Sunni community. But he was also a Salafi insurgent. Ulayan had been one of the many Baathist officers to become a Salafi during Saddam's Faith Campaign, and as the Baathist-Salafis went to war in 2003 he had become a senior commander in the Salafi resistance. For several years, Ulayan covertly fought against the Iraqi government at the same time that his party was in it.

In the Salafi insurgent movement, Baathist officers like Ulayan joined with "pure" non-Baathist Salafis to form a formidable

network. Ulayan's most significant "pure" Salafi comrade was
Mahmoud Mashhadani, a former Islamist militant who had been
imprisoned for conducting armed attacks against the Baath in
the 1990s. Like Ulayan, Mashhadani was a government official
and an insurgent at the same time. Technically, Mashhadani was
the government's most senior Sunni leader, having been elected
speaker of parliament in April 2006. According to one member
of Iraq's Sunni Islamic movement, a year after becoming speaker
Mashhadani allegedly, and bizarrely, colluded with Ulayan to
carry out a terrorist attack against his own parliament building
in April 2007, in which a suicide bomber was able to enter the
building supposedly using credentials from Mashhadani's entourage before detonating a bomb that killed eight people. The plot
also may have involved the parliamentarian Nasir al-Janabi, a
Sufi who was secretly a senior figure in Izzat al-Douri's Naqshbandi army and who later fled Iraq ahead of charges of involvement in a massacre of Shiites in Babil province.

Along with the Salafis and Sufis, some Iraqi Muslim Brotherhood members also acted as militants within the system, reflecting
the split between militant and non-militant wings of the Muslim
Brotherhood that had emerged in 2004. Adnan al-Dulaimi, the
Muslim Brotherhood leader who had patched together the movement's members after their release from Saddam's jails in 1991,
was elected to parliament in 2005 as head of the Tawafuq bloc.
But from this position, he allegedly helped to direct insurgent
attacks and assassinations designed to thwart the political process.
The most notable of these was a February 2005 attack in Baghdad
in which assassins narrowly missed independent Sunni politician
Mithal al-Alusi, killing Alusi's two sons instead. For Dulaimi,
insurgency was a family affair: in 2007, one of his sons was arrested
for assassinating a Sunni Awakening leader, and in the course of
the arrest U.S. troops found two car bombs parked in Dulaimi's

driveway in the Green Zone. In 2008, another of Dulaimi's sons was arrested while emplacing a roadside bomb.

These examples of senior leaders of the Iraqi Islamist groups represent only the Baghdad-based manifestation of the insurgents' subversion of the government from within. In the Sunni-majority provinces, there were far more numerous examples of insurgents who were able to acquire positions at all levels of local Iraqi government while continuing to carry out insurgent and terrorist operations against the government they had joined.

AL QAEDA'S OVERREACH

The native Iraqi insurgency that was subverting the political process from within had initially welcomed Al Qaeda and its pipeline of mujahideen from throughout the Arab world as useful allies in its difficult battle against the U.S. military and the new government. But by late 2005, the guest-worker insurgents had come to the verge of overwhelming their hosts.

The Iraqi insurgents had underestimated the strength of the regional Salafi network that fed Al Qaeda with great quantities of fighters and cash from the Persian Gulf, Levant, and North Africa. Al Qaeda's Syria-based facilitation network was capable of pushing large numbers of mujahideen across the porous Syrian-Iraqi border. With relative ease, foreign suicide bombers and fighters could move from the Damascus airport through a network of safehouses and friendly Salafi mosques to the Iraqi frontier, all under the eyes of supportive or bribeable Syrian officials. Sunni tribes who spanned the Iraq-Syria border also helped mujahideen move into Iraq just as they had smuggled goods and people of all kinds along the routes into Anbar and Ninewa for centuries. This ancient smuggling trade thrived in the absence of a strong Iraqi border security force after the Baathist regime's collapse in 2003.

The trove of Al Qaeda records captured by U.S. troops at the ancient town of Sinjar in Ninewa province in September 2007 casts light on this flow of Al Qaeda fighters. In the one-year period from August 2006 to August 2007, Al Qaeda documented almost seven hundred mujahideen passing through western Ninewa alone, a heavy enough flow to prompt Al Qaeda to appoint a "Border Emir" to supervise their passage. At its height in early 2007, this "Border Emirate" ushered more than a hundred twenty fighters a month from Syria to the front lines in Iraq. From the Sinjar area most of these fighters would make their way to the Tigris valley to be directed by Al Qaeda commanders against mainly Kurdish, Shia, or American targets.

Along with foreign manpower, Zarqawi and his Al Qaeda commanders enjoyed the advantage of foreign funding, which enabled them to outspend native Iraqi groups that were often cash-strapped in the blighted Iraqi economy of the post-Saddam years. One Sunni insurgent leader south of Baghdad told a typical story in 2008 when he explained that "Al Qaeda came in 2005 and hired all the young men away" from local insurgent commanders, adding that in doing so "Al Qaeda turned a nationalist insurgency into a sectarian one."

REGIONALIZATION OF THE IRAQ JIHAD

The flow of Al Qaeda mujahideen was not a one-way matter. As Zarqawi was attempting to expand the Iraqi insurgency into a sectarian civil war in 2005, he was also attempting to open new fronts outside Iraq. He focused particularly on exporting the Iraq jihad to his home country of Jordan, where he had once been imprisoned for attempting to start a terror campaign before the Iraq war. In November 2005, Zarqawi dispatched suicide operatives who bombed three western-owned hotels in Amman, killing more than sixty people, including dozens of wedding guests and the Hollywood producer Moustapha Akkad, who had once made a popular movie about early Islam starring Anthony Quinn. The bombings horrified Jordanians and produced a popular backlash that temporarily derailed Zarqawi's hopes. A poll taken a few weeks after the bombing showed that the percentage of Jordanians who viewed Al Qaeda in Iraq as a "legitimate resistance group" had plummeted from 67 to 20 percent.

Elsewhere Al Qaeda veterans of the Iraq jihad were returning to their home countries with the aim of establishing Al Qaeda franchises of their own. In Lebanon, Al Qaeda returnees carried out a string of bombings in Beirut and Sidon in early 2006, briefly declaring themselves "Al Qaeda fil Bilad ash-Sham" before much of their network was rounded up by Lebanese authorities. The support base for Lebanese mujahideen endured, however, particularly among the Sunni Salafis of Tripoli in northern Lebanon, who would later fight the Assad regime in nearby Hams. Al Qaeda supporters could also be found among the radicalized residents of Palestinian refugee camps, such as Ain el-Hilweh in southern Lebanon and Nahr al-Barid in the north. Both camps contained recruiters for Al Qaeda in Iraq, some of them connected to the Fatah al-Islam militant group that fought a pitched battle against the Lebanese Army in the rubbled Nahr al-Barid in 2007. Al Qaeda was drawing into Iraq, and then feeding back into circulation outside Iraq, a region-wide network of militants who intended to make war every-where between the Mediterranean and the Persian Gulf, far beyond the aims of the Iraqi Sunni insurgents who had begun the jihad in the first place.

THE RIFT WITHIN THE JIHAD

Back in Iraq, Zarqawi's explicit targeting of Shia noncombatants ran increasingly afoul of native insurgent groups who had other priorities in mind. Though many Iraqi Sunni insurgents believed a war against Iranian-backed Shia parties and militias would eventually be necessary, they believed the first order of insurgent business should be the expulsion of the U.S. troops backing the new Iraqi government. Without U.S. military support, many Sunni insurgents believed, the nascent government could be defeated relatively easily and the pre-2003 order restored. Among some Muslim Brotherhood members and even some Salafis, Zarqawi's indiscriminate attacks against the Shia also created a backlash, alienating less extreme Islamists who might otherwise support the insurgency. Even at the height of sectarian tension in Iraq, the Iraqi Salafi insurgents tended to avoid the kind of all-out confrontation with the Shia that Zarqawi was undertaking. Nor did they generally share Zarqawi's affinity for *takfir*, a doctrine formulated by the medieval Sunni extremist Ibn Taimiyyah that held that Islam required believers to actively denounce nonbelievers, or even to kill them. On these points, the moderates were in accord with Osama bin Laden's deputy and later successor, Ayman al-Zawahiri, who from his refuge in Pakistan sent letters to Zarqawi in 2005 urging him to soften his brutality toward the Shia. Wrote Zawahiri:

[M]any of your Muslim admirers amongst the common folk are wondering about your attacks on the Shia. . . . My opinion is that this matter won't be acceptable to the Muslim populace however much you have tried to explain it, and aversion to this will continue.

Among Iraqi Salafi insurgents, distrust of Zarqawi had been building for some time. The naturally paranoid Iraqi insurgents had been astonished when Zarqawi released back to Iran an Iranian diplomat kidnapped in Karbala in October 2004, and many Iraqi Salafis had taken the incident as evidence that Zarqawi was somehow cooperating strategically with the Iranian regime. From that point forward, many Iraqi insurgents interpreted Zarqawi's actions as intended to weaken Iraq on behalf of outside powers by sowing civil strife. By the fall of 2005, the tension between Zarqawi's organization and the main Baathist-Salafi insurgents had intensified to the point of intermittent warfare between them, especially in Mosul.

This fighting between fellow Sunni insurgent groups was about more than a mere turf battle or distrust of foreigners. As argued earlier in this chapter, the Sunni insurgency in 2005 was finding itself split by the political process. Having forced the Sunni boycott in January, native insurgent groups had decided not to block the vote for the referendum of October and the parliamentary elections of December. Since suppressing the Sunni vote had done nothing to stop the political process and writing of a federal constitution, they seem to have reasoned, perhaps the process could be derailed by fully turning out the Sunni vote. As the December polls approached, Zarqawi and Al Qaeda continued to warn that any Iraqis who were "overly active in promoting" the elections would be targeted. But in doing so, Zarqawi was suddenly far out of step with not just the Sunni mainstream, but also the Baathist-Salafi rejectionists who had once been his allies. The high Sunni turnout for the election exposed the fact that Zarqawi's native Iraqi support was slipping. In Ramadi, turnout in December 2005 was approximately 80 percent, after having been only 2 percent in January 2005. Similar turnout changes were registered elsewhere in Anbar and in Ninewa.

Something had to be done to shore up Al Qaeda's popular legitimacy. Zarqawi's solution was the announcement of the Mujahideen Shura Council (MSC), an umbrella group consisting of Al Qaeda and several smaller Salafi insurgent groups, all of which except Al Qaeda were native Iraqi. The council's strategy and operations would ostensibly be directed by a consensus among the groups, with Al Qaeda theoretically just one member of the mainly native insurgent front. In putting an Iraqi face on the Salafi insurgency, Zarqawi and Al Qaeda hoped to insulate themselves from criticism that they were a foreign group with a domineering non-Iraqi leader and a non-Iraqi agenda. For most of 2006, as Iraq slipped into sectarian civil war, Al Qaeda would mask its activities behind the Shura Council, but behind the scenes Zarqawi and his *takfiri* followers would continue the attacks that had caused many Iraqis to turn against them.

Zarqawi and Al Qaeda have often been credited with provoking the sectarian civil war phase of the Iraqi conflict by their iconic bombing of the al-Askaria mosque and its beloved "Golden Dome" in Samarra in February 2006. That attack against one of the most important shrines in Shia Islam, housing the remains of the tenth and eleventh imams, does appear to have precipitated a massive response from Iraq's Shia Islamist militant groups, who greatly accelerated the ongoing sectarian cleansing of greater Baghdad after the mosque was bombed. But the Samarra attack came after, not before, the main Sunni Islamist insurgent groups had restarted the war they had suspended to allow voting in late 2005, and a look at the violence statistics shows that insurgent activity was already rising significantly in the weeks prior to the Samarra attack. The euphoria of the December election had been premature. Outside observers believed the high election turnout indicated that the Sunnis had bought into the political process and that the insurgency was therefore fated to wither on the vine.

But this judgment was based on a reading of the political process rather than its political outcome. Simply put, when Sunni voters did not get the result they wished for at the ballot box, many picked up their weapons again. The fact that Iraqi Sunni insurgents had already opted to restart their war, and that Shia Islamist militants had already opted to carry out the sectarian cleansing of the country's center, explains why Zarqawi's killing by U.S. troops in June 2006 had no appreciable effect on the large-scale sectarian violence underway at the time.

As controversial and divisive as Zarqawi had been inside the Sunni resistance, Al Qaeda's next initiative after his death would prove even more so. In early October 2006, the Mujahideen Shura Council, Zarqawi's thinly disguised tool for asserting control over the Iraqi insurgency, announced that it and a handful of other jihadist groups would form the "Islamic State of Iraq," an emirate meant to be the first Islamic government in post-Saddam Iraq. The Islamic State would be a study in Sunni chauvinism and sectarian partition. It would encompass the Sunni-majority provinces of Anbar (already under extensive Al Qaeda control), Ninewa, and Salahadin, as well as Diyala, where Sunnis were a plurality among sizable Shia and Kurdish minorities. But it would also claim Kirkuk, Baghdad, and portions of Babil and Wasit in the south, where Sunnis were a clearly dwindling minority. Since the Shura Council was little more than an Al Qaeda front, the plan called for a dissection of the country with Al Qaeda ruling everywhere Sunnis lived while leaving the far northeast to the Kurds and the far south to the Shia.

The formation of the Islamic State of Iraq was a strategic error for Al Qaeda. After a year of steadily losing Iraqi popular support, Al Qaeda's leaders hoped the Islamic State would put an Iraqi face on the jihad and attract Iraqi Sunni nationalists to their cause. For Sunni nationalists, even those in the Salafi and Sufi insurgencies, the Islamic State was an unwelcome political competitor. Most former Baathists wanted to restore the Baathist state, not create a new foreign-led Islamic one, while almost all Sunnis viewed with horror the idea that Iraq should be partitioned at all. The desire to thwart partition had, after all, been the reason Sunnis had flocked to the polls in October 2005 to try to vote down the federal constitution.

The announcement of the Islamic State of Iraq also created tension within Al Qaeda's core constituency, the Salafi communities of the Persian Gulf, Levant, and North Africa. Salafi purists who believed they must fight to restore a universal caliphate also believed national states were an abomination that artificially divided God's umma. How, then, could they support the establishment of a national state in Iraq, even if it were an Islamic one? For those Salafis who were willing to entertain the idea of an eventual Islamic state in Iraq, there was also the religious argument that an Islamic state should not be established under occupation.

Backlash

Al Qaeda's actions and politics produced a three-pronged backlash among Iraqi Sunnis, devastating the group that had appeared poised in mid-2005 to become the strongest Sunni force in the country.

The tribal uprising against Al Qaeda in Sunni areas in Iraq has been well documented. In general terms, the Iraqi tribes rebelled against Al Qaeda's heavy-handed tactics and its encroachment on the sources of tribal power, such as control of smuggling and transit trade between Anbar and Jordan. Anbaris also chafed under Al Qaeda's Taliban-style enforcement of strict Islamic rules. The Iraqi tribal areas may have been home to many devout Sunnis, but they tended to be unenthusiastic about the puritanical requirements of

Salafism, which frowned on the rather materialistic lifestyle Iraqi tribal leaders had long enjoyed. By early 2006, Al Qaeda was regularly assassinating Anbari sheikhs who defied Al Qaeda authority, and some Al Qaeda commanders even engendered tribal hostility by demanding the privilege of marrying into tribal families.

The second aspect of the Sunni backlash was the war between Al Qaeda and other Islamist militant groups, especially in the north. The intra-insurgent battle there grew in scale after its first signs in Mosul in the fall of 2005. In early April 2007, Jaish al-Islami, the largest Baathist-Salafi militant group, publicly accused the Islamic State and Al Qaeda of violating Islamic law by killing fellow Muslims and appealed to Osama bin Laden to reassert control over his wayward affiliate.

Beyond these power struggles, there was by mid-2007 a growing popular revulsion at the sectarian violence that the Islamist militants had wrought. Al Qaeda found itself impugned by the same popular outrage the Sadrists encountered after the August 2007 shootout in Karbala. Two days before the massive street celebrations that greeted Iraq's Asian Cup championship victory over Saudi Arabia, similar but smaller celebrations had taken place after Iraq's semifinal victory, but a tone-deaf Al Qaeda had aroused deep popular anger by bombing two victory parties in the streets of Baghdad. The attacks killed fifty soccer fans, including a small boy named Hamza whom the football team dramatically declared to be their martyr-mascot before the final game.

Not all Sunni Iraqi leaders were happy with the backlash against Al Qaeda. From his refuge in Jordan, Harith al-Dhari argued that the Awakening had become an un-Islamic alliance with "occupiers" against fellow Iraqis. "We reject the actions of Al Qaeda," al-Dhari told al-Jazeera television, "but they are still part of us." Ninety percent of Al Qaeda members were Iraqis, Dhari claimed, meaning that "Al Qaeda is of us, and we are with it."

The Amman-based Dhari, however, was out of touch. The popular Iraqi mood was swinging in the opposite direction. In an environment where Al Qaeda relied on the support of Iraqi youths for its local strength, the terrorist group was hurt by its loss of the "coolness factor" in late 2007. It was one thing for young Iraqi Sunnis to support Al Qaeda when the group was apparently winning its war, but quite another when the U.S. military, Iraqi Army, and Awakening councils were proving themselves more powerful in local battles. One police commander in Habbaniyah recounted an illustrative case. Stepping from his home on Christmas Eve, 2007, he had been astonished to find the young men of his neighborhood setting off fireworks, dancing with their girlfriends, and drinking alcohol—all distinctly "Christian" activities that Al Qaeda had banned. The bemused policeman had teased the youths, "You're celebrating like Christians, but last year you were all Al Qaeda!" The young men had laughed, the police officer later recalled, answering, "Al Qaeda? That was last year!"

The appearance of U.S. and Iraqi forces in places that had been security vacuums also dried up another, less recognized pool of Al Qaeda support. One tribal sheikh in a Diyala town that had been under Al Qaeda control in 2007 recalled the following year that the townspeople had been terrorized by the "Al Qaeda kids." Al Qaeda in his area, the sheikh explained, had been essentially street gangs composed of fatherless late-teenage boys (of whom there were many in Iraq after years of war and crackdowns) commanded by a few twenty-year-old "imams" sent from Jordan or Fallujah. When the adult U.S. and Iraqi soldiers had arrived, the Al Qaeda boys had melted away.

These local attitude changes were amplified by a new explicitly anti-Al Qaeda tone in the Iraqi media, where a pall of fear had made news outlets reluctant to criticize Al Qaeda by name before 2007, lest they be targeted for retaliation. By the fall of 2007 that taboo was breaking, as even the Sunni-associated media outlet Sharqiyah was running anti-Al Qaeda public service announcements urging Iraqis to reject Al Qaeda's sectarian message. After Al Qaeda bombed Baghdad's famed Mutanabi book market, one ad showed Iraqi booksellers pulling treasured volumes of Iraqi literature from the rubble, delivering the message that Al Qaeda was attacking Iraq's cultural heritage. In another of the most powerful ads, audiences heard excerpts from speeches by Abu Omar al-Baghdadi (spoken over video of a wild dog scavenging in a dark wasteland) in which the Al Qaeda leader pronounced words with a Najdi accent, leaving Iraqis to infer that "al-Baghdadi" was actually from the Wahhabi heartland of central Saudi Arabia. The impact of these popular responses was unmistakeable: by 2008, Al Qaeda had become unpopular, an object of disdain on Iraqi TV.

THE 2009 ELECTIONS AND THE ECLIPSE OF THE MUJAHIDEEN

Meanwhile, the regional jihad was becoming less relevant inside Iraq. In late 2006, Al Qaeda had still been strong enough to attempt to seize Sunni political leadership outright, but by the end of 2008 Sunni politics had passed Al Qaeda by. The secular Sunni political groups that had turned against the foreign-led Al Qaeda during the Awakening were preparing to contest the provincial elections of January 2009 with a view to regaining the local political control they had ceded by boycotting the January 2005 elections. In Anbar, the Awakening had evolved into a local political party, while in Ninewa, Arab politicians had formed a unified front against the Kurds. In Diyala, Baghdad, and Sunni areas in the south, secular Sunni politicians such as Saleh al-Mutlaq and Tariq al-Hashemi had garnered a strong mainstream following.

Practically everywhere, the calls of Sunni rejectionists had begun to fall on deaf ears.

If the December 2005 parliamentary vote had been, in the words of Iraqi political analyst Nibraz Kazimi, "not an election, but a census" in which Iraqis had voted overwhelmingly according to their sect or ethnicity, the provincial polling of January 2005 had been only a partial census. Millions of Sunni voters had boycotted the process altogether, meaning that in the Sunni-majority provinces of Ninewa, Salahadin, and Diyala coalitions made up of minority Kurdish and Shia parties had easily won control of local governing bodies. The 2005 boycott was a disaster for local Sunni interests that created deep grievances that terrorists like Zarqawi could easily exploit. In the Iraqi north, the Al Qaeda campaign— and that of other Sunni insurgent groups—was aimed against the Kurdish parties as well as the Shia, since many Sunni Arabs viewed the Kurdish political and military presence as an encroachment into Arab lands. Whatever the merits of this grievance, the near-total absence of Sunni Arabs from the northern provincial governments exacerbated the Kurd-Arab competition. Sunnis who perceived themselves as having little stake in a Kurd-Shia-dominated government were at best ambivalent about insurgent and terrorist attacks against that government, and many were in fact outright supporters of such violence.

The January 2009 elections changed these political arrangements wholesale. In Anbar, the new provincial council was dominated by the tribal groups that had comprised the Anbar Awakening against Al Qaeda. Prominent among the province's new governing coalition was Sheikh Ahmed Abu Risha, the brother of Sattar Abu Risha, the original Awakening leader whom Al Qaeda had assassinated in 2007. The Awakening groups aimed above all to deny a share of provincial power to the Islamic Party, and the Awakening sheikhs' rhetoric against the Islamic Party was at least as vitriolic as their rhetoric against either Al Qaeda or the Iranians. In Diyala, where a coalition led by ISCI had controlled the provincial council since 2005, a new Sunni-majority coalition led by allies of Vice President Tariq al-Hashemi and Saleh al-Mutlaq won control of the provincial council and governor's seat. In Salahadin, meanwhile, a Sunni-led coalition replaced a Kurdish-led one.

The most significant change, however, took place in Ninewa, where a Sunni coalition won a majority in the government council, reversing the basic power relationship between Kurds and Arabs that had prevailed in the province since the 2003 invasion. Probably not coincidentally Ninewa, among Iraq's most violent areas for several years, began to stabilize, and a number of Sunni insurgent groups active in the province began seeking to enter into peace and amnesty talks.

THE IRAQIZATION OF AL QAEDA IN IRAQ

The one place where the January 2009 elections did not change the political dynamics between Arabs and Kurds was in Kirkuk, where elections were not held in January 2009 due to the inability of the competing parties to agree on who should be allowed to vote there. Among the Arabs and some Sunni Turcomans of the Kirkuk region, Izzat al-Douri's Naqshbandi Army had benefited from Al Qaeda's weakening position, moving into the militant space that severe military pressure from U.S. and Iraqi troops was forcing Al Qaeda to cede. By 2009, western officials in Iraq were coming to view the Naqshbandis as a more potent long-term threat in the north than Al Qaeda, meaning that the mujahideen who had once swamped the Iraqi resistance had been superseded by natives on both a political and a military level.

Years of military operations, combined with tightened Iraqi government control of Iraq's borders, reduced the infusion of foreign mujahideen in Al Qaeda in Iraq. These factors also contributed to a long process in which native Iraqi militants gradually supplanted the foreign element in the organization. In retrospect, Al Qaeda in Iraq can be said to have gone through three stages of "Iraqization," or as Iraqi insurgents have referred to it, three "generations." The first Al Qaeda generation consisted mainly of foreigners under the command of the Jordanian Zarqawi who pledged their allegiance to bin Laden. The second generation was characterized by partnership between foreigners and Iraqis, under the Egyptian Abu Ayyub al-Masri and the Iraqi Abu Omar al-Baghdadi. Since those two leaders were killed in April 2010, the third generation of Al Qaeda has been mainly Iraqi, with mainly Iraqi leaders except for the "minister of war" in Al Qaeda's political front, the Islamic State of Iraq. Al Qaeda's ministers of war have continued to be foreigners because the group's Iraqi leaders have considered it important to maintain strong links with foreign mujahideen networks outside the country. Al Qaeda leaders have also cynically considered that foreigners will be unconstrained by Iraqi social restrictions on violence or emotional ties with Iraqis, and therefore more willing to attack Christians and other Iraqi targets.

OBSERVATIONS ON SUNNI CHAUVINISM

Rend Rahim, an Iraqi scholar who became Baghdad's first post-Saddam ambassador to the United States, has observed that before 2003 Iraqi Sunnis considered Shia religious practices to be somewhat "quaint." But from 2003 onward, with the emergence of Shia Islamist militias, many Sunnis would come to view Shiism as a dangerous heresy practiced on a menacing scale. Among Sunnis, Salafis were especially repulsed by Shiism's ceremonies and worship of the family of the Prophet Muhammad, but even mainstream, secular Sunnis tended to view Shiism as a Persian form of Islam whose adherents were not to be fully trusted as patriotic Arabs.

Yet beyond the question of whether Sunnis considered the Iraqi Shia fit, in religious terms, to govern Iraq, the simple fact in post-Saddam Iraq was that many Sunnis could not accept that the Iraqi Shia outnumbered them. Shia practice had been so suppressed in Baathist Iraq that it probably had not felt as though Shia were a majority among the population. In addition, before 2003 millions of lower-class Shiites had lived mainly out of the sight of middle-class Sunnis, cooped up in huge slums like Sadr City, which by 2003 had a population—more than two million—almost equal to the rest of Baghdad put together. The same situation obtained in other major cities such as Basra, where the neighborhoods of Qibla and Hayyaniyah were packed with the Shia poor. These vast slums had been perched on the outskirts of cities where the median family was closer to the middle class, away from the more prosperous neigborhoods where the Sunni-heavy professional classes and government officials tended to live. For its average citizen, then, pre-2003 Baghdad would probably not have felt like a Shia-majority city. And for many urban Iraqis, sectarian identities were simply not relevant before 2003. "When people started talking about Sunni and Shia in 2003, we had to go and ask our parents which we were," recalled one young Baghdadi woman of mixed-sect middle-class parentage. "Before 2003 we thought to be Sunni meant you were from the north and to be Shia meant you were from the south."

The Sunnis of Iraq also seem not to have recognized fully the huge demographic shifts that had taken place in southern Iraq

under the Baath, when industrialization and the growth of a rent-
ier economy had prompted hundreds of thousands of southern
families to move from small farms into the cities to either find
work or become wards of the state. These influxes had swelled the
south's urban population, so that by 1987, outside of Kurdistan,
seven of Iraq's ten largest cities were in the south. This process had
undergone a final acceleration after 1991, when Saddam had ordered
the draining of the southern marshes that Shia rebels had used as
safe havens, forcing thousands of "marsh Arab" families to move
into the cities.

When the long-contained Shia population began to emerge in
2003, many Sunnis simply could not believe their eyes. A curious
conspiracy narrative began to develop among this Sunni minority
that had always felt it was at least a plurality, as Sunni community
leaders began to question the internationally cited statistics: the
number of southern Shiites was overestimated, some claimed, and
included many southern crypto-Sunnis forced to live as Shia out
of fear after Saddam's fall. Sunni chauvinists also claimed the population estimates included hundreds of thousands or even millions
of Iranians sent into Iraq by the Iranian regime after April 2003 in
a bid to colonize the country. There were some meager grounds for
this argument, since a large number of Shia Iraqis chased into exile
by the Baath had flooded back into the country after Saddam's
fall, but these were hardly Persians. Nevertheless, Sunni community leaders in Baghdad kept their own population charts asserting
that fully 42 percent of the country was Sunni Arab, and used
them to claim that international estimates showing Iraq as 55 to
60 percent Shia were part of a secret American-Iranian plot to
weaken Iraq and make it an Iranian satellite. When the first Iraqi
elections resulted in a large Shia majority in parliament, these
Sunni chauvinists would claim that a fraud had been perpetrated

and that the results showed the political process was purposely skewed to exclude Sunnis from their rightful share of power.

Despite these intricate arguments, for many Sunnis the ethno-sectarian balance inside Iraq was not really the issue. The major motivation behind Sunni rejectionism was not the wish to honor Iraq's true demographics or to preserve Baathism (which most Salafis did not fervently espouse anyway) but rather a desire to preserve the Sunni political ascendancy that had prevailed since Iraq's creation in 1921—a motivation that the Iraqi-born historian Elie Kedourie once called "the traditional anti-Shiite policy of the Ottomans" entrenched in Iraq by "centuries of Sunni domination." After all, Sunni Iraqis had long celebrated historical images of Baghdad as the seat of the Sunni Arabs' greatest empire, the Abbasid Caliphate, and post-2003 Sunni insurgent propaganda repeatedly declared that to surrender control of the city to the Shia would be to undo the first Muslims' holy victory over the pagan Persians in the monumental battle of Qadisiyah south of Baghdad in 636.

This historical imagery almost certainly resonated with the majority of Iraqi Sunnis who believed their country was but a component of a broader Arab nation subdivided by borders that Arabs had not chosen for themselves. Even if Sunnis were not technically a present majority inside Iraq's foreign-made boundaries, they were an overwhelming majority in the Arab nation, a fact they believed gave them a natural right to rule in Iraq. "*Lana al-hukum; wa lakum al-latum*," went an old Sunni political expression directed at the Shia: "For us, political power; for you, self-flagellation." To preserve this political birthright after 2003, Iraq's Sunni chauvinists had become willing accessories to mass murder and the destruction of the country. If they could not own Iraq, they would ensure that no one could.

CHAPTER SIX

The Kurdish Maximalists

F AR TO THE NORTH of the sectarian cleansing in Baghdad, a different civil war was playing out, one only marginally connected to the struggle for power among Sunni and Shia factions in the center of the country but every bit as sectarian. As it had done for the Shia Islamist parties in Baghdad, the collapse of Saddam's regime offered a golden opportunity for Kurdish nationalists, particularly those who wished to expand the Kurdistan region to annex the strategic city of Kirkuk; to extend Kurdish control to the isolated Kurdish enclaves that lay on the Arab side of the Green Line; and perhaps even to seize enough Arab territory to build a land bridge to Syrian Kurdistan. Kurdish nationalists also wished to punish the Sunni chauvinists of the north who had supported decades of suppression of the Kurdish community, including Saddam's brutal campaigns to stamp out the Kurdish cause. Accordingly, in the chaotic immediate aftermath of Saddam's fall, Kurdish political parties, peshmerga, and asayish intelligence services poured into the vacuum left in the Baath's wake.

The Arabs of Mosul and the upper Tigris valley, initially thrown off balance by the disappearance of the Baathist state in which they had been a core constituency, would pull out all the stops to defeat these Kurdish aims, ultimately employing the worst of the

133

Sunni sectarian terrorist groups in their cause and international-
izing the conflict by bringing in support from Syria, Turkey, and
beyond. The ensuing conflict was a messy one, taking place in a
region so demographically complex that the violence took on many
dimensions beyond the main Arab-Kurdish one: conflict among
tribes, within tribes, between rural and urban, between Islamists
and non-Muslims, and even between Sunni and Shia groups that
had never before thought of themselves in those sectarian terms.
Through it all, the Kurds would struggle mightily to hold onto
what they had grabbed in 2003, in hopes of keeping the Kurdish
maximalist dream within reach.

THE KURDISH JERUSALEM

The Arab-Kurdish struggle for power took place mainly in what
became two theaters of war: the ancient region of Assyria and the
medieval city of Kirkuk. Kirkuk's strategic adjoining oilfields made
it the key to the viability of any future Iraqi Kurdish state, while
its centuries-old Kurdish community made it a symbolic center of
Kurdish history and culture. Iraqi Kurdistan's two principal leaders, Jalal Talabani of the Patriotic Union of Kurdistan (PUK) and
'Massoud Barzani of the Kurdish Democratic Party (KDP), had
both explicitly spoken of Kirkuk as Kurdistan's future capital, and
Talabani labeled Kirkuk "the Jerusalem of Kurdistan." Even Barham Salih, a younger technocrat most known among Kurdish
leaders for his willingness to work within the framework of an
Iraqi state in Baghdad, would declare that Kirkuk was "a bench-
mark by which most Kurds would define their legitimacy in Iraq."
For Kurdish nationalists, the idea of Kurdistan without Kirkuk
and its sprawling metropolitan area of more than one million people was unthinkable.

Sunni Arab chauvinists felt equally strongly in the opposite direction. If the Kurds were to gain Kirkuk, Sunnis judged, they would be on an irreversible path toward independence. Baghdad, Mosul, Ramadi, Tikrit, and Kirkuk had been the great cities of the Iraqi Sunni world, the very basis of Iraqi Sunni power in the region. If Baghdad were lost to the Shia and Kirkuk lost to the Kurds, what would be left for the Sunnis? A similar question was asked by the more than one million Iraqi Turcomans, an ethnic community that was both the residue of the Ottoman Empire and a former majority in Kirkuk city. Like the Kurds, the Turcomans considered Kirkuk their cultural center and symbolic capital, and if Kirkuk were to disappear behind the Green Line, the Iraqi Turcoman population would be cut into communities separated by a virtual international boundary.

Of course, the question was far more than a local Arab-Kurd-Turcoman matter. Kirkuk's ultimate ownership was central to the question of whether there would be one Iraq or two. If the government in Baghdad were to lose control of Kirkuk, it would be near certain the Iraqi state would lose all of Kurdistan along with its 45 billion barrels of oil, proven reserves equal to those of Libya. Furthermore, once detached from Arab Iraq, what would prevent an oil-rich Kurdish state from becoming an ally, client, or satellite of either Turkey or Iran, enabling either of those energy-hungry former empires to project power mere miles from the Tigris valley? No government in Baghdad, whether led by King Faisal, Saddam Hussein, or Nuri Maliki, wanted to look north and see a new foreign country where four Iraqi provinces had been.

Taken together, these considerations meant that for Kurdish nationalists, Sunni Arabs, Turcomans, and the Shia leaders of the new Iraqi government, the stakes in the Kirkuk question were high enough to fight over, and for more than a decade after April 2003 that is exactly what they did.

THE WAR OF DEMOGRAPHICS

As with so many of the internal conflicts in Iraq, the Kirkuk dispute had its roots in longstanding rivalries that the policies of
Saddam Hussein and the Baath made much worse. A great deal of
the Iraq conflict resulted not from natural strife among Iraqi communities, but from jarring local changes wrought by thirty-five
years of Baathist social engineering. U.S. troops who deployed
across Iraq in 2003 were surprised to find just how extensive
Saddam's schemes had been, and how thick were the human flot-
sam and jetsam of clans and communities resettled here and there,
expelled from traditional homelands or invited to new ones. This
had been the case in Ninewa, where Saddam had forced Kurds to
move to the highlands of Kurdistan and had built new Arab settlements on the eastern perimeter of Mosul to make it a more
fully Arab city. He had resettled trusted clans from his home
region to the Iranian border to guard the Diyala valley approaches
to central Iraq. He had Arabized the Turcomans of the north to
make them more loyal to his pan-Arab regime. He had expelled
to Iran at least fifteen thousand Shia families or individuals at
the outset of the Iran-Iraq War on the grounds that they were
of Persian descent. He had famously drained the southern
marshes after the uprising of 1991, forcing the marsh Arabs who
had lived there for thousands of years into cities to expunge once
and for all a traditional rebel sanctuary, much as Charles II had
drained the fens of southeast England to break Puritan rebellions there.

Nowhere in Iraq were the Baath more ambitious in their social
engineering than in Kirkuk. The British army that occupied Kirkuk
in 1918 had described it as a Turcoman city, and the last credible
census of the city, taken in 1957, the final year of the Iraqi monarchy, had shown a Turcoman plurality in a Kirkuk town of a hun-

dred twenty thousand people, situated in a province that was about half Kurdish on the whole. But after the Kurdish revolt of 1974–75, when peshmerga rebels had been supported by the Shah of Iran, the Baath had taken steps to dramatically alter the ethnic balance of 1957, aiming to pull Kirkuk firmly into Arab Iraq and reduce the threat of Kurdish nationalism to the Baathist state.

To begin with, the Baath had redrawn the map to cut Kurdistan down to size, stealing portions of Baghdad and Kirkuk provinces in 1976 to create Salahadin province in the mid-Tigris region and make Saddam's hometown of Tikrit a seat of local government for the first time. They had dramatically shrunk Kirkuk province, chopping away a good deal of its territory and appending to it the Sunni Arab district of Hawijah, naming the amended province Ta'mim rather than Kirkuk. Saddam and the Baath had then diluted the new Ta'mim province's Kurdish character, partly by the Arabization of Kirkuk's Turcomans and Kurds, but also by resettling thousands of southern Shia Arab families in the city, and finally by expelling thousands of Kurdish families, particularly those who had supported the revolt of 1974–75. By the time the Baathist state claimed to conduct a census in 1997, Iraqi government records showed an Arab majority of 58 percent in Ta'mim. The number is highly suspect, but even if that census had been credible, it would have reflected vast forced migration of as many as two hundred thousand Kurds, including probably more than a hundred thousand in the aftermath of the 1991 northern uprising. The 1997 numbers would also have included an unknown number of Kurds involuntarily reclassified as Arabs, along with perhaps two hundred fifty thousand southern Arabs brought to Kirkuk as settlers, most of them Shia. This was the demographic situation in Kirkuk and its surrounding region when the Baath, which had made so many changes to Kirkuk, suddenly collapsed in 2003.

THE KURDISH EXPANSION

In Iraq's military geography, Kirkuk guards central Iraq's lowlands against invaders from the highlands to the northeast and Iran. Conversely, the huge Kani Domlan ridge against which the city sits is the high ground that protects Kurdistan from invaders issuing forth from central Iraq, as many Iraqi armies have done over the past century. The terrain on the Arab side of the Kani Domlan consists of extraordinarily rugged sandstone hills nearly impassible to a mechanized army, but beyond the ridge lies an open plain, perfect country for tanks all the way to the Kurdish capital of Irbil. In Arab hands, Kirkuk could always pose a military threat to the very heart of Iraqi Kurdistan.

It was no surprise, then, that Iraqi Kurds moved quickly to seize Kirkuk when the Baath fell in 2003. As Saddam's divisions melted away in the war's first days, an army of seventy thousand peshmerga and five thousand U.S. troops advanced from the Green Line into the Kirkuk area. In the ensuing chaos, U.S. advisers were shocked to see the peshmerga looting the city once Saddam's troops had fled. The new Kurdish forces in the city seized property from the old regime and its prominent followers and began laying the groundwork for the return of thousands of Kurds the Baath had expelled. When the pillaging subsided, Kurdish authorities set up new government mechanisms for restoring property the expelled Kurds had lost, some of which was in Arab hands. The peshmerga seizure of the city enabled future Iraqi President Jalal Talabani's allies to take control of the municipal government. Coalition officials prevented Talabani himself from setting up his headquarters in the disputed city, but they did not prevent Talabani's Patriotic Union of Kurdistan from remaking its administration and security forces into a virtual extension of the Kurdistan Regional Government (KRG) that has remained in place ever since.

Cementing the Kurdish Gains

With the long-coveted Kirkuk in their hands at last, the Kurds took measures to make their control permanent. To eliminate any doubt about the new strategic arrangement, the new Kurdish owners emplaced an enormous billboard of a Kurdish flag on the ridge above the city, where it dominated the skyline in a fashion akin to Los Angeles' Hollywood sign. The Kurds changed the physical boundary between Arab and Kurdish Iraq as well, as a line of military blockhouses on the Kani Domlan ridge behind the city became a peshmerga defensive line barring the way to the Kurdish country beyond. The same was happening all along the Green Line: not only had the Kurds pushed the line westward into formerly Arab territory; they had also rendered it permanent with forts, fences, and checkpoints, making it into a de facto international border that Arab Iraqis could not easily pass through without KRG-issued authorization documents.

In Kirkuk city, from the spring of 2003 onward the Kurdish authorities began reversing the demographic changes that Saddam had wrought, bringing back Kurdish families the Baath had expelled and ringing the city with vast new housing settlements. These steps would increase the city's population to nine hundred thousand by 2011, more than double the population that Saddam's regime had recorded in 1987. The province's new Kurdish authorities also began to pressure Arab families that Saddam had settled in the area to return to their places of origin, especially the thousands of Shia Arab families the Baath had brought from the south.

Having created new facts on the ground, the Kurdish authorities' next step was to codify them in the Iraqi constitution being drafted in 2004–05. The task was not easy, considering the hopelessly confused demographic picture and unreliable vital statistics the Baath had left behind. With nothing else to go on, the non-Arab claimants

to the city settled on the 1957 census as the last valid record of
what Kirkuk's natural population should look like, and began to
use that outdated survey to judge who should rightfully govern
Kirkuk and rightfully live there. This reliance on half-century-old
records was rife with problems. A city that held a hundred twenty
thousand people in 1957 had grown to more than seven times that
size, and no one could say what the natural growth of the city's
population would have looked like had it been left alone. There
was also some suspicion that the Baath had tampered with the
1957 records in any case.

These factors made establishing the pedigree of each family in
Kirkuk a near-impossible task. Yet that is precisely what the framers of the Iraqi constitution of 2005 decided to require. Article 140
of the constitution decreed a three-step process for settling the
disputed territories and internal boundaries of the country. First
would come "normalization" of the disputed areas, an undoing of
Saddam's demographic alterations and the displacement of population caused by war that would involve both the resettling of
those who had been expelled and the expulsion of those who had
been resettled—exactly the process Kirkuk's new Kurdish governors had set in motion. Next would come a census of the "normal-
ized" areas that would double as a registration of voters. Finally,
having counted the rightful residents of the disputed territories,
the Iraqi government would hold a referendum in which those
residents would vote, by a simple majority, to remain part of Arab
Iraq or join Iraqi Kurdistan. Simply put, the constitution called for
the government to rejigger the ethnic balance and then vote a new
map of the country.

This constitutional process heavily favored Kurdish claims,
reflecting the Kurds' advantage over Sunni Arabs at the national
level of Iraqi politics. But even at the local level, the political process was trending against the Kurds' rivals as time passed. When

the Coalition Provisional Authority established an interim governing council for Kirkuk in 2003, Kurds held only eleven seats of thirty, with Sunni Arabs, Turcomans, and Christians holding six each. The misguided Arab and Turcoman boycott of the parliamentary and provincial elections of January 2005 had reversed this Arab-Turcoman advantage, yielding a provincial council in which Kurds held twenty-six of forty-one seats. By the time of the October 2005 constitutional referendum, a vote that would govern Kirkuk's political fate, the pro-Kurdish vote in favor of a federalized constitution stood at more than 60 percent, completing the political eclipse of the anti-Kurdish parties in the province.

THE ARAB AND TURCOMAN RESISTANCE

From an early stage after Saddam's fall, Kirkuk's Arab sheikhs had begun to organize angry protests against the new political arrangement that had made the Kurds masters of the city and its province. In demonstrations covered by Al Jazeera television in 2003, thousands of Arabs marched through Kirkuk's streets, chanting against the Kurdish move to "annex" the city, since, in the words of one Arab organizer, "Kirkuk is an Arab town." But when nothing changed, political violence took the place of demonstrations, and local tribes such as the Obeid became the core of a resistance movement in the region between Kirkuk and the Tigris. Sheikh Abdul Rahman Munshid al-Assi was perhaps the most prominent of the Obeidi leaders who had adopted a militantly anti-Kurdish stance. "Most important of all, Kirkuk must never become part of Kurdistan," he told a western reporter in 2006; "It is an Iraqi city, and we will take all routes to prevent the division of Iraq," implying by "all routes" that his tribe was involved in militant resistance. He was hardly alone. The entire upper Tigris was a region that could not but reject the new political order. For the three decades of Baathist rule, Tikrit and the central north had taken increasing control of the entire country as Saddam drew from his home region to staff his state and army. "We ran this country for thirty-five years," the deputy governor of Salahadin defiantly reminded American officials in 2007. With the collapse of Saddam's state, the Sunnis of the upper Tigris were losing power not just in Baghdad, but also in their home territory.

The resistance also included Turcoman militants who rejected the new ascendancy of Kurdish parties in what Turcomans considered to be a Turkish homeland in Kirkuk. Sunni Turcomans also resented the new power held by Shia tribes in mixed-sect Turcoman towns of the Kirkuk region such as Tuz Khormato, Qara Tepe, and Suleiman Beg. In Kirkuk and these Turcoman towns, the Sunni-dominated Iraqi Turcoman Front, a party formed in the 1990s with the aim of carving out an autonomous Turcoman region, encouraged political and militant resistance against the Kurds and Shia around them. Iraqi Turcoman Front leaders in Kirkuk coordinated their activities with branches in Tel Afar and Mosul, making their resistance campaign a far-reaching one. The Kirkuk-based Turcoman Front may also have enjoyed a close relationship with Turkish intelligence, a factor that would have allowed the Turkish government to reach directly into the Kirkuk dispute.

The Sunni-Shia rift in Turcoman towns added a layer of complexity to an already complicated landscape. As the Iraqi Turcoman Front drifted toward resistance in 2003–04, Shia Turcoman politicians created the competing Turcoman Democratic Movement and allied with the Kurdish parties. Meanwhile, Shia Arabs of Kirkuk, whom Kurdish officials were pressuring to return to southern Iraq, went in a different direction by joining the Sadr movement, so that a city already thick with ethnosectarian militias would have a contingent of Sadr's Jaysh al-Mahdi as well. Whereas the leading Shia parties of Baghdad acceded to Kurdish control of Kirkuk, Sadr and his party emphatically rejected it.

Rounding out the militant picture were Al Qaeda and Ansar al-Sunna, which, though relatively minor political players in Kirkuk, would take advantage of the many Arab-Kurd and Sunni-Shia fissures in the Kirkuk region to carry out terrorist attacks for years on end.

THE NATURE OF THE KIRKUK WAR

By 2004, the Kirkuk region was in the throes of a brutal local war among potent warring parties. The Kurdish political parties were firmly in control of Kirkuk's police forces, the local Iraqi Army division, and local offices of the asayish, the Kurdish secret police. Arrayed against them were the many Arab and Turcoman resistance groups, most of them linked to political parties and tribal groups. The fighting between these two sides resulted in the deaths of more than three thousand Kirkuki civilians between 2003 and 2009, about half of them in the intense war years of 2006–07. The most serious violence was political. Suicide bombers often attacked the Kurdish police headquarters or gatherings, such as an April 2007 attack that killed and wounded more than two hundred near a police station, including dozens of children leaving a nearby girls' school. Bombers and assassins repeatedly attacked Kurdish political offices and gatherings in the province, as in the July 2007 truck bombing of a PUK office in Kirkuk that killed and wounded more than two hundred fifty, or the July 2008 suicide bombing of a Kurdish political rally that caused more than two hundred casualties.

Al Qaeda and other takfiri groups, meanwhile, explicitly targeted Kurdish and Shia civilians as part of a jihad that was less a political campaign than a cosmic ideological struggle against what they considered heretical sects of Islam. These attacks were meant to terrorize the civilian population and discourage them from interacting with the state, such as a June 2005 suicide bombing that killed and wounded more than a hundred Kirkukis lined up to receive pensions, or the more than a hundred forty killed and wounded by a suicide bomber in a Kirkuk market in June 2009. Al Qaeda was also likely responsible for attacks such as the massive truck bombing that killed or wounded almost three hundred worshippers leaving a Shia mosque in the Turcoman town of Taza in June 2009, the largest terrorist attack in the entire country that year.

The battles between the warring parties in the Kirkuk region—where security forces associated with the Kurdish parties targeted insurgents, and the insurgents carried out guerrilla and terrorist attacks against the Kurds and Shia—were part of a broader system of conflict across the north, including the adjacent Salahadin province, where more than six thousand civilians were killed in 2003–09. A favorite insurgent target during this period was state-owned infrastructure, particularly the pipelines that carried oil the short distance from Kirkuk's oilfields to northern Iraq's only major refinery, at Baiji, and to an export line that ran to Turkey. By disrupting the flow of oil, insurgents could depress the Kurdish parties' revenues and discredit the new Iraqi government at the same time, a political objective indicating that the Naqshbandis or other Baathists were most likely to blame. By contrast, the frequent suicide bombings against the foreign workers' quarters near the Baiji refinery bore the hallmark of Al Qaeda or other takfiri militant groups. The worst attacks at Baiji in 2007 were probably linked to the major role the refinery had come to play in the financing of the militant groups fighting in the north. Western officials estimated that up to $2 billion in the Baiji refinery's profits disappeared into the black market in 2007, with a significant portion funneled to

Al Qaeda and other insurgents by refinery administrators who were either corrupt or intimidated.

These patterns of violence were consistent throughout 2003–09. The result was the devastation of the upper Tigris region and its population, with tens of thousands killed and wounded and hundreds of thousands displaced. But despite the physical damage the six-year insurgent campaign caused, it made virtually no impact on the Kurdish parties' fundamental control of Kirkuk.

THE CONSTITUTIONAL TIME BOMB AND THE TURKEY-PKK WAR

Having established a procedure whose likeliest outcome was the annexation of Kirkuk to Kurdistan, the Iraqi constitution had not afforded the potentially losing parties much time to get used to the idea. The constitution approved by referendum in October 2005 called for the three steps of normalization, census, and referendum in the disputed territories to be completed by December 31, 2007. As that date approached, it began to look more like the scheduled kickoff of a civil war than the lasting resolution of a political dispute. Sunni Arabs and Turcomans of Kirkuk and Hawijah had bitterly protested the Baghdad government's decision in 2005 to allow displaced Kurds outside Kirkuk to vote in Kirkuk's election, and they claimed the resulting Arab-Turcoman share of only fifteen of forty-one provincial council seats underrepresented their real strength in the province. Arab-Turcoman objections culminated in a November 2006 Arab and Turcoman withdrawal from the Kirkuk council, paralyzing the local government.

With the local Article 140 process frozen, the national government intervened. In February 2007, three months after the Arab-

Turcoman boycott, a committee appointed by Prime Minister
Maliki to oversee Article 140's implementation announced that
Arabs settled in Kirkuk by Saddam would be given $12,000 each to
move back to their original homes. The committee also announced
that a Kirkuk census would be conducted in July 2007, followed by
a referendum in November. This impractically short timeline caused
the committee's collapse, as its Sunni Arab chairman, Maliki's own
justice minister, resigned his post, signifying that no national Sunni
Arab leader could afford to be associated with a process that was
ceding Arab control of the disputed territories. By July 2007, it
was clear no census could be held, since "normalization" had
barely begun, and western and Iraqi officials quietly floated pro-
posals to postpone the process indefinitely. Kurdish President
Massoud Barzani responded by warning in August that delaying
the Kirkuk referendum would lead to "a real civil war," and his
allies in parliament declared their intention to hold the plebiscite
unilaterally if the Baghdad government would not do it.

This brinksmanship was overcome by events in October 2007,
when the Kurdistan Workers' Party (PKK) restarted its long-
running insurgency against Turkey. From bases inside Iraq, PKK
fighters attacked Turkish military and police targets across the
border and carried out terrorist bombings in some civilian areas.
The Turkish military responded with an aerial bombardment campaign inside Iraqi Kurdistan that caused an Iraqi political crisis
at precisely the time the Kirkuk issue was meant to be settled.
Kurdish popular anger at the Turkish bombing of Kurdish territory ran high, forcing Barzani and his allies to threaten to withdraw from the Maliki government if Iraqi leaders did not demand
an immediate end to the Turkish offensive on "sovereign Iraqi territory." The withdrawal of Kurdish support would have caused
the Maliki government's collapse at exactly the time that Adel

Abd al-Mahdi's ISCI and other parties were seeking to orchestrate Maliki's replacement anyway. That Kurdish separatists should insist upon Baghdad's intervention to protect Kurdistan was ironic since Kurdistan Regional Government (KRG) leaders for years had prevented the central government from deploying any troops into KRG territory at all, and had worked to limit Baghdad's authority in security and foreign policy writ large.

For their part, the Turks seemed to use their retaliatory strikes not just to neutralize the PKK, but also to signal to Iraqi Kurdish leaders that Turkey was powerful enough to prevent an autonomous Kurdistan if it wished to do so. Turkish warplanes and artillery were imperfectly careful about hitting strictly PKK targets, as when they destroyed four bridges used by Kurdish civilians near the border area. The Turkish offensive weakened the KRG's position in the debate over Kirkuk taking place in the Iraqi parliament. Among other things, the crisis made clear that the United States could not choose to support Kurdish nationalism over the legitimate security interests of Turkey, a NATO member state. Within weeks of the start of their offensive, Turkish military leaders told journalists that Turkey was receiving intelligence from the United States to help the Turks target the PKK more effectively, presumably to dampen Iraqi Kurdish anger at the Turks' previously blunt attacks. Consequently, when the Turkish Army mounted a limited ground offensive into Kurdistan in early 2008, KRG leaders in Irbil were forced to accede to the Turkish invasion and to take steps to limit the PKK's logistics base inside Iraq. Massoud Barzani's nephew Nechirvan Barzani, the KRG's prime minister, went so far as to declare that the KRG was "against the PKK existence inside the Kurdistan Region and its attacks on Turkey" and to call on the PKK to declare an unconditional cease-fire.

THE NATIONAL DISPUTE

Back in Kirkuk, the most recalcitrant Obeidi sheikh, Abd al-Rahman Munshid al-Assi, had led the Arab boycott of the provincial council, but he had also strayed too far into militancy, and in November 2007 he was jailed on terrorism charges. His removal enabled the paramount Obeidi sheikh, Anwar al-Assi, to strike a deal with local Kurdish leaders to get the council back to work. The Arabs' return to the local Kirkuk council, taking place at exactly the time that the Arab-Kurd power struggle was causing such national-level turmoil, illustrated a paradox about the Kirkuk dispute. Despite several years of local warfare and a constant war of words, Arab-Kurd relations within the city were good enough that Kirkuklis, left to their own devices, could work out a modus vivendi allowing local governance to proceed. It was at the national level that Arab-Kurd relations over Kirkuk seemed irreconcilable, as the Iraqi parliament made clear in the months following the Turkey-Kurdistan crisis. In January 2008, when the parliament debated the division of Iraqi oil profits—a question that would probably determine the future balance of power between Kurdistan and the central government—Arab members combined to reject a Kurdish proposal that would have given Irbil control over most of Kurdistan's oil. Though it came in the midst of a Sunni-Shia sectarian war, the Kurdish proposal nonetheless joined Sunni and Shiite Arab parties, with 150 of 275 parliamentarians signing a declaration against it, the largest parliamentary bloc formed on any issue. The petition even united the Shia Sadrists and Sunni Tawafuq, whose militiamen were engaged in street warfare across Baghdad at the time. The same Arab parties later rejected a Kurdish electoral proposal that would have allowed displaced Kurds to vote in Kirkuk while excluding resettled Arabs. The parliament ultimately approved the electoral law for the January

2009 elections only by agreeing to keep Kirkuk out of the voting altogether.

These parliamentary debates were sober reminders of the depth of Arab distrust of the Kurds' quest for autonomy. The decision to delay elections in Kirkuk indefinitely meant that Kirkuklis were stuck for the long term with the results of the partially boycotted election of January 2005, and also signified that all measures to address the basic Arab-Kurd political relationship were slowing into paralysis.

THE STRUGGLE FOR ASSYRIA

Far northwest of the Kirkuk and Diyala battlefields, Sunni chauvinism and Kurdish maximalism collided in a violent, high-stakes contest for the city of Mosul and the plains of Ninewa. The war in Ninewa played out on many levels—ethnic, sectarian, tribal, and others—owing mainly to Mosul's particular geography and demography. Modern Mosul, a city of almost two million people, lay adjacent to the ruins of the biblical city of Nineveh, the imperial capital of Assyria for which the surrounding province is named. For thousands of years, the city had sat at a crossroads of great empires and cultures, giving it an unusually cosmopolitan nature, with a Sunni Arab majority living mainly peacefully alongside large minorities of Kurds, Assyrian and Sabean Christians, Turcomans, and a dizzying array of smaller sects and ethnicities. Since Roman times, the east-west Silk Road had run through Mosul, connecting the region to both the Mediterranean and China, making the city's livelihood more dependent on the flow of goods and people west to Aleppo than south to Baghdad. For much of its modern history, Mosul was not so much an Iraqi outpost on the southern edge of Ottoman Anatolia—and eastern Syria—as it was an Ottoman outpost on the edge of Arab Iraq, a province equal in stature to Baghdad and Basra, ruled directly from Constantinople.

Mosul's inclusion in the modern Baghdad-centered Iraqi state had been somewhat accidental. When the European powers met in Paris in 1919 to divide the Arab lands of the Ottoman Empire, Mosul and its region were originally meant to be part of French Syria, and were only transferred to British control as the result of a personal agreement between Lloyd George and Clemenceau. Even then, it was not clear that Mosul would be permanently incorporated into the new post-Ottoman Iraq. British armies had entered Mosul days after the Anglo-Ottoman armistice of 1918, not before, and Kemalist Turkey continued to claim it as an Ottoman city. Ataturk and his forces periodically threatened to seize the city until the League of Nations formally awarded it to Baghdad in 1925, dashing the hopes of a substantial portion of Mosulawis who did not relish the idea of being subordinated to a new British-dominated government in Baghdad.

The annexation of Mosul into the new Iraq was not the last time the powerful men of Mosul would find themselves unhappy with a newly established political arrangement. A few months after the leftist military dictator Abd al-Karim Qasim seized power in Baghdad in 1958, the pro-Nasser military garrison of Mosul mutinied against the new regime and its communist allies, aiming to take power and join Iraq to the new United Arab Republic of Egypt and Syria. Though the revolt collapsed in short order, it indicated the underlying support for Arab nationalist parties in Mosul, and it also established a pattern: when power changed hands in Baghdad, Mosulawis would not necessarily accept the new order.

The practical consequence of this history is that when the Sunni Arabs of Ninewa found themselves pushed out of power in Mosul after April 2003, they would quickly and naturally turn toward Syria and Turkey, using old ties to seek material and political support in rejecting the new political order that threatened to exclude them.

THE MOSULAWI MILITARY ELITE

Events in early post-invasion Iraq signaled to many Mosulawis that they might be on the cusp of another unwelcome political arrangement. The most significant sign was the Coalition Provisional Authority's disbanding of the Iraqi Army. Iraqi regimes had come and gone, but throughout the country's existence Mosul had remained the heart of the army, without doubt the strongest of Iraq's national institutions. Mosulawis could point to a number of native sons who had served in the senior ranks under the Iraqi monarchy, the Qasim regime, and the Baath. Nicknamed by Iraqis "the Officer City," Mosul was home to so many retired generals that one American commander referred to it as the Iraqi equivalent of Alexandria, Virginia. Mosulawis dominated the upper ranks of Saddam's army, including the Republican Guard, and also figured prominently in Saddam's security apparatus.

The disbanding of the army and dissolution of the Baath Party would have a serious material impact on the city's elite, depriving retired and serving Mosulawi generals of salaries and pensions, and would have an ideological impact as well. From an early stage, the Mosulawi-led army had been to Iraq what the Prussian-led army had been to early Germany. Iraq's founding fathers, such as Jafar Pasha and Nuri al-Said, were military men who had dreamed of Iraq as an Arab Prussia or Piedmont whose army would be the instrument through which the Arab nation eventually would be united. This dream had been passed down through generations of Iraqi officers, including the Iran-Iraq War generation that considered itself to have saved the Arab world from a Persian onslaught.

The officers of Mosul could imagine themselves as not just the central pillar of the state, but as keepers of a sacred mission to liberate all Arabs someday from the partition the west had imposed upon them.

THE GREEN LINE AND THE CONTEST FOR THE JAZEERA

In the chaotic days after Saddam's fall, these thousands of Mosulawi military men watched in alarm as they were supplanted by expatriates and Kurdish politicians who intended to wrest Mosul from its traditional elite. As Saddam's armies melted away in the spring of 2003, Kurdish peshmerga moved forward from the "Green Line" that had divided Baathist-controlled Iraq from the Kurdistan region, taking up positions in the Kurdish neighborhoods of east Mosul and on the major roads leading into the city, ensuring that no Arab could approach Kurdistan without going through peshmerga checkpoints. Peshmerga units also established outposts astride the route to the main Syrian border crossing at Rabiah, Mosul's economic lifeline.

The forward movement of the Green Line represented long-standing Kurdish ambitions, as well as, in the Kurdish view, the righting of wrongs they had suffered under Saddam. In the offices of Kurdistan Regional Government (KRG) officials in Irbil, Dahouk, and elsewhere, the walls were covered with maps depicting Kurdistan's borders where Kurds believed they ought to be, extending from the outskirts of Aleppo in the west almost to Kut in the south, with large swaths of southeastern Turkey, northwestern Iran, and the Diyala valley included. These aspirational maps showed Kurdish control not just where Kurdish majorities lived, but also where Kurdish minorities lived, including the traditionally Sunni Arab–controlled lands of western Ninewa, and they imagined an Iraqi Kurdish region contiguous with Syrian Kurdistan. Inside Mosul, opportunist allies of Massoud Barzani and the Kurdistan Democratic Party (KDP) set up political offices and prepared to contest Sunni Arab control of the city and province.

The territories the KDP coveted were in an Arab region that the peshmerga would not subdue easily. The vast arid plains west of Mosul were part of the Jazeera, the region bounded by the Tigris and Euphrates rivers and extending from the outskirts of Baghdad in the southeast almost to Aleppo in the northwest. In pre-modern times, the Jazeera had effectively been a separate Arab country, distinct in both geography and politics from the country the Arabs knew as Iraq to the southeast. The British diplomat and orientalist Sir Mark Sykes noted this distinction when he visited the region in 1907, remarking that Iraq "is as different a country to the Jazirah as is Castille to Normandy." Sykes had recorded his observations of a country peopled by seminomadic tribes and farmers, or *fellahin*, who scraped out a living on dry farms, and of powerful tribes who had long preyed upon caravans transiting the old Silk Road that passed under Sinjar Mountain, defying the rule of Ottoman officials in large towns like Deir ez-Zour and Tel Afar.

It was an irony, then, that when Sykes and other British and French officials partitioned the Arabic-speaking Ottoman lands after the First World War, they had drawn a geometric boundary right down the middle of the Jazeera, bisecting these tribal lands, giving half to British Iraq and half to French Syria. The lines had naturally meant little to the tribes that had long ranged from one end of the Jazeera to the other but were suddenly told in 1920 they were living across an international border from their tribal kinsmen and their seasonal grazing lands.

The tribes in question were powerful ones. The Iraqi-Syrian branch of the enormous Shammar tribe had invaded the Jazeera two centuries before, migrating north from their tribe's ancestral home in Jebel Shammar in central Arabia to defeat the potent Tai and Obeid tribes in a long series of wars over water and grazing lands. As a result, the Shammar considered the Jazeera theirs by right of conquest, and the most powerful Shammar sheikhs had even claimed the title of emirs of the Jazeera, strong enough to collect tolls from travelers on the roads between Mosul and Aleppo. The Shammar had profited from trans-Jazeera commerce up to contemporary times, when Saddam had allowed smuggling with Syria to evade UN sanctions in the 1990s. Jazeera Arabs had facilitated this trade across the lightly guarded border that was marked by little more than an easily crossed earthen berm running for hundreds of kilometers.

The Shammar and other Sunnis of the Jazeera were unsurprisingly displeased by the appearance in 2003 of Kurdish peshmerga bases and checkpoints in their midst. Sinjar, 120 kilometers west of Mosul, was the site of ancient Singara, once an important Roman outpost city of twenty thousand people, but it was also home to two ethnic Kurdish communities, the Shabak and the Yezidis, that had lost their Kurdish identity after centuries of isolation. Both groups practiced unique religions distantly related to Islam, factors that would later make them targets of takfiri terrorists. The Shabak practiced a mystical religion similar to Sufism, while the Yezidis observed a mysterious creed allegedly built around devil-worship. The Yezidis had often revolted against their Ottoman and Iraqi rulers, and neither group relished the idea of Kurdish authority, but when KDP officials arrived in Sinjar in 2003 it was clear they meant to reclaim the Yezidis and Shabak for Kurdistan. These dynamics doomed Sinjar to being an ethnic battlefield for the better part of a decade.

The Mosulawi Opportunists

Back in Mosul, the disappearance of the Saddam regime had created an open moment not just for Kurdish opportunists, but for Arab ones as well, some of whom hoped to seize a greater share of power for their families or tribes by working with the Kurds and Americans who had taken the city. Most notorious among the Arab opportunists was Misha'an al-Jabouri, a member of the large Jabour tribe whose heartland lay south of Mosul. In a time of rampant opportunism, Misha'an stood out for his chameleon-like nature. He had begun his career as a Saddam loyalist and business partner of Saddam's son, Udai, until forced to flee to Jordan after allegedly cheating Udai of profits. In Jordan, Misha'an had joined the anti-Saddam opposition, eventually serving as chief of staff to Saddam's treasonous son-in-law Hussein Kamal when the latter joined the opposition in Amman in the early 1990s. But in Amman Misha'an had hedged his bets by working for both opposition and regime, reportedly becoming an informant for the Iraqi secret police. He had even provided the regime with evidence against members of his own tribe and family, resulting in the executions of dozens of Jabouris, even though Saddam had earlier hanged Misha'an's own brother for treason. Later, as the Iraqi regime headed for war with the United States, Misha'an had changed his stripes once again, becoming an ally of Massoud Barzani and the KDP, even though the Kurds had killed Misha'an's father when the latter had commanded a regime-sponsored paramilitary unit in Saddam's war against the Kurds in the late 1980s.

As the Baathist regime collapsed in 2003, Misha'an reappeared in Mosul alongside the KDP, negotiating his way onto the city's interim council and establishing a power base in the city. Though he would later change sides again and become an insurgent warlord, in the disorganized early days that followed the regime's collapse in 2003 he was able to become a near–de facto governor of the province. Like the Kurds, Misha'an and other returning expatriates posed a threat to the traditional Mosulawi power structure. These many precursors for civil war—the supplanting of the traditional Sunni ascendancy, the Kurdish grab for territory in the Jazeera, the meaningless border partitioning the Jazeera between Iraq and Syria, the disenfranchisement of a potent military community—would cause Ninewa to explode in 2004 and provide fuel for the fire to burn for years afterward.

THE FALL OF MOSUL AND FAILURE OF ELECTIONS

At first, the new expatriate-led order in Ninewa enjoyed some semblance of stability. Though close to the KDP, Osama Kashmoula proved an effective governor in Mosul, credible enough with the Arab population and preserving enough of the pre-2003 apparatus to keep the city from slipping into outright revolt. But after insurgents assassinated Kashmoula in July 2004, the situation steadily deteriorated. The murdered governor was succeeded by his erratic cousin, who effectively turned over the running of the province to his Kurdish deputy Kesro Goran, head of the KDP in Ninewa and a close ally of Massoud Barzani. Under Goran, the provincial government gradually became an extension of the KDP and a coalition of minor Arab tribes, while Kurdish troops in Mosul often carried out heavy-handed antiterrorism operations against the city's Sunni neighborhoods.

The Kurdish soldiers were responding to a serious problem, as hundreds of Sunni mujahideen entering Iraq—with Syrian regime complicity—used Sinjar and Tel Afar as staging bases before proceeding to Mosul and the Tigris valley. By late summer of 2004, Tel Afar was in open revolt, with fighters of groups such as Ansar al-Islam—Abu Musab al-Zarqawi's hosts in northern Iraq before 2003—in control of the city's streets, operating with the complicity of policemen drawn from the local Sunni Turcoman population. Among the insurgent groups that flocked to Tel Afar, Turkish officials played an ambiguous role, drawn to the city out of a sort of pan-Turanian concern but offering material support to Turcoman radicals who were willing to work in turn with Sunni terrorist groups.

Though U.S. and Iraqi troops retook Tel Afar in September 2004, the revolt spread to Mosul a few weeks later. On November 10, less than forty-eight hours after U.S. troops began an assault on the insurgent stronghold of Fallujah in Anbar, insurgents overran Mosul, causing the collapse of its five-thousand-man police force in a single day. The insurgent offensive, apparently timed to relieve pressure from the besieged insurgents in Fallujah, indicated that the insurgency's leaders were capable of a coordinated strategy reaching across wide expanses of Iraq.

As they did in Tel Afar, Iraqi and U.S. troops reestablished government control in Mosul by the end of 2004, but the insurgents had succeeded in irreversibly damaging the political process in the province. Amid the chaos, virtually all Arab Mosulawis heeded calls from Al Qaeda and from Harith al-Dhari to boycott the January 2005 elections for provincial council and national parliament. The virtually unopposed KDP and its allies swept the election, so that of thirty-seven provincial council seats, only two went to Sunni Arabs, cementing the political reversal the Kurds of Ninewa had sought since Saddam's fall.

THE SUNNI-SHIA WAR IN TEL AFAR

As the Arab-Kurd war in Ninewa intensified in 2005, the Sunni-Shia sectarian war that was raging far to the south in Baghdad began to spill into Ninewa as well. About halfway between Sinjar and Mosul, Tel Afar was home to two hundred thousand Sunni and Shia Turcomans, a community that had migrated south from Anatolia centuries before and had been left behind when the Ottoman Empire fell, like the till left behind by a glacier. In modern Arab Iraq, the Turcomans were truly a marooned people, speaking a virtually dead medieval Turkish language in which no textbooks were written. The only route to improvement for Tel Afaris was to Arabize or to join the Iraqi Army, and they had done both, meaning the town had a disproportionate number of men with military expertise. Sunni-Shia sectarianism had been unknown in Tel Afar before 2003, but the arrival of Sunni militants had led the city's Shia Turcomans to seek the protection of Shia supremacists in Baghdad. Deputy Interior Minister Ali Ghaleb, himself a Shia Tel Afari, had hired hundreds of fellow Shia Turcomans into Tel Afar's police, some of them loyalists of the Sadrists or Badr Corps. Similarly, SCIRI parliamentarian Muhammad Taqi al-Mullah, a former Badr Corps commander from Tel Afar, sought to use his political position to direct state resources to his fellow Tel Afari Shia.

By early 2005, the city was split between warring sectarian parties, with Shia militant police fighting a Sunni-insurgent-allied mayor. The battles between the two parties polarized the town, leading Sunni Turcomans to invite Abu Musab al-Zarqawi and Al Qaeda to join their local war as reinforcements. As the Sunni tribes of Anbar would later discover, those who invited Al Qaeda into local disputes invariably got more than they had bargained for, so that by the summer of 2005 it was Al Qaeda and the non-

Tel Afari mujahideen who controlled the Sunni quarters of the town, terrorizing the locals they had been meant to rescue.

THE SHAMMAR VERSUS THE KDP

On the periphery of the war in Tel Afar, the Sunnis of the Jazeera engaged in a struggle of their own with Kurdistan Democratic Pary (KDP) officials and peshmerga who had projected Kurdish power into western Ninewa. They had also been largely hostile toward the new Iraqi Army division stationed in the western half of the province, a majority Kurdish unit commanded by a former peshmerga officer. From an early stage the Sunni Arab towns west of Mosul had served as willing waypoints for the mujahideen that Al Qaeda facilitators were sending into Iraq from Syria, and the region had grown thick with foreign fighters. The leaders of the peshmerga outposts of western Ninewa had been overbearing in their own right, occasionally cut off the water supply for Arab townspeople to punish them for allowing mujahideen to use their towns as staging bases.

The Kurds' main political opposition among Ninewa's Sunnis came from Abdullah al-Yawar, the leading sheikh of the Shammar and a first cousin of Ghazi al-Yawar, the Sunni politician who had been Iraq's first interim president in 2004–05. A tall, stocky man in his early forties, Sheikh Abdullah wielded a great deal of authority among his fellow tribesmen, a rare dynamic among the Iraqi tribes. The Yawars also enjoyed strong tribal ties beyond Iraq, westward into Syria and southward into the central Arabian highlands from which their Shammar ancestors had come in the eighteenth century. The Yawars considered themselves an extension of a vast Shammar "nation" extending from Mosul all the way south to the Jebel Shammar, from which their Rashidi cousins had once ruled most of central Arabia. The Rashidi Shammar had lost their central Arabian empire to Abdul Aziz Ibn Saud in 1906 and then had backed the wrong horse in the First World War, siding with the Ottomans against the invading British in hopes of regaining their lost emirate from the pro-British Ibn Saud. By 2003, however, the old Shammar-Saudi feud had long since been repaired. Saudi King Abdullah was himself born of a Shammar mother, making him Abdullah al-Yawar's kinsman. In their battle with the Kurds, the Yawars would be able to call upon powerful friends.

Despite their wealth and regional connections, however, the Yawars and their Ninewa Sunni allies were at a political disadvantage in 2005, having foolishly frozen themselves out of power by boycotting the January elections. Sheikh Abdullah had recognized his disastrous mistake in boycotting the political process, and he worked to assemble an anti-Kurdish political coalition in anticipation of the next round of elections, whenever they might be held. The Yawars particularly sought an alliance with Ninewa's Yezidis, as many as two hundred thousand of whom lived in concentrations near Mosul and Sinjar. Though Kurds claim Yezidis as part of the Kurdish ethnic group, Yezidis were periodically subjected to attacks and discrimination in Kurdish territories, particularly by Kurdish Islamists. The Kurds responded by aligning with a rival clan of the Shammar, the Jarba, to blunt the Yawars' influence.

THE RESURGENCE OF AL QAEDA IN NINEWA

The Jarba rivalry might disrupt the Yawars' plans to create an anti-Kurdish political front, but a greater disruption was the ongoing Al Qaeda insurgency, which flared up again in Ninewa in 2007. The reemergence of Al Qaeda in western Ninewa and Mosul in that year reignited the civil war in the province, overturning the military victory the Iraqi government and U.S. forces had won in Tel Afar and Mosul in 2005 and crowding out peaceful political initiatives. Al Qaeda's return was driven in part by the Anbar Awakening of late 2006, in which the major tribes of Ramadi turned the upper Euphrates valley into a zone completely hostile to Al Qaeda's presence, leading Al Qaeda's Syria-based facilitators to shift their "pipeline" of mujahideen into the Jazeera to the north. Al Qaeda fighters were also drawn to Tel Afar because it offered them an easy opportunity to attack Shia Iraqis without risking forays into Shia strongholds in central Iraq.

The ensuing civil war in Ninewa was also fuelled in part by the release of prisoners from Abu Ghraib and the overreaction of Shia Tel Afaris. In late 2006, hundreds of insurgents who had been captured in the city in late 2005 were released after a year of detention and began drifting back into Tel Afar. Their sudden reappearance caused a panic among Tel Afar's Shia Turcoman leaders, who raised the alarm in Baghdad that their city was in danger again. The Interior Ministry responded by hiring hundreds of Shia Turcoman tribesmen into the police force and sacking almost a hundred Sunni policemen at the same time. With the police force turned back into a Shia militia, Tel Afar's Sunnis once again opened the city to Al Qaeda terrorists from Syria. On March 27, 2007, two massive truck bombs hit the main Shia marketplace of Tel Afar, killing or wounding five hundred Tel Afaris, almost all of them Shia. Within hours, the enraged Shia police exacted revenge by randomly executing Sunni men and boys in the street, killing seventy before Iraqi Army troops halted the massacre. A handful of Shia policemen were arrested for the killings but never went to trial.

The market bombings and subsequent massacre were only the opening salvo of a campaign that intensified through the summer. Under severe pressure in mid-2007 from the U.S.-Iraqi "surge" in Anbar, Baghdad, Babil, and Diyala, many Al Qaeda fighters migrated back into Ninewa, including Abu Ayyub al-Masri. To help fund their operations in the Mosul area, al-Masri and his Al Qaeda associates demanded protection money from local businesses, such as mobile phone companies, local cement manufacturers and construction companies, the state-run Northern Oil Company, and even local health clinics and pharmacies.

THE DESTRUCTION OF THE MINORITIES

Political support was harder for Al Qaeda to garner. The intrajihadi battle with native insurgent groups that Zarqawi had begun in 2005 had not been settled, and as Al Qaeda leaders and fighters reappeared in Mosul in late 2007, they found themselves in bloody turf battles with Jaish al-Islami and other Baathist Islamist groups. One way Al Qaeda and its allies attempted to polarize Ninewa's population and generate communal support was to target the non-Muslim religious minorities that had lived in Mosul for centuries. Estimates vary, but most sources agree that of the slightly more than one million Christians living in Iraq in 2003, more than half were forced to leave the country by 2010, with Christians accounting for about one of every five Iraqi refugees in the countries surrounding Iraq. The terrorist "cleansing" of Mosul's Christians accelerated in 2008. In February of that year, Al Qaeda shocked Christians by abducting Mosul's Chaldean Archbishop as he left his church, later murdering him and dumping his body. Later in the year, systematic terrorist attacks forced twelve thousand Christians to leave the city in a span of a few weeks.

The political effect of the attacks was to drive the Assyrians and other Christians away from Ninewa's Sunnis just as the Sunnis were hoping to assemble a broad anti-Kurdish front. Some Christian leaders in eastern Ninewa called for the creation of a separate autonomous Christian region, with its own regional guard force, while Kurdish leaders called for Christian areas to be annexed to Kurdistan, and the Kurdistan Regional Government (KRG) reportedly distributed millions of dollars to Christian villagers to establish a KRG-sponsored civil society network.

Al Qaeda had also stepped up its targeting of Ninewa's Yezidis after an incident in April 2007 in which Yezidi men in eastern Ninewa stoned to death a Yezidi woman who had taken a Sunni lover and supposedly converted to Islam. Days later, terrorists intercepted a bus with twenty-three Yezidi workers and shot them against a wall in Mosul. A few months later, the Sunni terrorist campaign against Yezidis intersected with a Sunni insurgent campaign against the peshmerga to devastating effect. In August 2007, Sunni terrorists near Sinjar carried out the most horrific terrorist act of the entire Iraq war. On August 14, Al Qaeda operatives detonated four massive car bombs in two Yezidi-Kurdish communities, causing whole apartment blocks to collapse on their residents and trap hundreds in the rubble. The final toll was an astonishing 796 killed and an additional fifteen hundred wounded. It was the single most costly attack of the long Iraqi civil war, taking more than twice as many lives in proportion to Iraq's population as the 9/11 attacks in the United States.

AL QAEDA AND SUNNI POLITICS

The terrible bombings against the Yezidis made the Yawars' hoped-for Yezidi-Sunni alliance unthinkable, ruining Sunni plans for an anti-Kurdish front in 2007. But by mid-2008, Al Qaeda's own overbearing behavior created openings for another Sunni centrist coalition. South of Mosul, Jabouri tribesmen formed an anti–Al Qaeda militia, limiting terrorist political influence in the upper

Tigris and Zab valleys. But the political coup de grace for Al Qaeda and other insurgent groups in Ninewa came with a shift of popular sentiment against Al Qaeda and the emergence of a credible Sunni political alternative. Abu Ayyub al-Masri's men in Mosul had worn out their welcome in 2008 by extracting heavy taxes from local businesses and killing or intimidating those who would not pay. Al Qaeda had murdered a popular Mosulawi pharmacist who defied them, as well as the popular director general of the Mosul city government, and angry Mosulawis had responded by offering the security forces greater intelligence on Al Qaeda's networks in the city.

As this popular backlash was underway, a broad Sunni coalition began to form in Mosul to reverse both Al Qaeda's control of the streets and the Kurdish takeover of the provincial government. Led by notables such as Abdullah al-Yawar and the parliamentarian Osama al-Nujaifi, the new Sunni bloc represented a rare alliance between Ninewa's rural and urban elites. The coalition had sweeping Sunni Arab support, not just because of traditional Sunni attitudes, but also because the Kurdish leaders of Ninewa had squandered five years in power in which they could have attempted to win popular support through public services and security. Instead, their heavy-handed approach had given Sunnis the impression that they meant to annex Mosul to an eventual Kurdish state, or at the very least to hold it until trading it back to the Sunnis in exchange for Kirkuk. The Kurds had failed to bring Mosul the kind of development and prosperity they had brought to Irbil and other KRG cities, so that after five years of KDP rule Mosul was in worse material condition than when the KDP had arrived in 2003. Even Ninewa's roads lagged behind those of Kurdistan, falling into such a state of disrepair that Mosulawis wishing to travel to Baghdad usually drove by way of Irbil. Ninewa

Arabs believed this reflected a Kurdish strategy to keep Mosul unstable so that the city's traditional trade with Turkey and Syria would naturally migrate behind the Green Line. These perceptions helped fuel a huge Sunni victory in the provincial elections of 2009, when the Yawar-Nujaifi-led bloc won control of the provincial council and replaced the KDP in power.

THE ARAB-KURD STALEMATE

After five years of Kurdish ascendancy, Ninewa's Sunni elite had succeeded, by a variety of violent and political means, in arresting the Kurdish advance across the Assyrian plains. In 2009, these Sunni leaders had fully reversed their disastrous 2005 rejection of the political process and were poised to potentially retake Mosul's share of national power in the parliamentary elections in 2010. Along the way, they had squeezed Al Qaeda out of mainstream Sunni politics. But though the Sunni elite had broken KDP control of western Ninewa and Mosul city, they were not strong enough to push the KDP back to the pre-2003 Green Line, and Kurdish leaders had no intention of allowing the Kurdish presence to be rolled back to its Saddam-era limits.

Like the Kirkuk dispute, the local Sunni-KDP dispute also had national implications and prompted national-level intervention. As the local Kurdish parties lost ground to the reinvigorated local Sunnis, the Kurdish parliamentary bloc in Baghdad would repeatedly use its powerful position to reinforce the Kurds in Ninewa, such as in the Kurdish parliamentarians' insistence that the peshmerga presence there was necessary as part of a Baghdad-sponsored project to allow the more than a hundred thousand Kurds that Saddam had displaced from the Mosul area to return to their homes safely. And in a sign of things to come, Maliki and his Dawa allies had increasingly become referees in the ongoing Sunni-Kurdish dispute, with Maliki's army commander in Mosul using his troops as a political balancer between Sunnis and the KDP.

Thus had Arabs, Kurds, and Turcomans fought a brutal six-year war over Kirkuk, Ninewa, and other disputed territories in the north with practically no political result. Arabs and Turcomans had not succeeded in pushing the Green Line physically back eastward, whence it had been advanced by the Kurdish offensive of April 2003, while the Kurds had failed to secure a permanent land bridge to the Kurdish enclaves of Ninewa and Syria. The intense ethnic conflict in these areas had resulted in a sort of paralysis, with the rival local parties frozen in place until national-level politics could tip the balance. But at the national level, too, the opposing sides had made little headway in pressing their claims. The Sunni Arab and Turcoman parties had made a terrible mistake in boycotting the January 2005 elections, something they had done largely to try to halt the political process that was heading toward the KRG annexation of Kirkuk. Conversely, that same process, written into the new Iraqi constitution by the Kurds and their Shia allies, had fallen apart in 2007 as a result of its own un-workability, diplomatic pressure, and the Turkish campaign against the PKK.

In short, none of the fundamental disputes that had led to violence had been resolved. The disputed territories along the Green Line would remain potential flashpoints, ripe for exploitation by militants who relished conflict or by divisive, opportunistic politicians aiming to draw political support from polarized Arab or Kurdish constituencies. The warring parties had accomplished little since 2003 other than devastating northern Iraq's cities and towns, killing or wounding tens of thousands, and driving hundreds of thousands from their homes—all while radicalizing and polarizing communities that had coexisted for centuries, making it highly probable that future losers in the political struggle would simply return to violence, and would find an ample base of support in doing so.

THE RESISTANCE

CHAPTER SEVEN

The Iraqi Shia "Resistance"

ONFERENCES ARE COMMON in Beirut, but in late October 2011 a peculiar one took place at the four-star Tamar
Rotana hotel. Ten days after the United States announced
its troops would leave Iraq by the end of the year, a motley mix of
militants and political activists gathered to mark the opening of
the "Ahl al-Haqq Center for Studies," a new Beirut think tank
affiliated with the Iranian-sponsored Iraqi insurgent group Asa'ib
Ahl al-Haqq. Representatives from Hezbollah and Hamas gave
speeches hailing Asa'ib Ahl al-Haqq's "victory" over the United
States in Iraq. A Hezbollah media spokesman equated Asa'ib Ahl
al-Haqq's fight against the United States to the Hezbollah and
Hamas "victories" over Israel in 2006 and 2008. A radical Lebanese
university professor detailed a supposed American plot to control all of Europe and Asia. A Lebanese general who spent more
than three years in jail under suspicion of helping to kill former
Lebanese Prime Minister Rafiq Hariri spoke about the "U.S.-
Zionist security system." For their part, the Iraqi speakers from
Asa'ib Ahl al-Haqq stressed the need for all the region's "sons of
resistance" to band together against their common foes. The event
was covered by Lebanese state media, with its proceedings posted
to a government website.

The Tamar Rotana gathering was a splashy coming-out party
for an Iraqi group that had started as a small offshoot of Moqtada

171

Sadr's Jaysh al-Mahdi six years before, headed by former top deputies to Moqtada himself. Asa'ib Ahl al-Haqq's reception in Beirut
signified that after eight years of local fighting against American
troops in Iraq, the Iraqi Shia militants had graduated into full-
fledged membership in the regional "Axis of Resistance" that was
engaged in a wide-ranging conflict against the United States and
its allies.

ROOTS OF THE RESISTANCE: THE SADIQ SADR MOVEMENT

Asa'ib Ahl al-Haqq's reception in Beirut was the culmination of
thirty years of radicalization, during which the Iraqi Shia militants' forebears had evolved from social movement, to insurgent
army, to Iranian-sponsored political parties. They had been born
among the remnants of the grassroots movement that Dawa left
behind when it fled Saddam's Iraq at the outset of the Iran-Iraq
War. With Dawa leaders gone and Muhammad Baqir Sadr executed, Baqr Sadr's cousin Muhammad Sadiq Sadr had stepped
into the leadership vacuum, eventually building a following of
millions of Iraqis during the war-torn decade of the 1980s. Learn-
ing from the mistakes that had decimated the Shia Islamists of the
1970s, Sadiq Sadr kept a lower profile than Muhammad Baqir and
Dawa had done. He was less hostile to the Baathist regime, developing a working relationship with Saddam during and after the
Iran-Iraq War. For Saddam, engaged in an existential war against
the Iranians, Sadiq Sadr was a useful Iraqi counterweight to the
Iranian clerics and their doctrine of *wilayet al-faqih*, and the Baath
gave Sadiq Sadr room to operate.

Sadr made good use of the space the regime gave him, cultivating
a network of laymen professionals across Iraq, as the Muslim Brotherhood had done elsewhere. He paid particular attention to Iraq's

colleges of engineering and sciences, where loyal teachers identified talented undergraduates who might make good candidates to study religion under Sadiq Sadr in Najaf. When the party led by Sadiq Sadr's son Moqtada joined the post-Saddam Iraqi government years later, some of these same laymen academics and engineers would become Sadrist government technocrats or even parliamentary leaders, such as the senior Sadrist politician Baha al-Araji.

A more important aspect of Sadiq Sadr's networking was his installation of Friday prayer imams in Shia-majority areas, a practice that was not traditional in Iraqi Shiism. Sadiq Sadr's Friday imams built a massive following during the period of Saddam's Faith Campaign, particularly among the lower classes packed into Sadr City and others slums, where Communism had thrived in the 1950s. It was a step that put Sadiq Sadr at odds with the Shia religious establishment in Najaf, where leading clerics such as Grand Marja Abul Qasim al-Khoei and Ayatollah Ali al-Sistani had favored the traditional quietist approach toward politics and governance. Sadiq Sadr's Friday mosque gatherings became a means of directly engaging his followers in a way that the quietist *marjaiyyah* had seldom done, and it represented a continuance of the activist approach Muhammad Baqir Sadr had advocated.

Most important to the network Sadiq Sadr was building, however, was its nerve center: the *hawza*, or religious college, that he headed in Najaf. Each of Najaf's *marjaiyyah* had their own college, each following a well-defined curriculum. In Sadiq Sadr's *hawza*, Sadr himself could be considered dean of faculty, with a bevy of associate professors and graduate assistants. There were also brilliant graduate students, some of whom studied in the same class of 1998 as Muqtada Sadr himself, such as Adnan al-Shahmani, later an influential member of parliament, and Qais al-Khazali and Akram al-Kabi, who would one day command the Jaysh al-Mahdi "Special Groups" before striking out on their own to found Asa'ib

Ahl al-Haqq. Sadiq Sadr invested deeply in these young men, bringing the brightest of them to deliver sermons at the grand mosque in Kufa, where Sadr served as the senior Friday imam and where the Prophet Muhammad's grandson Hussein had been bound when he was famously intercepted and killed at Karbala in the year 680.

Throughout the 1980s and '90s, Sadiq Sadr's public speeches were a study in anti-Americanism and anti-Zionism, and videos still circulate on YouTube of the white-haired ayatollah, looking two decades older than his fifty years, delivering fiery sermons in Kufa that echoed the anti-western and anti-Israeli themes of Saddam's foreign policy. Nevertheless, at some point in the late 1990s, the détente between Sadiq Sadr and Saddam had unraveled, leading to Sadiq Sadr's assassination in Najaf along with his older sons and leaving Muqtada as the sole survivor among the politically active Sadrs.

Sadiq Sadr's killing prompted outbursts that, in retrospect, indicated that the ayatollah had spawned a popular movement strong enough to survive him. In the days after his death, a series of spontaneous protests by Sadrist followers erupted across southern Iraq and Baghdad, large and turbulent enough to lead the regime to deploy security forces against Sadr-loyalist neighborhoods. In al-Thawra, the huge Shia-majority neighborhood of Baghdad that would be renamed Sadr City in 2003, regime security forces clashed with enraged Sadrists, killing somewhere between forty and three hundred of them. The scene was repeated in Basra, where opposition sources claimed that after four days of intense fighting, the Baath had executed as many as five hundred Shia rebels.

There were disturbances outside Iraq as well. In Jordan, two thousand Iraqis protested Sadiq Sadr's killing outside the Iraqi embassy in Amman. In Iran, a memorial ceremony for Sadr in

Qom turned into an unruly fiasco when a large Sadrist crowd tried to attack SCIRI leader Muhammad Baqr Hakim as he unwisely entered the mosque to pay his respects. Hakim and the Iran-based SCIRI had been bitter rivals to Sadr during the 1990s, with the former accusing Sadr of collaborating with Saddam against the Shia cause. The assault against Hakim showed the depth of Sadrist anger over SCIRI's criticisms of Sadr, as well as Sadrists' resentment against Shia expatriates who had not shared in the harsh conditions of 1990s Iraq.

Back in Iraq, Sadr's assassination led to the scattering of his *hawza* to the four winds, with some of his top followers disappearing underground. Some of Sadr's street following undoubtedly migrated into the Baathist regime's camp, because some Shia neighborhoods that had responded violently to Sadr's killing had become Saddamist strongholds by 2003. This was especially true in Sadr City and the other Shia areas of east Baghdad, which provided thousands of young men to Udai Hussein's Fedayeen Saddam militia. The Fedayeen recruited heavily in Shia neighborhoods, partly because Saddam and his regime did not trust Udai with the command of more important Sunni-majority units, and partly because the high unemployment level of the Shia slums meant many were willing to join Udai's forces to receive training and pay. Later some of these Shia Fedayeen would become members of Muqtada's Jaysh al-Mahdi, bringing their paramilitary skills with them.

At the leadership level, however, little is known of how the Sadrists spent the years between 1999 and 2003. One Sadrist later estimated that a hundred twenty Sadrist clerics were arrested or executed at the time of Sadiq Sadr's killing. Spared such a fate, Muqtada al-Sadr seems to have continued clerical studies in Najaf under the Afghan quietist ayatollah Muhammad Ishaq al-Fayadh. Otherwise, almost nothing is known of how much the regime

learned about their network, whether the Sadrists sought help
from the Iranian regime, or what future Sadrist leaders, including
Muqtada, did or said to survive.

All that is certain is that the western armies that invaded Iraq
in 2003 had virtually no idea the Sadrists were there.

THE STRUGGLE FOR NAJAF AND MURDER OF
ABDUL MAJID AL-KHOEI

The first post-Saddam manifestation of Sadiq Sadr's movement
came in Najaf in April 2003, where three Shia clerical factions
sought control of the city. The stakes were high, since the group
that gained control of the *hawza* and shrines in the city would be
in a strong position to use clerical authority to direct the political
behavior of the Iraqi Shia community. The expatriate Hakims and
SCIRI represented the *wilayet al-faqih* faction closest to Iran and
most identified with the idea that Iraq should be an Islamic republic on the Iranian model. The Hakims hoped to make Najaf the
real political center of Iraq, with a clerical veto over whatever government would form in Baghdad. The Sadrists represented a more
nationalist and populist opposition to the Hakims, advocates of
clerical activism but wary of Iranian influence, especially after the
Iranian regime had spent the 1990s vehemently criticizing Sadiq
Sadr. Yet a third faction represented the clerical establishment
already present in Najaf, aligned behind Sistani, somewhat wary
of Iranian influence but more quietist than the Sadrists were prepared to be.

Aside from Sistani, the most prominent figure in the Najafi
faction was the young cleric Abdul Majid al-Khoei, son of the
beloved Ayatollah Abul Qasim al-Khoei, who had preceded Sistani as Grand Marja before dying under Baathist house arrest in

1992. Abdul Majid had left Iraq after the Shia uprising of 1991, settling in London to run his father's charitable foundation and become a prominent member of the Iraqi opposition. Abdul Majid advocated a rapprochement between the Iraqi Shia and the West, a position that put him at odds with both the Iranian regime-sponsored Hakims and the Sadrists, and he particularly sought to repair the Iraqi Shiites' distrust of the United States after the perceived American "betrayal" of the 1991 uprising. When Abdul Majid arrived in Iraq in early April 2003, transported by American officials, the battle for Baghdad was still going on, and he quickly attempted to establish a presence at the Imam Ali shrine. While meeting with Hayder Kelidar, the Iraqi government official whose family had long been the shrine's custodians, Abdul Majid and his entourage were attacked by a Sadrist crowd that dragged Kelidar and Khoei into the street, stabbing and shooting the men to death near Muqtada Sadr's home. Eyewitnesses recounted that the badly wounded Abdul Majid had been dragged to Muqtada's door, where Sadr had refused his pleas for mercy, and that it was Sadr's top lieutenants who had actually done the killing.

In the Iraqi Shia community, Abdul Majid's murder was a shocking crime that deprived the brand-new political process of a rare Shia leader who was both credible in his community and interested in a partnership with the West. "Had Abdul Majid lived, he would have been a major player," a senior Shia politician later recalled. "Things would have been very different in that case." The murder was also an indefensible attack by fellow Shia clerics against one of the most respected *marjaiyyah* families, and in the years after 2003, the killing would repeatedly come back to haunt Muqtada and his lieutenants. The Sadrist uprising of early 2004 was partly begun to preempt a warrant an Iraqi court and the Coalition Provisional Authority had issued for Muqtada's arrest on the murder charge. Later, the Maliki government subtly threatened several times to reopen the case in order to gain political leverage over the Sadrists, and it was not until Maliki needed to secure Muqtada's support during the political crisis of late 2011 that the Iraqi government dropped the charges, though advisers to Maliki privately indicated they could be resurrected if necessary.

Nevertheless, for Muqtada and his lieutenants, the murder had served its purpose, making the unmistakable political statement that the Sadrists were a force to be reckoned with, willing to use brutal political violence, unwilling to let the expatriate political elite fashion a new order without giving the Sadrists their share of power.

THE JAYSH AL-MAHDI

After killing Abdul Majid, the Sadrists' next major step was to revive their long-dormant popular following and convert it into an armed presence on Iraq's streets, thereby taking advantage of the security vacuum caused by the collapse of the Iraqi state and giving the movement the means to protect its interests by force. The resulting Sadrist militia, the Jaysh al-Mahdi, or Mahdi Army, was a loose paramilitary club whose initial raison d'être was not armed resistance against foreign troops, but rather the protection of Shia pilgrims during the annual processions honoring the martyrdom of the Imam Hussein in Karbala and Najaf. The first of these took place just days after Saddam had been toppled, held fully in the open for the first time since the 1970s. The fact that the Mahdi Army grew to a presence of tens of thousands within just a few months of Saddam's fall indicated that the Sadiq Sadr network had survived the regime's 1999 crackdown intact. The militia also grew by absorbing some of the thousands of Shia Fedayeen that Saddam left unemployed after the Coalition Provisional Authority dissolved the organization in May 2003. The number of Fedayeen who became Sadrists is not known, but former Jaysh al-Mahdi leaders later estimated it in the thousands, referring to the Fedayeen joiners as "Baathists" within the Sadr movement.

In social terms, the Mahdi Army represented a mobilization of lower-class Shia Iraqis, often from tribal families who migrated from southern Iraq to the slums of Sadr City in the 1950s to '70s. Their grandfathers were more likely to have been followers of the leftist Abdul Karim Qasim than conservative Islamists. The Sadrist militants of 2003, by contrast, were mainly aggrieved Shia men who, having suffered grievously under the Saddam regime, were capable of shocking violence against Baathists and Sunnis in mixed-sect areas, and they would play a major role in the sectarian cleansing of 2005–07. They were also deeply ignorant of the wider world. Having grown up as the most disadvantaged social group in an isolated police state, the Sadrists had generally led sheltered, poorly educated lives, with few of their number venturing beyond Iraq. One senior Iraqi politician illustrated the Sadrists' insularity by describing his journey to Amman, Jordan, in 2007 with a Sadrist leader who had never been outside Iraq. Unused to advanced infrastructure, the Sadrist was alarmed by the streetlights lining the highway from the airport into Amman, demanding of his fellow traveler, "Is there an emergency? Why are all the roads lit at night? Tell me what has gone wrong!"

Sadrist characteristics like these left other Shia political leaders with mixed feelings about the Mahdi Army and often a reluctance to use force against them: on one hand, they posed a threat to Shia leaders who had come from outside the country, but on the other hand, their general state of ignorance and poverty was what the Shia opposition to Saddam had striven to redress.

In the absence of worldly experience, the Sadrists were ideologically driven, steeped in the narrative of Shia victimization (especially over the "betrayal" of the Shia uprising of 1991) and conspiracy theory promoted by their clerical leaders. Sadrist leaders described their movement as ranged against an evil America bent on destroying Islam and the Arab world, and their turn to insurgency against the U.S.-led Coalition was unsurprising. The events leading to the Sadrist uprisings in Baghdad and southern Iraq in early 2004 have been well documented elsewhere and need not be recounted here. The Mahdi Army would later field hundreds of death squads against Iraqi Sunnis, but at the outset of the insurgency it behaved in a more cross-sectarian fashion, fighting primarily against foreign troops. They had even sent Shia fighters to Fallujah in 2004 to assist the Sunni insurgents there, and Sunni insurgents had returned the favor by sending fighters to Najaf to assist the Mahdi Army militiamen fighting U.S. troops in the shrine city.

Despite the cross-sectarian support the Sadrists enjoyed during their first uprisings, the clashes with the U.S. military in April and August 2004 resulted in a crushing defeat for the Mahdi Army. The Sadrist military disasters of 2004 set in motion a chain of events that eventually fractured the original Sadiq Sadr movement, set Sadrist leaders against each other, and opened the movement to co-optation by outside powers. After 2004, what had been for two decades an indigenous Shia Iraqi movement would increasingly resemble a client of the Iranian regime that Sadiq Sadr had once defied.

THE SADRIST RESISTANCE AND IRAN

The August 2004 battle in Najaf had been particularly costly for the Mahdi Army, leaving several hundred fighters killed and wounded. The defeated Sadrist militia leaders realized they had little hope of besting either U.S. troops or the Iraqi Army in pitched battles as long as the Mahdi Army was nothing more than a lightly armed and disorganized rabble. A few key Sadrist militia commanders believed the solution was to transform their popular resistance movement into smaller, more disciplined, and better-equipped "special groups" that could wage a more effective irregular war against U.S. troops. The foot soldiers of the Mahdi Army could continue to be a force on the streets of Iraqi cities, but the leading role in the Shia insurgency would fall to the more capable Special Groups.

The Najaf fighting had exposed more than just the Sadrists' military weakness. It had also revealed deep fractures among the Sadrist leaders. Muqtada Sadr had been erratic as a militant leader, dictatorial and mercurial with his subordinates. Some of the favored students of his late father grew resentful of Muqtada's assertion of sole control over his father's vast network. After all, Sadiq Sadr had brought top students such as Qais al-Khazali into his councils while Muqtada and his friends had reputedly busied themselves elsewhere playing video games (earning Muqtada the derisive nickname "Mullah Atari"). It was entirely possible that Sadiq Sadr's acolytes considered themselves more worthy heirs of the old man's legacy than Muqtada could be.

To create a truly effective insurgent force and operate independently of Muqtada, however, these militants needed a new patron who could provide military assistance and resources. They therefore decided to place themselves in the hands of Iran's most dangerous man.

HAJJI QASSEM

The would-be commanders of the Special Groups sought assistance from Brigadier General Qassem Soleimani, head of the Quds

Force, the branch of Iran's Islamic Revolutionary Guards Corps responsible for covert operations and subversion in the places that mattered most to Iran's national security strategy: Afghanistan, Syria, Lebanon, the Palestinian territories, the Arabian peninsula, and, above all, Iraq. In U.S. terms, the Quds Force functioned as a cross between the CIA, Special Operations Command, and State Department, with Quds Force officers in the aforementioned countries responsible for intelligence, military, and political affairs there. Its commander since 1996, Soleimani—known to Arabs as Hajji Qassem—was a product of Iran's Islamic revolution who as a young man had commanded a front-line Revolutionary Guard division in the Iran-Iraq War, joining a tightly knit group of Guards commanders with the same experience. Like other veterans of that costly war, Soleimani would have come away from the conflict with the conclusion that Iraq must be the top priority among Iranian security interests, never again allowed to pose an existential threat to Iran and its revolution. The sudden removal of Saddam, therefore, had presented an unexpected chance to permanently reshape Iraq into a friendly client state, an opportunity the Iranians surely had no intention of missing.

In this context, the Special Groups' entreaty for support came at a good time for Soleimani and the regime. In the years before 2003, Soleimani had been the Iranian regime's point man in dealing with the Iraqi opposition groups, but by late 2004 his longtime Iraqi Shia clients were becoming increasingly problematic. They had grown too friendly with the United States for Iran's taste, participating too unreservedly in the U.S.-led political process and developing what seemed to be a strategic partnership with the Americans. The Sadrists who approached Soleimani for help in 2004–05 were potentially an additional proxy whom Soleimani could use as a rejectionist counterweight in Iraqi Shia politics, a force that could help accomplish the Iranian regime's near-term goal of expelling the U.S. military from Iran's doorstep—a goal that SCIRI and Badr did not appear to share.

The open rift inside the Sadrist leadership was also a golden opportunity for the Iranian regime to co-opt part of a Sadr movement that had long posed a potentially dangerous challenge to the authority of Iran's Supreme Leader in the Shia world. Sadiq Sadr's grassroots movement had been in many ways a reaction against Iranian Shiism and the Iranian regime itself, particularly the Iranian assertion that under the doctrine of *wilayet al-faqih* Iran's Supreme Leader was the rightful leader of the Muslim world. Sadiq Sadr had undercut the Supreme Leader's authority by claiming to be the rightful *faqih* for Iraq's Shia Muslims himself. The Iranians had exerted great influence over the Shia expatriate parties, but little over the Iraqi Shia populace, which tended to be anti-Iranian, especially in the areas hardest hit by Iranian offensives during the Iran-Iraq War. Working with the new Sadrist rivals to Muqtada's leadership could at last give the Iranians access to the broader Sadrist base. In the years after 2004, the Quds Force would work hard to gain direct control of portions of Muqtada Sadr's military organization as a means of bringing the grassroots Sadrist following into the Iranian regime's sphere of influence.

Soleimani was well equipped for the task of molding the Sadr movement into an Iranian proxy. Answering to no one but the Supreme Leader, he was free to act without sharing his plans with other Iranian agencies. He also knew Arab politics well. Arab politicians recounted that he received a constant flow of visitors from Iraq and the Levant, either in Tehran's Istiqlal Hotel—where he kept guests from different factions sequestered from each other on different floors—or in his heavily guarded, multistory headquarters near the intersection of tree-lined Naderi and Ayatalia streets, opposite the Foreign Ministry's strategic studies center. "He speaks Arabic only haltingly," one Arab visitor to the headquarters recalled. "He frequently has to turn to an interpreter to give him the Arabic for a Persian word he is thinking of. And he speaks very classical Arabic, not the colloquial style Arabs use." Yet despite approaching Arabs as a foreigner, Solemani's influence was obvious. His ability to deploy violence against his political enemies in Iraq left the entire Iraqi political elite intimidated. "He is the most powerful man in Iraq without question," former National Security Adviser Mowaffaq al-Rubaie told an Arabic newspaper in 2010. "Nothing gets done without him." The Iranian general could inspire fear in the most senior Iraqi officials.

Beyond an intimate knowledge of Iraqi affairs, Soleimani could, in his outreach to the Sadrists, draw upon his long experience as Iran's interlocutor with the Arab world's most potent Islamist resistance groups, especially Hezbollah and Hamas. He had forged deep relationships with Hezbollah's political chief Hassan Nasrallah and its militant kingpin Imad Mughniyah, with the latter ultimately enjoying de facto status as a senior Quds Force commander and a direct relationship with Supreme Leader Khamenei until Mughniyah's death in a Damascus car bombing in 2008. Part of his appeal to Arab Islamists, an Arab politician observed, was his ascetic personal manner. Dressing in simple, almost worn-out clothes, Soleimani gave his Arab guests simple working-class-style Persian meals preceded by group prayers, quite unlike the feasts served to guests in Arab capitals. In person, he was understated, speaking softly with all visitors and displaying a physical frailty that made him appear, in one visitor's words, "So thin that he looked like he was wasting away, with pale skin that made him look much older than he actually is—like Dracula or some kind of ghost."

SOLEIMANI'S PROXIES IN IRAQ

Soleimani's ghostly appearance notwithstanding, his men's presence among the Sadrists in Iraq was no apparition. Soleimani dispatched Quds Force officers to train the Special Groups in camps inside Iran, to funnel arms to them through southern Iraq, and to act as military advisers on the ground inside Iraq as well. He had a cadre of senior Arabic-speaking Quds Force officers with extensive networks inside Iraq, including Iran's ambassador in Baghdad.

The reason the Quds Force presence in Iraq became known is that a relatively large number of Quds Force operatives were exposed or captured by U.S. troops between 2006 and 2008. Though all were eventually released or allowed to continue their work, their exposure showed that Iraq with more than a hundred fifty thousand Coalition troops was a risky place for Soleimani's Persian officers to directly operate. By late 2006, then, Soleimani and the Iranian regime began to rely heavily on more effective Arab middlemen in their relationship with the Sadrist militants.

The first of these middlemen was Lebanese Hezbollah, whose experienced, native Arabic-speaking militants could perform functions inside Iraq that had become too dangerous for Quds Force men to do themselves. Hezbollah played a critical role in the Iranian regime's outreach to Sadrist factions. The Iraqi militants who traveled to Iranian training camps found themselves in the hands of Hezbollah instructors, whom Quds Force leaders used in much the same way the Soviets had used Cubans to train Spanish-speaking Communists during the Cold War, a factor that at once took advantage of Hezbollah's solid credibility in the Arab world and mitigated the natural tension that might ensue from the Iraqis' interaction with Persian trainers. These Hezbollah instructors no

doubt drew upon their combat experience against Israel as teaching points, and one can imagine the young, inexperienced Iraqis
gathered around grizzled Hezbollah commanders telling war stories of their "victories" over the feared Israelis and occasionally
expressing their adherence to *wilayet al-faqih*. It was surely no
coincidence that the Special Groups and other Sadrists after 2005
began to model themselves after Hezbollah, seeking to establish
themselves inside Iraq as both a political party and an armed resistance movement beyond the Iraqi state's control.

By early 2007, Hezbollah had moved into an even more active
relationship with the Sadrist militant groups, as the Lebanese
organization's operatives entered Iraq to work directly with Iraqi
Shia militant groups to plan and conduct attacks against U.S. and
Coalition targets. The most egregious example of Hezbollah's
involvement in the war against the United States was senior Hezbollah commander Musa Daqduq, who in January 2007 helped
Asa'ib Ahl al-Haqq plan a bold raid against U.S. military advisers
in Karbala that resulted in the abduction and execution of five
American soldiers. Daqduq was captured in Basra a few weeks
later, but feigned being a mute for the first few months of his
detention in order to hide his Lebanese nationality from his
Coalition captors.

Hezbollah's role among the Iraqi militant groups went beyond
military activities as well. The Lebanese organization had preexisting relationships with members of the Sadiq Sadr movement that
enabled Hezbollah to play a political role in Iraq. Most notably,
Hezbollah leader Hassan Nasrallah could use senior Lebanese
cleric and Hezbollah official Muhammad Kawtharani as a liaison
to the Sadrists and their offshoots, owing to the years Kawtharani
had spent studying and teaching in Sadiq Sadr's *hawza* in Najaf.
Among Hezbollah's political officers, Kawtharani would repeatedly
handle the Iraqi political portfolio for Nasrallah.

The period of deeper Hezbollah involvement also coincided with the growing role of another Arab Quds Force middleman: the former Badr Corps commander Abu Mahdi al-Muhandis, who after 2003 became known among Iraqis as Soleimani's favored Iraqi representative. Muhandis was actually elected to the Iraqi parliament in 2005, but was ultimately suspended from parliament for his militant activities. As some Special Groups factions began to break from the main Sadr movement in 2005–06, Abu Mahdi was able to gather some of the breakaway Sadrists into a new Special Groups–type organization, Kata'ib Hezbollah, which resembled other Sadrist offshoots but was wholly controlled by the Quds Force and received the best training and arms the Iranians could offer. Throughout 2007 and 2008, Kata'ib Hezbollah routinely conducted attacks against Coalition targets and then contributed video of the attacks to be aired on Lebanese Hezbollah's Al-Manar television channel, illustrating again the close relationship among the Quds Force, Lebanese Hezbollah, and the Iraqi militants whom Soleimani sponsored.

With the rise of Muhandis' militants, there were now three different categories of "Special Groups" operating in Iraq. The first were Special Groups still controlled by Muqtada Sadr and his organization, which were generally Mahdi Army groups that had received better training and arms than the rest of the militia and had remained loyal to Muqtada, thereby earning the label of "Muqtada Groups" among other Shia militants. The second were the Asa'ib Ahl al-Haqq groups that had broken from Muqtada's control to work closely with the Quds Force, but were commanded by Iraqis who considered themselves allied with, but not bound to, the Iranian regime. The third were those groups controlled directly by the Quds Force and loyal to the Supreme Leader, such as Kata'ib Hezbollah, which other Shia militants called the "Khamenei Groups." These three different collections of militants sometimes acted in concert—especially against Coalition targets—but just as often at cross purposes, and occasionally fought one another for control of territory or in political disputes. But despite their political differences, they would join together against the Iraqi government in the Shia civil war of 2007–08.

The "Resistance" versus the Iraqi Establishment

At the same time the Special Groups were beginning to challenge Muqtada al-Sadr's leadership of the Sadr movement, Muqtada and his political representatives were challenging the new Maliki government's leadership of the country. The Sadrists had enjoyed excellent relations with Dawa's Prime Minister Ibrahim al-Jaafari, the Iraqi leader considered to be closest in sentiment and ideology to the Sadiq Sadr movement, and had remained in support of Jaafari's Dawa in the premiership contest of 2006, when the Sadrists had cast the deciding votes for Dawa's Maliki over SCIRI's Adel Abd al-Mahdi. But the Sadrists had turned against Maliki when the new prime minister cooperated with Coalition forces against both Sunni and Shia insurgents. When Muqtada angrily withdrew his ministers from Maliki's cabinet in late 2006, Maliki began a quest to retain the support of some of the Sadrist constituency by finding other Sadrists who could be brought into Maliki's coalition.

By 2006–07, the Malikiyoun had several Sadrist splinter parties to choose from. The most prominent was Fadhila, the Basra-based party and militia led by Sadiq Sadr's former deputy Muhammad al-Yaqoubi, whose own son had been a classmate of Muqtada in the Sadiq Sadr *hawza*. Fadhila had done surprisingly well in the provincial elections of 2005, capturing the Basra governorship and gaining enough local government power to hire a large number of its militia members into police positions, especially among the police units that were supposed to guard Basra's oilfields and pipelines, which were the lifeblood of the entire Iraqi state. Maliki's relationship with Fadhila, however, was too turbulent to allow for a counter-Muqtada alliance, particularly after the Fadhila governor of Basra attempted in 2007–08 to make Basra an autonomous region beyond the Maliki government's control.

More to Maliki's liking than Fadhila were Qais al-Khazali and Asa'ib Ahl al-Haqq. The Malikiyoun believed Qais was a more mature and strategically minded leader than Muqtada who might deliver enough of Sadiq Sadr's grassroots base into Maliki's camp to neutralize the opposition from Muqtada's parliamentary bloc. Accordingly, Maliki aides negotiated with Khazali for the militia's public disavowal of violence in return for Maliki's support for Asa'ib Ahl al-Haqq as a political party.

Maliki and his aides were understandably dismayed, then, when Coalition troops arrested Qais with Hezbollah commander Musa Daqduq in early 2007 for masterminding the murderous raid against U.S. soldiers in Karbala. Maliki was further dismayed to see the Coalition's damning evidence that Qais and his men had carried out numerous attacks on behalf of the Iranians, a fact that led to Maliki's reluctant agreement to Qais's incarceration.

In truth, Khazali was a thin reed for Maliki to lean upon. Appearing younger than his thirty-four years in 2007, Qais was a charismatic speaker but politically inexperienced and unrefined, having been exposed, like many Sadrists, to little of the wider world. He often spoke with a broad grin and broken front tooth that made him look more like a young Sadr City hoodlum than the leader of a real political movement, though his followers treated him with an affected deference. The prospects for such neophytes operating independently of the formidable Qassem Soleimani were meager. Nevertheless, Qais's detention by U.S. troops in 2007 opened a six-year effort by the Malikiyoun first to free Qais and hundreds of Asa'ib Ahl al-Haqq operatives from captivity and then to set them up as peer competitors to Moqtada Sadr.

THE SADRISTS IN CRISIS

The Malikiyoun's quest for a Sadrist alternative took place as two other major developments for the Sadr movement were playing out in 2007–08. The first was that the Sadrist militia's disorganization had grown so great that it threatened the credibility of the broader Sadrist political movement. The militiamen whose protection had been welcomed by Shia pilgrims in 2004 had made themselves unwelcome by mid-2007. The Mahdi Army, as this book has discussed, bore much popular blame for the sectarian cleansing of greater Baghdad in 2005–06, and as Al Qaeda's power in the Baghdad region waned in 2007, the Shia populace questioned why the militia was still needed on the street, given the Iraqi Army's restored presence in much of the country. In truth, many Mahdi Army groups had long since ceased to serve a security purpose and instead had become a self-serving mafia that intimidated the Shia communities they were supposed to be guarding. In Sadr City, Mahdi Army commanders controlled the essentials of daily life, including electricity and cooking gas, distributing the latter from Sadrist mosques and forcing competitors out of business. The militia commanders also came to control the provision of housing, serving essentially as apartment brokers and landlords for Sadr City residents who wished to move out of the slums. The militias placed Shia families in the vacant homes of Sunnis whom the militias themselves had driven away, especially in west Baghdad neighborhoods like Sh'ula and Hurriyeh. Where the militias were most powerful, they often took steps to impose strict Islamic law, punishing, sometimes by death, residents who committed violations of what militia leaders considered proper Islamic behavior, such as prostitution, homosexuality, or the sale of alcohol or music.

In short, the Sadrist militias imposed a heavy hand on Shia communities by 2007, and popular resentment against them ran deep. It was in this context that the country viewed the disastrous shootout between the Mahdi Army and government police at the Imam Hussein shrine in Karbala in August 2007 that left dozens of pilgrims dead in the crossfire. For the Sadrists, the clash had been a simple turf battle with Badr Corps rivals who happened to be wearing government uniforms. For the Iraqi public, it was final evidence of a militia gone amok. Muqtada Sadr's immediate announcement of a six-month "freeze" on Mahdi Army activities could be seen as an attempt at damage control, to preserve the popular support the Sadr movement had enjoyed since the 1980s and to stave off the many forces attempting to fracture his political base.

The Karbala incident led Muqtada and his allies to launch several initiatives to reassert control of a militia network that had clearly slipped out of Muqtada's grasp. After announcing the Mahdi Army "freeze," Muqtada dispatched a committee of trusted commanders from Najaf to Baghdad to purge rogue Mahdi Army men who had committed embarrassing abuses of the population or defied orders. Along with the purge, Muqtada ordered the vast majority of the Mahdi Army to convert itself into a social welfare organization called the *Mumahidun* ("Those Who Pave the Way"— sometimes translated tongue-in-cheek by American officials as "The Steamrollers") that would be engaged in religious classes and activities to prepare for the return of the Mahdi. Future militant resistance activities, Muqtada announced, would be reserved only for an elite portion of the Mahdi Army that would be renamed the Promised Day Brigade, which would continue the war against American troops. With the establishment of the Mumahidun and the Promised Day Brigade, Muqtada's organizations would more closely resemble Lebanese Hezbollah's division into political, social welfare, and military wings. Like Hezbollah's military wing, the Promised Day Brigade would have a close relationship with the Quds Force and would send its fighters to Iran for training and equipping.

Another major development was the onset of outright civil war among the Iraqi Shia parties and their associated armed wings in 2007–08 (described in chapter 2), intra-Shia battles that signified that Iran's military strategy in Iraq had failed. In an effort to empower Iraqi proxies to fight and hopefully expel U.S. troops from Iraq, Soleimani and the Quds Force had armed and trained as many Shia factions as possible. But in doing so, they had given those factions the means to make war upon each other, ruining the Shia political unity that was the core of Iran's longer-term strategy to ensure that the new Iraqi order would be Shia-dominated and friendly to Iran. In retrospect, giving the Iraqi parties arms without being able to control the direction in which they were aimed was a colossal blunder by Soleimani and his deputies, one that would take them years to overcome.

THE RESISTANCE AND IRAN VERSUS SISTANI

Meanwhile, as Iran's various armed Iraqi clients were battling for supremacy after 2004, another more subtle—and successful—line of Iranian strategy was playing out, in which the Sadrists and their offshoots played a significant role. One of the greatest dangers for the Iranian regime in post-Saddam Iraq was that a reinvigorated Iraqi clerical establishment in Najaf might challenge the Iranians for religious leadership of the Shia world, which had traditionally been centered in Najaf and Karbala until the appearance of Iran's Islamic Republic in 1979. During the decades in which the Baath had suppressed the Shia clergy in Najaf and Karbala, the Iranian clergy had become the intellectual center of Shiism for the first time, a distinction they would be loath to surrender back to a resurgent Najaf. In addition, Supreme Leader Ali Khamenei's legitimacy rested on the idea that he was God's supreme representative on Earth, a proposition that could be shaken if he, with his middling credentials as an Islamic scholar, were seriously challenged by more eminent Islamic authorities outside Iran such as Lebanon's Grand Ayatollah Muhammad Hussein Fadlallah, one of Dawa's cofounders, or, more significantly, Najaf's Grand Marja Ali Sistani, originally Iranian himself. Khamenei and his supporters thus took active steps after 2003 to prevent Sistani and the Iraqi clerical establishment from using their post-Saddam freedom to build a clerical infrastructure that might overshadow Khamenei's own in the Arab world.

The Iranian regime's first move was to establish a presence in Iraq that would not have been possible during Saddam's rule. Iranian businesses and developments sprang up in Najaf and Karbala to cater to the pilgrimage trade, some of them reportedly linked to the Quds Force, and Quds Force officers reportedly operated under the guise of a foundation for the "Reconstruction of Iraq's Holy Sites." The Iranian regime also invested heavily in expanding the supreme leader's clerical infrastructure throughout the Arab world, opening well-resourced offices and providing student and clergy stipends the Iraqi marjaiyyah could not match. In recent years, the Iranian regime also seemed to position itself to challenge for the post-Sistani leadership of Najaf by opening up new offices in the city for Ayatollah Mahmud Shahrudi, an Iraqi loyalist of the supreme leader who had long served as the head of Iraq's judiciary, and Dawa insiders had signaled they might eventually recognize Shahrudi as their party's official marja.

But it may be that the most direct Iranian measures were aimed at Sistani himself. The grand marja's clerical network in Iraq came under severe pressure after 2004, a fact that some Sistani loyalists attributed to his rivalry with the supreme leader. Sistani's aides eventually came to believe that the Iranians posed a physical threat to their leader, and they discouraged Sistani from leaving his Najaf home due to their belief, reasonable or not, that he might be targeted by snipers emplaced by the Iranian regime. In this light, it is unlikely to be merely coincidental that Sistani's network in Baghdad and southern Iraq came under attack in 2005–07, with the grand marja's offices attacked in several cities and more than a dozen of his representatives assassinated, including at least seven in the summer of 2007 alone, five of them in Najaf. As had been the case in the immediate aftermath of Saddam's fall in 2003, a violent power struggle was taking place in Najaf, with high stakes for both the Iraqi Shia and the Iranian regime.

Other Shia factions aimed to limit Sistani's influence as well. There were strange millenarian cult figures who denounced Sistani, such as Mahmud Hasani Sarkhi, who claimed to speak directly for the Mahdi and whose thousands of followers occasionally attacked Sistani's offices, or the "Soldiers of Heaven," a secretive, supposedly anti-Sistani cult that came from nowhere to fight pitched battles against Iraqi troops in the south in 2007–08. Of course, the entire Sadiq Sadr movement had been in many ways a backlash against the quietist marjaiyyah whom Sistani typified, and Muqtada Sadr's ill-fated attempts to seize control of Najaf in 2003–04 had been acts of defiance against Sistani himself, though some of Muqtada's rank-and-file followers privately considered Sistani their source of emulation. A great many Sadrists, however, considered Muqtada their marja, despite his inexperience and the fact that he lacked the scholarly credentials to be an ayatollah. Muqtada's loyalists referred to him as "Sayyid al-Qaed," or "Sayyid Leader," and he frequently published statements, usually posted on his website, that amounted to fatwas, despite his lack of formal standing to issue them. For a prominent cleric to bypass the *hawza*'s entire rigorous education process in this way was in itself a challenge to the establishment that Sistani headed.

The broad array of Sistani's religious oppponents indicated that it would not be easy for the ayatollahs of Najaf to reclaim the mantle of worldwide Shia religious leadership from the Iranian regime, as so many pre-2003 observers had predicted would happen naturally once Saddam Hussein was gone.

THE SADRISTS' POLITICAL COMEBACK

By the end of the summer of 2008, the Sadr movement seemed on the verge of political extinction, with its militant army defeated and many senior commanders fled to Iran. But a series of political developments, combined with adroit maneuvers by the Sadrists themselves, allowed the Sadrists to reenter the Iraqi political mainstream, eventually to become the largest single party in the Iraqi parliament.

The initial factor in their revival was Prime Minister Maliki's initiative to reconcile with the Sadrists in order to gain their political support against Abd el-Aziz Hakim and ISCI, Maliki's only remaining peer competitors—with whom, of course, he had formed a temporary alliance in order to prosecute the Iraqi government's war against the Sadrists just months beforehand. Accordingly, the Malikiyoun worked during the fall and winter of 2008–09 to reach an agreement under which Sadrist prisoners would be released and Sadrist candidates could compete in the 2009 provincial elections as independents, provided that the Sadrists dropped their resistance to the government. This agreement allowed the Sadrists to escape the decree the other major Iraqi parties had issued just a few months before, during the height of the Shia civil war, banning any party with an illegal militia from participating in elections—a decree that had been explicitly aimed at the Sadrists.

The Sadrists quickly made clear, however, that dropping their resistance to the Maliki government was not the same as dropping resistance to the U.S.-led Coalition. As the Iraqi government and parliament took up the question of whether and how to extend the U.S. military presence in Iraq beyond the expiration of the UN mandate at the end of 2008, the Sadrists used the issue to regain political leverage and reenergize their demoralized base. Within the government itself, the twenty-nine-member Sadrist bloc led the parliamentary opposition to the proposed Status of Forces Agreement (SoFA) that would allow U.S. troops to remain in the country, with Sadrist leaders making fiery speeches against any continued U.S.-Iraqi security relationship. From his sanctuary in Iran, and no doubt encouraged by his hosts, Muqtada Sadr railed against the idea of a SoFA, drawing comparisons to other military agreements with western powers, such as the U.S.-Iranian SoFA of 1964 against which Ayatollah Khomeini had led a protest movement, and the Anglo-Iraqi treaty of 1948 that had guaranteed British bases in the country but had sparked violent protests that collapsed the Iraqi government at the time. Though the Sadrists ultimately could not prevent the parliament's ratification of the agreement, which passed with slightly more than half of the parliament's approval in November 2008, they had succeeded in solidifying their position as the "anti-occupation" front in Iraqi politics, a stance that had a good deal of popular appeal. The Sadrists' vocal opposition to the SoFA also may have influenced the Malikiyoun to severely restrict the operations U.S. troops could conduct, as in the provision that U.S. troops should exit Iraq's cities by June 2009.

In both the national and local governments, the Sadrists had appeared to follow a Hezbollah-like strategy of gaining control of public services, with the aim of making themselves a necessary part of Iraqis' daily lives and receiving credit for providing for their constituency's welfare. In joining the Maliki government in 2006, the Sadrists had sought control of service ministries such as Health, Agriculture, Water, and Transportation and had emplaced technocratic Sadrist laymen atop them. In Lebanon, Hezbollah had used this method to create a state-within-a-state in which the party controlled state resources in Shia areas alongside a parallel party-controlled structure of clinics, schools, and so on. The Sadrists would have less success with this formula in Iraq, however, mainly because the Iraqi state was too powerful to be easily marginalized as the Lebanese state had been. Nor could Sadrist foundations and mosques hope to compete with the largess of the oil-rich Iraqi state in the same way that Hezbollah could outspend the Lebanese government. Hezbollah had built up its autonomy largely by staying out of the Lebanese state, but in Iraq the Sadrists could only compete with other parties by participating in the state and claiming a share of state resources.

Where the Sadrists had greater success in emulating Hezbollah was in participating in politics as both a party and a militia. By mid-2009, the Sadrists had a parliamentary bloc of almost thirty along with forty-one local council seats, but continued to deploy the Promised Day Brigade to attack U.S. troops. The party paid virtually no political price for the violence its armed wing perpetrated, and its political wing was able to parlay its modest 2009 provincial election success into a much greater showing in the national elections of March 2010. Though they were members of the third-finishing electoral coalition, they won forty seats, more than any other single Iraqi party. Their key was party discipline:

they made the most of their followers' votes by ensuring that pro-Sadrist candidate lists did not compete against each other in any province, a practice many other parties were not organized enough to follow. The Sadrists were the only single party to poll in double digits in the popular vote, gaining slightly over 10 percent of the almost twelve million votes cast, a huge following in a country whose political movements were so fragmented.

ASA'IB AHL AL-HAQQ'S DETENTION AND ESCAPE

As the Sadrists were reestablishing themselves as a major political party in 2009, hundreds of Asaib Ahl al-Haqq (AAH) leaders and fighters languished in U.S. detention centers near Baghdad and Basra, sidelining the group as a political factor. Yet pressure came from several directions in 2009 to push ahead with a plan to strike a reconciliation agreement with AAH under which the group would be released from prison in return for laying down its arms. As they had hoped to do in 2006, the Malikiyoun still aimed to bring Qais al-Khazali and his followers into politics as Dawa clients and peer competitors to the Sadrists. Qassem Soleimani, too, frequently pressed the Malikiyoun to push for Qais's release, presumably so the AAH leader could return to the battlefield as a Quds Force proxy. The British government also had an interest in pushing ahead with a "reconciliation" initiative with the imprisoned AAH leaders, because it was AAH members who had abducted five British citizens from the Ministry of Finance in March 2007, just weeks after Qais al-Khazali's capture, in an apparent attempt to procure hostages who could be eventually traded for Khazali and other AAH members.

The capture of the five Britons—four security guards and a Bearing Point computer technician whom they were guarding—

illustrated that AAH was operating much as Hezbollah and Iran's Revolutionary Guards had done in Lebanon in the 1980s, viewing western hostages as strategic assets. AAH members had taken the Britons in broad daylight, dressing as Iraqi police and carrying the British men away in police vehicles, whisking them away to Iran within hours. In their "reconciliation" negotiations in 2009–10, AAH leaders consistently pledged to release the men, failing to reveal until late in the release process that they had executed the four security guards shortly after capturing them, leaving only the technician, Peter Moore, still alive. Thus the negotiations eventually became a matter of trading a large number of AAH members for the bodies of AAH's murder victims, similar to Hezbollah's practice of trading Israeli dead for the release of living Hezbollah operatives.

Throughout the negotiations, Qais al-Khazali agreed that in return for his freedom he would ensure AAH lay down its weapons and rebrand itself as a political organization. Qais himself insisted upon remaining in captivity as his various subordinates were released, making him the final AAH member set free. U.S. troops handed Qais over to Iraqi officials on December 30, and after a brief stay in Iraqi custody, Khazali escaped to Iran. Rather than lay down its arms as its leaders had pledged to do, AAH, with its ranks swelled by the members who had been in U.S. custody, soon restarted kidnappings and attacks against U.S. targets.

HAJJI QASSEM'S SPOILERS

As the Sadrists moved into the political mainstream and AAH emerged from U.S. imprisonment, the third major resistance faction, Kata'ib Hezbollah, raised its profile in Iraq as well. More than any other Iraqi militant faction, the group had become a direct extension of the Quds Force in Iraq, used to further the Iranian regime's interests there. Its overall chief, Abu Mahdi al-Muhandis, was more than a military commander: he was Qassem Soleimani's Iraqi political envoy, the man whom Soleimani used to relay messages to Iraqi politicians and militant leaders of every rank, including the prime minister.

Abu Mahdi had a long "resistance" pedigree that made him ideal for the job of representing the Iranian regime's external arm. As a young man, he had been one of the Dawa movement's Iran-sponsored terrorist operatives who carried out the attacks against the U.S. and French embassies in Kuwait in 1983. Two years later, in 1985, he had participated in an unsuccessful plot to kill the emir of Kuwait, and had joined the Badr Corps at about the same time. Convicted of the assassination plot in absentia by a Kuwaiti court, Abu Mahdi had eventually wound up on death row in a Kuwaiti prison in 1990, when he was miraculously saved from execution by invading Iraqi troops who let the emirate's prisoners go free. Escaping to Iran, he spent the 1990s as a senior Badr Corps leader conducting clandestine operations against Saddam's regime in southern Iraq.

Abu Mahdi had spent the first few years of the post-Saddam era working in the open in Baghdad, where he was elected to parliament on the SCIRI-Badr list in 2005. Though the Badr Corps later declared it had expelled him as a result of his militant activities, he seems to have continued to enjoy some official Iraqi government privileges even as he became a fugitive suspected of terrorism. After he was forced to flee Iraq when his role in supporting militant activities became known, Abu Mahdi lived a relatively ascetic lifestyle in Tehran, much as his commander, Qassem Soleimani, did. One visitor to his home in a gated Revolutionary Guards neighborhood noted that the house was sparsely furnished, not luxurious, and Abu Mahdi himself spoke at length about the decadence and disrespect for Islam prevalent in his hometown of Basra. Throughout this period of exile, Iraqi government officials treated him with kid gloves, presumably to avoid angering his Quds Force superiors. In 2010, though he was widely known to be engaging in terrorist activities, Abu Mahdi was apparently treated administratively as a "retiree" from parliament, awarded a full parliamentary pension that he continues to receive to this day. As he drew his Iraqi government retirement pay, he became a ubiquitous Quds Force envoy, showing up in Lebanon, Syria, and even Iraq to coordinate with the Iranian regime's proxies. An Iraqi delegation to Damascus in 2010 was surprised to find Abu Mahdi awaiting them with Assad regime officials, as was a later Iraqi delegation that visited Bashar al-Assad in 2012. By the late summer of 2012, after the departure of U.S. troops, Abu Mahdi was comfortable enough to return full-time to Baghdad. In other words, Abu Mahdi has moved freely throughout the Quds Force's region since 2003.

Kata'ib Hezbollah's members, probably numbering in the hundreds, are far fewer than the low thousands that comprise Asa'ib Ahl al-Haqq and the tens of thousands who make up the Sadrist organization and militia, but they appear to enjoy more extensive military support than other Shia militant factions. In exchange, they are counted upon to act according to Iranian regime interests. Iraqis, for example, have little interest, for good or ill, in the fate of the Mujahideen-e Khalq (MeK), the aging Iranian militant group and quasicult that split from the Iranian regime shortly after the Islamic revolution and spent the 1980s and '90s inside Iraq as favored clients of Saddam, who used them as fighters in the Iran-Iraq War and in the crushing of the 1991 uprising. Since 2003, the MeK have been bottled up on compounds not far from Baghdad, guarded first by U.S. troops and more recently by the Iraqi Army, rendering the group essentially powerless. The Iranian regime, however, has found the MeK to be a dangerous intelligence and political threat, and frequently has used Kata'ib Hezbollah to conduct attacks against MeK encampments. Against the MeK, Kata'ib Hezbollah resembled other proxy "spoilers" the Iranian regime had cultivated elsewhere in the Arab world: militants who can afford to ignore local political considerations because their means come entirely from Iranian regime patronage, enabling them to violently upset local politics when it serves Iranian interests to do so.

THE RESISTANCE AFTER "OCCUPATION"

This spoiling influence was on clear display in 2011, when the Maliki government and the resistance groups were at odds over the question of a continued U.S. military presence in Iraq. As the U.S. and Iraqi governments entered into talks on a potential arrangement for U.S. troops to remain in the country beyond the expiration of the U.S. Security Agreement at year's end, Shia militant groups intensified their attacks against American troops, with fourteen U.S. soldiers killed and dozens more wounded by Iranian signature weapons in June 2011 alone. If the Americans were to withdraw, the Shia militants apparently hoped to gain political clout by claiming credit for driving them out, as Hezbollah had claimed credit for the Israeli evacuation of Lebanon in 2000.

The 2011 attacks also indicated the Shia resistance was targeting more than just the U.S. military. When the U.S. State Department opened a Basra consulate in June at the old British base that had been targeted heavily in 2007–08, Shia militant groups attacked the new facility with rockets and mortars several times a week, making the work of U.S. diplomats exceedingly difficult. The Shia militants also returned to their practice of kidnapping Americans. The same month the Basra consulate opened, Sadrist militants in Baghdad abducted American businessman Randy Hulz and held him incommunicado for nine months before releasing him at a press conference where they forced the civilian Hulz to wear a U.S. military uniform, an act that was by definition a war crime. For the Iraqi Shia militants, the kidnapping of westerners was a means of gaining strategic leverage by "storing" hostages (or their remains) for long periods and producing them when they were most valuable as bargaining chips, as the Iranian regime and its proxies had done in 1980s Lebanon.

As the U.S. military presence wound down in late 2011, the Shia militant groups were expanding their original objective of expelling the U.S. military from their country, seemingly aiming to break the relationship between the Iraqi and U.S. governments. Muqtada Sadr and his parliamentarians, for example, viewed the huge U.S. Embassy in Baghdad as an unnecessarily large and menacing American presence, and Sadr himself declared that the U.S. diplomatic mission in Iraq should be no larger than the meager Iraqi diplomatic mission in Washington. He also tried to block Prime Minister Maliki's visit to Washington in December 2011, warning that Maliki would be betraying his country by making a trip to America. "If my little finger were an [American] occupier, I would chop it off," Muqtada Sadr had told an al-Arabiyah interviewer in November 2011, a full two weeks after the United States announced the decision not to retain troops in Iraq past the end of the year. Asked whether his forces intended to continue fighting the United States now that American troops were leaving, Sadr replied that he and his party would not accept an American presence in Iraq of any kind, civilian or military, warning that "if they remain, we will fight." But the Sadrist leader also indicated that it was not enough for the Americans to leave just Iraq:

Muqtada Sadr: . . . But of course, the Americans aren't occupying Iraq only. They are occupying Islamic countries with which we have ties of friendship, religion, denomination, and

so on. We have Islamic and human ties with them. It is not
occupying Iraq only. True, the main concern has been Iraq
and the U.S. withdrawal from it. But the U.S. is an occupying
imperialistic country around the world, not only in Iraq. . . .

Interviewer: If the Americans withdraw, will the Mahdi
Army lay down its arms?

Muqtada Sadr: Who would we use these weapons against?
As long as there is occupation, we use weapons against it, but
if the occupation leaves, and *if the Mahdi Army is not needed
for other matters,* such as defending Iraq's borders and so on,
we will maintain only cultural, social, and religious activities.

In this way did the most important Shia militant leader signal that his armed movement might carry the fight against the
United States beyond Iraq's borders, while also hinting at a
future Hezbollah-type role for his armed followers inside Iraq,
in which his militia would remain armed after the "occupiers"
had departed.

Life under the "Resistance"

By the time of the U.S. military withdrawal from Iraq—the originally stated raison d'être for the resistance—Sadiq Sadr's mass following had differentiated itself into several distinct political and
militant groups, among which his son Muqtada had created Iraq's
largest political party and his former disciple Qais al-Khazali had
founded Iraq's closest analogue to Lebanese Hezbollah, with the
latter poised to enter into a political partnership with the Maliki
government. The Iranian regime had succeeded in neutralizing the
Sadiq Sadr movement's natural anti-Iranian bent, even carving
out some of the movement for the Quds Force to control directly

as a tool of Iranian regional strategy. Along the way, Sadiq Sadr's followers had made Iraq a thoroughly hostile place for Americans, both military and civilian, and had signaled their intention to disrupt U.S.-Iraqi interstate relations. They also had not shied from turning their weapons on fellow Iraqis, in the purported interest of either driving out the "occupiers" or enforcing a strict Islamic code in a society unused to it.

The weeks following the departure of U.S. troops in December 2011 indicated what average Iraqis could expect from the resistance in the "post-occupation" era. The day the U.S.-Iraq security agreement expired, December 31, 2011, gunfights broke out between Sadr's men and Asa'ib Ahl al-Haqq in several Baghdad neighborhoods, including Sadr City and Kadhimiyah, in what looked distinctly like a turf war between rival mafia syndicates.

There were early signs that Iraqi life under the resistance would be stifling. Iraqis who had worked closely with the Americans found themselves in a precarious situation, and in the Iraqi south and Baghdad U.S.-funded NGOs and civil society groups began to curtail their activities, relocate to Kurdistan, or shut down entirely in early 2012, citing intimidation by local Shia Islamist groups and even government officials. Anecdotes abounded of Iraqis who had worked for the U.S. military being forced to hide their identities and employment histories or to leave the country and seek asylum.

Meanwhile, in neighborhoods where the Shia resistance groups had a significant presence, a reign of terror began to unfold against Iraqis whose behavior they deemed un-Islamic. In several cities militants routinely attacked the owners of liquor stores and other "sinful" establishments, even though Iraqi society had traditionally allowed their trades to thrive, especially those owned by or catering to non-Muslim minorities. An even worse fate befell the thousands of young Iraqis who had adopted the "Emo" clothing and hairstyle fad (a successor to the "Goth" phenomenon among teens in the United States), which Shia Islamist groups denounced as sinful because of its supposed association with a homosexual lifestyle. In the first few weeks of 2012, Shia militants reportedly murdered at least seventy "Emo Youth" in the Baghdad area alone, with an unknown number of additional "Emo" victims wounded or simply missing. Weighing in on the matter, Iraqi government spokesmen ominously referred to the victims as "devil worshippers," while government security forces took little action to stop the killings. The conclusion was hard to miss: now that they had cleansed Iraq of the "occupiers" by force of arms, the Shia Islamist radicals intended to purify their morally polluted society, market by market, street by street.

THE POST-AMERICAN IRAQ

CHAPTER EIGHT

Interregnum, Crackdown, and Spillover

THIS BOOK HAS ATTEMPTED to trace how three political trends—authoritarianism, sectarianism, and "resistance"— came to dominate Iraqi politics in the post-Saddam era, as well as how, after five brutal years of war, the Iraqi political factions reached an accommodation, with U.S. support, that allowed for the tamping down of violence and the emergence of cross-sectarian or nationalist political coalitions in 2008–09. In subsequent years, however, the dominant trends of authoritarianism, sectarianism, and "resistance" would unravel the cross-sectarian accommodation of 2008–09 and lead the country on a grim course back to conflict. Through the bitterly contested election year of 2010, the Malikiyoun would prove they could lose an election and yet hold onto power—power they would use in 2011 to crack down on a popular opposition movement and rival political parties. And in 2012–13, the Syrian civil war would spill over into Iraq, merging the sectarian power struggles in the two countries.

2010: THE INTERREGNUM

The March 2010 Elections
As the pivotal national election year of 2010 dawned, the nationalist coalitions that had swept the provincial elections of 2009—at

209

the expense of sectarian Islamist parties whom Iraqis held responsible for the worst of the civil war—looked to repeat their success
in the elections for national parliament scheduled for March. As
the election approached, three coalitions were likely to dominate
the next parliament: Nuri Maliki's State of Law coalition, which
hoped to benefit from the prime minister's perceived leading role
in reestablishing law and order; Ayad Allawi's Iraqiyah coalition,
which had the support of the Sunni Awakening but enjoyed significant support in the Shia south as well; and the Kurdistan Alliance, a coalition encompassing the major Kurdish parties. For the
Shia supremacists who had dominated the 2005 elections, but
whose political appeal depended on the religious polarization of
the country, the outlook was a troubling one. The Shia parties and
militants—many of them aligned with the Iranian regime—who
had aimed to exclude Sunnis and Baathists from Iraqi politics and
government after 2003 now faced the likelihood that Iraqiyah, a
coalition dominated by those very same Sunnis and former Baathists,
would win a major share of the next government.

     Fortunately for the Shia sectarians, the parliamentary de-
Baathification committee aimed to prevent a Sunni-Baathist
resurgence. The committee had begun as an instrument to prevent
recalcitrant Baathists from undermining the new Iraqi democracy
from within, but in the 2010 election season it became an analogue to Iran's Guardian Council, an unelected body empowered
to exclude candidates from competing for office. This committee
issued a ban against more than five hundred candidates due to
their Baathist histories, though the committee's authority was
dubious since it issued from a soon-to-expire parliament whose
top leaders appeared to have no hand in what the committee was
doing. The ban took the Iraqi political class by surprise and threw
candidate lists into disarray just weeks before the vote. Nevertheless, the polling took place on March 7 with little violence and a

turnout of more than 60 percent to elect a 325-member parliament, expanded from the previous body's 275 seats.

The unofficial returns yielded several surprises, most of which spelled trouble for Nuri Maliki. The election was a broad rejection of the incumbents from 2005, with voters electing almost as many first-time parliamentarians (262) as the entire strength of the previous parliament. The Sadrists, the prime minister's biggest Shia rivals, surprisingly increased their seats from twenty-nine to forty, making them the largest single party in parliament and indicating they had made up much of the political ground they had lost in their war with Maliki two years before. This success instantly made the Sadrists the dominant component of the Shia Iraqi National Alliance (INA), since ISCI and Badr had won only seventeen seats, a shocking reduction from their 2005 total.

An even greater threat to Maliki's position was the unexpected success of Ayad Allawi and Iraqiyah, who finished first in the voting with a plurality of ninety-one seats, two more than Maliki's State of Law at eighty-nine. In hindsight, the results made sense: both Maliki and Iraqiyah had worked hard to attract candidates from the opposite sect, but while the Shia Allawi had succeeded in attracting strong secular Shia candidates across the south, Maliki had failed to attract Sunnis into the State of Law coalition, other than a few Awakening leaders. As a result, Iraqiyah was virtually unchallenged in Sunni-majority areas, so that for the first time in post-Saddam elections the Sunni vote would not be split.

In the Shia provinces and Baghdad it was a far different story. Since Maliki had stayed out of the broad Shia coalition, the Iraqi National Alliance, his Shia followers would be pitted against strong Shia competitors. If the provincial vote of 2009 was a reliable indicator, State of Law, the INA, and Iraqiyah all stood to poll well in the south, splitting the Shia vote among them and leaving no single coalition with much hope of winning enough seats to form a government without including their principal rivals.

For whatever reason, these indicators had escaped the Malikiyoun as they surveyed the electoral landscape. Before the election, Maliki's political advisers were privately confident that in the new parliament of 325 members, the prime minister's coalition would win between 110 and 120 seats, a number that would have enabled Maliki to easily form a government by picking among any of the other competing coalitions. This overestimate of Maliki's electoral prospects would haunt the prime minister in the months to come.

THE STALEMATE AND THE IRBIL AGREEMENT

By a literal reading of the Iraqi constitution, Iraqiyah's ninety-one-seat plurality would give Allawi the first chance to form a government. Maliki, however, seemed to have no intention of abiding by a literal reading of the constitution, and he and his allies pulled several levers of the state machinery to overturn Allawi's electoral victory. As election officials released the returns just days after the voting, the prime minister claimed the vote totals were fraudulent and demanded recounts in districts where his coalition had polled below the Malikiyoun's expectations. When the Iraqi Electoral Commission and United Nations officials in Baghdad found no evidence of fraud on a scale that would justify a recount, Maliki accused commission chief Faraj al-Haidari and the United Nations of colluding to unseat him on behalf of the western powers. The prime minister secured a court order for a limited recount, but the new count made no change in the balance of seats.

Maliki's next line of attack was against the constitutional underpinning of the electoral process itself, and it succeeded beyond expectation. On the eve of the Iraqi High Electoral Commission's announcement of the official results on March 26, 2010, Maliki asked Iraq's chief justice, Medhat al-Mahmoud, for a formal constitutional interpretation: when the Iraqi constitution directed the Iraqi president to ask "the largest bloc" to form a government, Maliki asked, did it mean the largest of the published electoral blocs that had contested the election? Or could it simply mean the largest bloc that could be cobbled together among the winning candidates? Medhat helpfully gave Maliki a ruling holding with the latter, which he announced the same day the Electoral Commission officially named Iraqiyah the winning electoral bloc.

Judge Medhat's decision opened the door for an extended competition among the Iraqi parties, because the "largest bloc" could now be composed of any collection of 163 or more parliamentarians, regardless of the lists on which they had contested the election—an interpretation that rendered the election itself nearly meaningless. Medhat's ruling also contradicted the stated intent of the Iraqi constitutional framers, who were all still alive and available to comment. The lead Shia drafter of the document, ISCI's Sheikh Humam Hamoudi, had told television interviewers that the drafters had intended "largest bloc" to mean the largest bloc contesting the election, and that had indeed been the interpretation applied after the December 2005 elections, when the United Iraqi Alliance had won a plurality and received the first chance to form a government.

Nevertheless, with Medhat's ruling in hand Maliki could claim to be in control of the government formation process, and he therefore began a long campaign to attract enough coalition partners to hold onto the premiership. He was aided by Iraqi President Jalal Talabani, who could have thwarted Maliki by formally giving Allawi the constitutionally mandated thirty days to form a government, but instead flew to Tehran the day after the election results were published to hold negotiations with the Iranian regime, Maliki's State of Law, and the Iraqi National Alliance on forming the next government—talks from which Iraqiyah was excluded.

The position of the various bargainers was clear from the beginning: Maliki was willing to form a governing coalition with the other Shia parties and Kurds, but only if they agreed to his return as premier. The Iranians, still unhappy with Maliki's 2008 crackdown on their Shia militant clients, seemed to prefer any other Shia Islamist premier, but apparently would accept Maliki's return if he agreed not to extend the U.S. military presence in Iraq beyond its scheduled expiration in 2011. Within the INA, the Sadrists, still smarting from their war with Maliki two years before, were willing to form a governing coalition with State of Law, but only if someone other than Maliki were premier. The Sadrists even held a "referendum" in which more than a million Sadr followers preferred Ibrahim al-Jaafari or Jaafar Baqir al-Sadr over Maliki by a wide margin.

With these redlines drawn, Iraq entered a nine-month period without a new government, the longest post-election gap in modern world history. Throughout this interregnum the competing blocs alternately courted and sought to fracture one another in desultory attempts to break the impasse. Frozen out of the Tehran-sponsored Shia process, Allawi and his Iraqiyah allies made high-profile visits to the regional Sunni powers, hoping to garner enough political support, and probably financial support as well, from the Gulf states, Syria, Jordan, and Turkey to entice other Iraqi parties to join him.

Maliki finally ended these challenges to his leadership only by securing Iranian support in reconstituting the Shia parliamentary bloc and persuading the Iranian regime to pressure the Sadrists to accept him as prime minister, which the Sadrists duly did in November amid news reports that Maliki might cede them several southern governorships in return. Having solidified his Shia and Iranian support, Maliki then secured Kurdish and Iraqiyah acquiescence by accepting specific power-sharing arrangements at a gathering of the major parties in Irbil in December 2010. Though the parties did not make the terms of the Irbil Agreement public, it was understood that Maliki had agreed that Allawi should head a government committee to control "strategic policy"; that the security ministries would be headed by independent technocrats rather than politicians; and that the Baghdad-Irbil dispute over oil jurisdiction would be decided mainly in the Kurds' favor. The parties who signed the Irbil Agreement with Maliki understood themselves to be forming a government of national unity in which the Malikiyoun would be but one of many sharers of power, but that idea would disintegrate in 2011.

The Fallout of 2010

The turbulent political struggle of 2010 halted the secular nationalist trend that emerged in 2009, as the exclusion of mainly Sunni parliamentary candidates began the repolarizing of Iraqi politics along sectarian lines. The same went for Maliki himself: having presented himself as a cross-sectarian leader in 2009, Maliki had returned to the Shia fold to hold onto the premiership in 2010, a shift that would deepen the country's sectarian struggle later. "We lost Maliki in 2010," a Sunni lawmaker later lamented. "To hold onto power he agreed to become a Shia champion again."

Maliki's return as premier also meant that his network of political appointees and clients seeded throughout the government agencies would remain in place, strengthening the Malikiyoun's hold on the machinery of the state. He had demonstrated that he could use that machinery to overcome even the loss of an election, a fact that would demoralize his opposition in the years to come. Maliki's victory also killed the idea of any alternate leader within

Dawa or the State of Law coalition and perhaps explained why the promising young politician Jafaar Baqir Sadr suddenly quit parliament for exile in Beirut just weeks after Maliki's reappointment as prime minister.

The months after the interregnum brought a settling of scores among some of the main characters in the 2010 drama. Still convinced he had been cheated out of an election victory, Maliki eventually punished the Iraqi electoral commission for its defiance, using a parliamentary investigation in April 2012 to briefly jail the commission's director for the "crime" of paying an $87 bonus to some commission workers, after which the director fled to Kurdistan. Meanwhile, the director of the de-Baathification committee was assassinated near Sadr City, shot in his car by professional hit men.

2011: YEAR OF THE CRACKDOWN

Maliki had held onto control of the state in 2010 by outlasting his major rivals. In 2011 he would use the state's power against them. In the spring and summer of 2011 Maliki's security forces broke up an Arab Spring–style protest movement of Sadrists, Sunnis, and small parties in the Baghdad region. In the late fall, Maliki cracked down on his main Sunni rivals, fragmenting the Iraqiyah bloc and pushing increasing numbers of Sunnis out of mainstream politics.

IRAQ'S SUPPRESSED SPRING

Since Maliki's ascent to the premiership in 2006, the Malikiyoun had worked hard to consolidate control of the institutions of the state. But after almost five years in power, the Malikiyoun's process of state consolidation collided with popular grievances in 2011.

The improving security situation of 2009–10 had raised Iraqis' expectations, as had the formation of a new national unity government after the Irbil Agreement. Iraqis had anticipated a "peace dividend" of development and public services, which had suffered from eight years of conflict stacked atop the dozen years of deterioration and neglect during the sanctions period of 1991 to 2003. The public had much to complain about. Iraq's electrical grid remained in shambles, with demand far exceeding the national grid's output. Iraq's growing youth population confronted a severe housing shortage, with the Iraqi government itself estimating a shortfall of over three million family housing units in a country of thirty-plus million people. The list went on and on. Iraq's deeply entrenched socialist system saddled the state with the responsibility for fixing these problems, but the weak Iraqi ministries were incapable of such fixes. Nor was there a private sector solution, since the Iraqi business community remained a weak offshoot of the massive public sector, dominated by crony capitalists competing for government contracts.

As 2011 opened with massive demonstrations in Egypt and other Arab states, the same phenomenon took shape in Iraq. As in Egypt—and later Syria—public anger over government corruption and inadequate services began to boil over in several major Iraqi cities. Friday demonstrations and "Days of Rage" generated crowds sometimes numbering in the tens of thousands. The crowds took on a different character in different cities, ultimately comprising a loose combination of activist Arab youth groups, liberal political parties, the Sadr movement, marginalized Sunnis, and Kurdish youth.

The urban protests also coincided with a Sadrist confrontation with the Maliki government that began almost as soon as the ink was dry on the Irbil Agreement. After the southern governorships Maliki had reportedly promised them did not materialize, Sadrist leaders began a public campaign to criticize the government's corruption and ineffectiveness in delivering services, a message that resonated with the thousands of angry young men on the street.

The demonstrations of 2011 were at their largest in Baghdad and Basra in late February and early March. In Baghdad, protesters rallied in the city's own Tahrir Square, consciously drawing comparisons to the square's famous Cairo namesake. In both cities, the size and anger of the crowds elicited a ferocious response from government security forces, which used a combination of lethal and nonlethal force to suppress the demonstrations. In the last week of February 2011, Iraqi security forces fired on crowds in several cities, killing about thirty protesters countrywide and producing scenes not unlike those in Egypt in early February. Also as in Egypt, the government deployed armed plainclothes loyalists to infiltrate demonstrations and beat or intimidate protesters, while uniformed security forces detained hundreds of demonstrators. Government troops raided political and civic groups suspected of organizing demonstrations.

Opposition groups subsequently alleged that the Iraqi security forces had been given orders to use deadly force, but the allegations prompted no serious government investigation and no senior Iraqi officials were charged with the killing of protesters. "It could have been much worse," one senior Iraqi official later confided. The Iraqi generals in Baghdad had made up their minds to stamp out the protest movement completely, the official recalled, and as ugly as the death toll had been, "they were prepared to do so much more."

Following the February–March crackdown, protests continued through the summer months in Baghdad, but on a smaller scale and often restricted to Sadrist neighborhoods—and always in a tense standoff with government security men and Maliki loyalists.

In political terms, the Arab Spring protests in Iraq never reached the critical mass that characterized protests in Tunisia and Egypt, and unlike their North African counterparts Iraqi demonstrators tended to call for reform rather than regime change. Iraq's shoddy electrical grid also hampered protest organizers: with unreliable electricity, Iraqis had poor Internet connectivity, meaning that demonstrators could not use social media to mobilize as Egyptians had. The international community also paid little attention to the Iraqi demonstrations and the ensuing crackdown, so that the killing of Iraqi protesters did not elicit the same outrage among the western media as the killing of Egyptian and Libyan protesters had done, and no western governments denounced the Maliki government for using lethal force.

In the absence of external supporters, the "Iraqi Spring" movement began to fizzle out by summer's end. Outside the protests, the activist organizers suffered intense pressure and intimidation from government officials and loyalists. The clearest example was the case of popular broadcaster Hadi al-Mahdi, who used his radio talk show to help organize antigovernment rallies and had previously been arrested for fomenting protests in February. On September 8, 2011, unknown gunmen shot al-Mahdi in his home with silenced pistols just hours after he posted on Facebook that he had received death threats from government loyalists.

Al-Mahdi's murder coincided with the end of large-scale protests. The Maliki government's strategy of using official force and unofficial intimidation had worked, at least for the time being.

The "Baathist Plot" and the Federalist Challenge

By the fall of 2011, the Maliki government's quelling of antigovernment protests began to expand into a broader crackdown against Maliki's political rivals. Days after the United States announced on October 21 that American forces would leave Iraq when the U.S.-Iraq security agreement expired in December, the

Maliki government arrested more than six hundred Iraqis for their roles in an alleged Baathist coup plot. The implausible scheme, which the Maliki government claimed had been revealed in intelligence shared by the new Libyan government, supposedly involved former Baathists in all the Sunni-majority provinces and Basra. Upon examination, however, the list of those to be arrested seemed to resemble "the usual suspects," including some Iraqis who had exited the Baath before 2003, some whose age or infirmity precluded involvement in any plot, and some who were already dead.

The Sunni community responded vehemently to the wave of arrests. Sunni-majority provincial governments in Salahadin and Diyala, two provinces with sizable Shia and Kurdish minorities, immediately initiated the constitutional process of becoming federal regions—like the Kurdistan Regional Government—in order to insulate themselves from what they considered an overreaching government in Baghdad. The Sunni federalist maneuvers represented an about-face from 2005, when virtually the entire Sunni electorate had voted against the Iraqi constitution precisely because of their opposition to federalism and the idea that Shia parties might create a federal "Shiastan" region in the oil-rich south. Six years later, the Sunni and Shia communities had reversed roles on the question, with the Shia-led government now treating Sunni federalism as a dangerous partition of the country. Accordingly, Maliki responded to the Sunni federalism bids of 2011 with force, sending troops to Salahadin to contain antigovernment protests and to Diyala to arrest the Sunni provincial governor. Shia towns in both regions hosted rallies denouncing federalism, and local Shia leaders promised to attach their sub-districts to Baghdad if the provinces sought autonomy.

As these events unfolded on the ground, Maliki deftly blocked the federalism initiatives on the political level, asserting that they were unconstitutional since they were "based on sectarian motives" and that he as prime minister had the power to review federalism initiatives in the first place. Maliki also weakened the Sunni federalists by playing competing Sunni factions against each other. When the Anbar provincial government signaled its intention to join Salahadin and Diyala in seeking federal region status, Maliki responded with carrots rather than sticks, offering to increase all-Sunni Anbar's share of the national budget and meeting with Anbari leaders to hear their grievances, something he had not done in mixed-sect Salahadin and Diyala.

THE HASHEMI CRISIS

The federalism dispute of October and November set the stage for an even more intense crisis in December. In the first ninety-six hours after the December 15, 2011 ceremony marking the departure of U.S. troops from Iraq, the Maliki government moved to detain the most senior Sunni government leaders: Vice President Tariq al-Hashemi, Deputy Prime Minister Saleh al-Mutlaq, and Finance Minister Rafi al-Issawi. Special troops and armored vehicles surrounded the men's Green Zone homes, raided their offices, and arrested dozens of their staff, prompting frantic phone calls to western officials from Sunni leaders who believed a "night of the long knives" was underway. Coming just three days after Maliki met with President Obama at the White House to hail the completion of the Iraq mission, the raids sparked a political crisis that has never subsided. The Iraqiyah coalition responded by boycotting the parliament and cabinet, while Allawi and Issawi cowrote a *New York Times* op-ed urging American intervention to stop Maliki's crackdown. Two days before the raid on Sunni leaders, Saleh Mutlaq had denounced Maliki as "worse than Saddam Hussein," adding that at least

Saddam "was a builder, but Maliki has done absolutely nothing."
Mutlaq told CNN that

The political process is going . . . toward dictatorship. People
are not going to accept that, and most likely they are going
to ask for the division of the country. And this is going to be
a disaster. Dividing the country isn't going to be smooth,
because dividing the country is going to be a war before that
and a war after that.

"There will be a day whereby the Americans will realize that
they were deceived by al-Maliki," Mutlaq predicted, "and they will
regret that." Maliki answered Mutlaq's charges and the Iraqiyah
boycott by asserting the power to sack both Hashemi and Mutlaq
from their positions without parliamentary approval. Mutlaq eventually apologized and was reinstated, but Hashemi fled to Iraqi
Kurdistan, where he sheltered for several months before fleeing
further to Istanbul, permanently.

Iraqi state television, meanwhile, aired "confessions" from
Hashimi's bodyguards, who alleged on camera that Hashemi—
who had himself lost three siblings to assassination since 2003—
had paid them to carry out assassinations and attacks. Criticized
for acting without judicial approval, Maliki formed a panel of
judges to consider the charges against Hashemi, though the panel,
headed by Medhat al-Mahmoud, predictably endorsed the government's charges—in keeping with Medhat's series of rulings
in Maliki's favor since 2009—and ordered Hashemi tried for the
capital crime of supporting terrorism. The confessions had an air
of coercion, and anonymous government officials later told western journalists that Hashemi's men had been severely beaten
before their interrogations. Skepticism of the case grew when one
of the bodyguards whose testimony was used to indict Hashemi

died in the custody of government security officials in March 2012, with postmortem photos indicating he had likely been beaten to death. Nevertheless, an Iraqi court eventually convicted Hashemi in absentia, creating the bizarre situation of an Iraqi government sentencing its own serving vice president to death and demanding that a neighboring state return him to Iraq to be hanged.

Unlike the suppression of popular protests in the spring of 2011, which had elicited little international response, the Maliki government's heavy-handed crackdown on political opponents in the fall led to sharp criticism from abroad. Typical was a January 2012 Human Rights Watch report that blasted the government's systemic human rights abuses, including secret prisons, warrant-less arrests, intimidation, and torture. Major western media outlets also began to document what they termed a return to authoritarianism in Iraq, blunting the idea that the country was a working democracy. Nevertheless, the timing of the Sunni leaders' arrests, just hours after Maliki had left Washington, left the conspiracy-theory-minded Iraqi political class convinced that Maliki had somehow secured American permission for the crackdown.

THE ACTING GOVERNMENT

The purging of Hashemi shocked the prime minister's political rivals and began to create a political backlash, not because of sympathy for Hashemi himself, whom some Iraqi politicians considered to be arrogant and acerbic, but rather because of the precedent of the case: if Maliki could purge the most senior Sunni government leader, then he could purge practically anyone.

By early 2012, it was also clear that Maliki did not mean to honor the Irbil Agreement, most notably the division of the security ministries among the main political blocs. Instead, for more than a year Maliki had named himself "acting minister" for Defense and Interior, while appointing his own security adviser Falah Fayadh as acting head of the Iraqi intelligence community. He similarly left Hashemi's vice presidential post empty, meaning that the previously powerful presidency council—meant to be composed of a Kurd, a Sunni, and a Shia—was left without Sunni representation.

Realizing Maliki was close to controlling all the formal branches of government, the other Iraqi political blocs spent the months following the Hashemi purge attempting to maneuver Maliki into a "national reconciliation" process to implement the Irbil Agreement and restore the power-sharing arrangement that had prevailed before 2010, an idea enthusiastically endorsed by UN and western diplomats. Rather than be forced into such a position, Maliki repeatedly found reasons to delay the much-anticipated "national dialogue," such as that the dialogue could not take place until after Iraq had hosted the important Arab Summit of March 2012, an occasion Maliki meant to use to show that the Arab powers had endorsed his rule and that Baghdad had returned to normality. But after reportedly spending half a billion dollars to beautify central Baghdad for the benefit of the visiting Arab delegations, the Maliki government was embarrassed when most Arab heads of state declined to attend, including every Gulf state leader but the emir of Kuwait.

MALIKI'S "DONKEYS"

Away from the paralyzed "national dialogue" in which they were expected to give up much of their power, the Malikiyoun busied themselves with the fracturing of their two main rival blocs, the Sadrists and Ayad Allawi's Iraqiyah, the only political coalitions that could present viable Shia prime minister alternatives to Maliki. Toward the Sadr movement, the Malikiyoun continued to pursue a strategy of raising up peer competitors for the Sadrist base. As U.S. troops left Iraq in December 2011, the Malikiyoun finalized their agreement with the Iranian-sponsored Asa'ib Ahl al-Haqq (AAH) militia to enter into politics, where they would presumably challenge Muqtada al-Sadr for votes from the Sadiq Sadr constituency. Within weeks, the Maliki government began granting AAH permission to hold public "victory" rallies in Baghdad and other cities, leaving the unmistakable impression that AAH would enjoy Maliki's sponsorship and largess throughout Shia Iraq.

Iraqiyah, meanwhile, posed a serious conceptual threat to the Malikiyoun because of its cross-sectarian appeal: of the ninety-one seats Iraqiyah had won in 2010, a dozen had gone to Shia secularists, and Allawi allies spoke openly of aims to expand that number exponentially in future elections. The Malikiyoun's strategy toward Iraqiyah became clear soon after the Irbil Agreement: to whittle Iraqiyah down to size by poaching its Shia members, rendering Iraqiyah a Sunni-only bloc that could be more easily attacked on sectarian grounds. This approach worked like a charm, as almost all of Allawi's Shia Iraqiyah members of parliament abandoned him under pressure or enticement from the Malikiyoun in 2011.

While robbing Iraqiyah of its Shia component, the Malikiyoun began promoting more malleable Sunni politicians who might rob Iraqiyah's Sunni "hardliners" of some popular support. The idea of using cat's paws to give the ruling faction a cross-sectarian appearance was a familiar one to Iraqis, since Saddam had used the method continually, especially with the Kurds. Kurdish nationalists had derisively referred to Saddam's Kurdish proxies as "donkeys," and some Iraqi Sunnis in 2012 began to apply the same epithet to

Maliki's would-be Sunni allies. One of the most prominent example of the Malikiyoun's new Sunni alternatives was, incredibly, the
Sunni insurgent kingpin Misha'an al-Jabouri, who after spending
seven years in Syria working to overthrow the Iraqi government
was brought to Baghdad in early 2012 and allowed to begin political activities in northern Iraq. Jabouri immediately proved useful
to the Malikiyoun by attacking Iraqiyah for encouraging Sunni federalism and announcing he would form a political party committed
to a unitary Iraq. On their own, Jabouri and other Maliki-sponsored
Sunnis had virtually no organic political following, but if they could
become conduits through which Maliki government resources
flowed into the Sunni-majority provinces, then they could plausi-
bly compete for some of Iraqiyah's popular base, opening up political space in the Sunni constituency that Iraqiyah had virtually
locked up in the 2010 elections.

   Determined not to deal on a partnership basis with the representatives Iraqi Sunnis had elected, the Malikiyoun meant to thrust
upon the Sunni electorate proxy leaders that Maliki had chosen for
them. But this strategy was a dangerous one for the Malikiyoun: by
fracturing the Iraqiyah coalition that had sat astride the Sunni
political center, the Malikiyoun might be creating opportunities
not just for prospective Maliki henchmen like Misha'an Jabouri,
but also for the radical Sunni rejectionists whom Iraqiyah had
eclipsed. The Malikiyoun had succeeded in ending Tariq Hashemi's political career, but what would happen to the nearly quarter
of a million Iraqis who had voted for him, or to the more than
four hundred thousand who had voted for Ayad Allawi, if the
Malikiyoun ultimately succeeded in driving Allawi out of politics? The Malikiyoun clearly wished this Sunni constituency to
drift toward Maliki's preferred Sunni proxies, but it was just as
likely that frustrated Sunni centrists would return to the militant
politics that had dominated Sunni Iraq before 2008. It was surely

no coincidence that the leader of the Saddamist state in exile, Izzat al-Douri, chose the spring of 2012 as the moment to break nine years of silence with televised speeches calling for a revolt against the Maliki government and for war against the "Persians" with whom he accused Maliki of making common cause. Though the odds of the septuagenarian windbag Douri regaining a political foothold were probably quite limited in a country that had decidedly moved on from the Saddam era, Douri would not be alone among Sunni rejectionists in gauging that the Sunni base might be up for grabs again, to the benefit of Sunni militant groups such as Al Qaeda. Simply put, the Malikiyoun were cutting the Sunni political base loose from its moorings with no way to control the direction in which it might drift.

The Elusive No-Confidence Vote

By June 2012, Maliki's beleaguered parliamentary opponents, including most of Iraqiyah, the Sadrists, Ammar Hakim, and Massoud Barzani, decided the time had come to remove Maliki through a no-confidence vote. The opposition parties began a series of meetings mainly in Irbil to accumulate the 163 votes needed for the measure, with Muqtada Sadr telling reporters in May 2012 that "I promised my partners that if they secure 124 votes, then I will provide the rest to reach 164 votes."

In the course of events, these pledges were never put to the test. When the opposition parties that gathered in Irbil took the formal constitutional step of asking President Jalal Talabani to convene a no-confidence vote, Talabani required the opposition to present a petition signed by at least 163 parliamentarians so he could be assured the measure had enough support to pass. Opposition leaders duly sent Talabani a list of 173 parliamentarians in early June, but they quickly realized their error: the list of those favoring Maliki's removal found its way immediately into the prime minister's hands, and within days more than ten parliamentarians had recanted, almost surely under Malikiyoun pressure.

The affair left Iraqiyah and other opposition leaders feeling that Talabani had betrayed them. But fate trumped these charges. On December 18, Talabani suffered a stroke and fell into a coma from which he has never recovered, ending a long political career that had taken him from the Kurdish mountain rebellions of the 1960s, to senior leader of the anti-Saddam opposition, to the once-unthinkable position, for a Kurdish patriot, of president of the Iraqi Republic. His sudden disappearance from the political playing field was a serious blow to Maliki's luckless opposition and their attempts to restore a balance of political power.

2012–2013: THE SPILLOVER

Outside observers lamented the seeming dysfunctionality of Iraqi politics after 2010, in which the parties that formed the government appeared to jockey constantly for position while neglecting the business of governance. In actuality, Iraq's political dysfunction and stalemate in 2012 were increasingly related to the wider conflict raging on Iraq's borders. As political efforts to defeat Maliki stalled, signs emerged that the long-running Iraqi political crisis was being regionalized, blending into the war next door. Syria was casting a great pall over Iraq's politics, society, and foreign relations.

MALIKI'S SYRIAN VOLTE FACE

Having sided with the revolution in Bahrain, the Maliki government quickly sided with the counterrevolution in Syria. Their decision required some sharp reversals in Maliki's foreign policy. Before 2011, the Syrian government behaved toward Iraq as though the Alawite regime was a Sunni power, harboring the remnants of the Iraqi Baathist regime and facilitating the movement of jihadis into Iraq to attack the Shia and Kurdish communities there. The Maliki government, accordingly, treated the Assad regime as an enemy: In August and October 2009, most notably, Maliki blamed Bashar al-Assad personally for the massive "Autumn bombings" of Iraqi ministries in Baghdad, and even called for a UN special tribunal to investigate the Assad regime's sponsorship of terrorist attacks in Iraq. Less than two years later, however, Maliki and his government expediently changed their tune. As popular and regional pressure on the Assad regime mounted in mid-2011, the Maliki government came to Assad's defense, with Maliki criticizing the Syrian opposition and declaring that the Syrian people should "use the democratic process" to resolve their grievances against the regime, as though a democratic process already existed in Syria. The change in the Iraqi government's stance was probably partly induced by the Iranian regime, which sought to use its regional leverage to preserve Assad's rule, but it was also likely a quid pro quo in which the Assads promised to abandon the senior Iraqi Baathists who had long used Syria as a base for warring against the post-Saddam Iraqi government.

But the most significant factor in the Maliki government's Syria policy change was the Iraqi Shia leaders' deep fear that Assad's fall could lead to the emergence of a Sunni Salafi regime in Damascus that would sponsor a renewed jihad against the Iraqi state. Consequently, from mid-2011 the Maliki government extended political, economic, and even security support to the Assad regime. Politically, Iraq largely abstained from international diplomatic actions against Syria, and in fact occasionally offered its own peace initiatives to compete with those of the Arab League or United Nations. In the economic arena, while much of the international community sought to isolate the Assad regime, the Maliki government renewed trade and oil agreements with the Syrian regime, while leaving the Iraqi Central Bank's foreign currency sales open to Syrian and Iranian figures seeking to evade international sanctions. In the security realm, the Iraqi government did nothing to impede the Iraqi Shia militants who deployed to Syria to fight on the side of the Assad regime, many of them traveling openly, and armed, through Baghdad International Airport. Iraqi officials also did little to prevent the Iranian regime's use of Iraqi airspace to deliver military aid to the Assad regime, despite frequent complaints from the United States and western powers. There were also signs that Iraqi government security forces meant to create "strategic depth" for the Syrian regime inside Iraq. Iraqi troops had reinforced the Syrian border zone in 2011 to disrupt Iraqi Sunnis sending arms and fighters to the Syrian rebels, but the Iraqi government was caught playing an even more direct role in the Syrian war in March 2013, when Sunni insurgents inside Iraq massacred a contingent of more than fifty Syrian government troops whom Iraqi officials were escorting from Ninewa to a border crossing in Anbar.

The Anbar incident and Maliki's own statements on Syria indicated that the Iraqi government had become closely aligned with the Iranian regime in its regional strategy, fully willing to use Iraqi state resources to preserve Bashar al-Assad's power. "It has been one year and the [Syrian] regime did not fall," Maliki declared in April 2012, "and it will not fall, and why should it fall?" The fall of Assad would trigger a wider war in the region, Maliki explained, including a civil war in Iraq itself, and he therefore intended to oppose any arming of the Syrian opposition. In the space of less than a year, Assad's regime had shifted, in Maliki's view, from a Sunni power to a Shia one.

THE MERGER OF THE IRAQ AND SYRIAN JIHADS

The Iraqi Sunnis had also concluded that the Assad regime was a Shia power, one they had a vested interest in toppling. After eight years of Shia ascendancy inside Iraq, Iraqi Sunnis in 2011 could envision the establishment of a Sunni state in Syria after Bashar al-Assad's defeat, and if Syria were to become a Sunni power, then the Iraqi Sunnis could dream of being able, with fifteen million Syrian Sunnis at their backs, to either regain control in Baghdad or at least renegotiate a greater share of power there. "Every Iraqi Sunni leader privately hopes for this," one Sunni expatriate confided in 2012. From an early stage in the Syrian rebellion, therefore, Iraq's Sunni tribes provided material support to the Syrian opposition, especially in eastern Syria, where large tribes such as the Shammar, Obeid, and Dulaim spanned the Iraq-Syria border. The Sunni tribes were reversing the flow of arms and fighters that had poured from Syria into Iraq during the Iraqi insurgency, while offering the same kind of safe haven to Syrian insurgents that their Syrian cousins had once offered to Iraqi insurgents.

By late 2012, Syrian opposition members reported that Syrian border towns like Deir ez-Zor and Albu Kamal were flooded with Iraqi fighters. But many of them were not mainstream Iraqi tribesmen. The most potent Iraqi militant groups in Syria were in fact part of Al Qaeda in Iraq (AQI) or its political front, the Islamic State of Iraq, both of which had become heavily involved in the Syrian war. It was a natural step for the Iraqi jihadi networks, since during the heyday of the Iraqi insurgency Al Qaeda's logistical "tail" had stretched from Damascus to the Iraqi border, where the operational "tooth" had extended down the Euphrates and Tigris river valleys to central Iraq. With the coming of war in Syria, Al Qaeda's "tooth" and "tail" had simply switched roles, so that the

Syrian Salafi mosques and networks that had been the Iraq jihad's logistical base had taken up arms, while the Iraqi jihadis had become the Syrian jihad's logistical network.

For Al Qaeda, Iraq and Syria had blended into one theater of jihad, a fact made plain when AQI's top leader, Abu Bakr al-Baghdadi, claimed in April 2013 that Syria's strongest Islamist rebel group, the Nusrah Front, was an extension of the Islamic State of Iraq, and that the Islamic State of Iraq would henceforth be known as "The Islamic State in Iraq and the Levant."

THE DEFENDERS OF ZAYNAB

Like their Sunni Iraqi jihadi enemies, the Iraqi Shia militant groups had decided the Syrian war was theirs to fight. As the Assad regime came under increasing military pressure in 2012, growing numbers of Iraqi Shia fighters made their way to Damascus and other Syrian battlefields, often by flying in groups to Iran, from which they would be dispatched to the Syrian front by Iran's Islamic Revolutionary Guards Corps or Lebanese Hezbollah. Early in 2012, uniformed Iraqi fighters began to circulate YouTube videos of themselves fighting in the streets of Damascus to defend the Shia shrine of Zaynab (daughter of the Imam Ali) against "terrorists." By late 2012, Iraqi groups such as Asa'ib Ahl al-Haq, Kata'ib Hezbollah, and, to a lesser extent, the Sadrists, openly sponsored fighters to join the "Defenders of Zaynab" inside Syria, where they were presumably thrown into the fight as auxiliaries of Lebanese Hezbollah and the Assad regime. Also by late 2012, those Iraqi Shia groups were regularly bringing home the bodies of slain Shia fighters to be buried as martyrs in their southern Iraqi hometowns, exactly as Al Qaeda had once delivered the bodies of slain mujahedin to be buried as martyrs in Jordan, Syria, and beyond.

GREATER KURDISTAN

Sunnis and Shiites were not the only Iraqis plunging headlong into the Syrian war. As the Syrian regime retreated from northeastern Syria to defend Damascus and the Alawite heartland, Syrian Kurds asserted their autonomy, and the Iraqi Kurdish parties helped them do so. After some initial infighting in 2011–12, Massoud Barzani's KDP and the Syria-based PKK worked together enough to enable Syrian Kurds to begin creating a Syrian version of the Kurdistan Regional Government. Visitors to Syrian Kurdish areas such as Hassaka could find local officials to welcome them to "West Kurdistan" and issue administrative documents and license plates on its behalf. Back in Iraq, meanwhile, Iraqi peshmerga began training Syrian Kurds to defend the new realm.

The appearance of an autonomous Kurdish region in Syria offered the Kurds a historic opportunity to possibly create the Greater Kurdistan their forefathers had been denied at the Peace of Paris almost a century before. But if Kurdish leaders were to take advantage, they would first have to ensure that the emergence of "West Kurdistan" did not provoke a war with Turkey. By the end of 2012, Massoud Barzani's Iraqi Kurdish allies had begun to broker peace talks between their former PKK rivals (including the imprisoned PKK leader Abdullah Ocalan) and the Erdogan government, a development that would have been unimaginable when the PKK and Turkish Army fought each other in Iraqi Kurdistan just five years before.

Back in Baghdad, Maliki and his allies did not relish the potential Kurdish expansion, and they took steps to contain Barzani's KRG. In October 2012, Maliki deployed a new Iraqi Army "Tigris Command" to bases near Kirkuk and Diyala from which Maliki's troops could encroach upon territories the Kurds claimed as their own. In late November, Maliki even sent troops to the edge of

Kirkuk city, where Iraqi battalions had not set foot since 2003. Though this military standoff between Arabs and Kurds eventually passed, Iraq's Arab parliamentarians asserted their financial leverage over Barzani's KRG soon after by reducing the Kurdish share of the annual Iraqi government budget. In response, the KRG and the Erdogan government pushed ahead with plans for a Turkey-Kurdistan pipeline that, once completed, would make Iraqi Kurdistan economically independent by giving the Kurds a secure means of exporting their more than forty-five billion barrels of oil, beyond Baghdad's control.

THE SYRIAN WAR, THE ISSAWI CRISIS, AND THE SUNNI PROTEST MOVEMENT

By 2012, the Maliki government, Iraqi Sunnis, and the Kurdish parties supported opposing sides in Syria, and militants from Iraq's three main communities were heavily involved in the Syrian fighting. The Syrian conflict, in turn, had a deeply destabilizing effect on Iraq's internal politics, further polarizing the Iraqi parties and rendering moot the talk of a new Iraqi power-sharing arrangement that had dominated the political discussions of 2011. In essence, the Iraqi civil war and struggle for power had been displaced to Syria, with all three Iraqi communities intervening there directly and banking on the idea that the outcome of the Syrian war would determine a new balance of power inside Iraq. Under those circumstances, it would simply be a matter of time before the war next door returned home.

The Baghdad political elite spent the end of 2012 almost exactly as they had spent the end of 2011: responding to a crisis provoked by Prime Minister Maliki's attempt to arrest the country's top-ranking Sunni politician. On December 15, 2011, Maliki's security forces had moved against Vice President Tariq al-Hashemi, arresting dozens of his staff on terrorism charges. On December 19, 2012, Maliki's men repeated the exercise against Finance Minister Rafi al-Issawi, whom Malikiyoun officials accused of supporting the Sunni Islamist insurgent group Hamas al-Iraq. As they had done against Hashemi, government troops rounded up Issawi's staff and bodyguards and began eliciting confessions as Issawi himself sought refuge in Anbar. It was a dubious step for the Malikiyoun to take, since they had leveled the same accusation against Issawi in 2010 only to have U.S. officials publicly rebut the charge. And the move seemed to signify a shift in Maliki's attitudes toward potential Sunni partners: during the Hashemi affair a year before, Maliki allies had privately described Issawi as the Sunni "moderate" with whom they planned to work once the more recalcitrant Hashemi and Saleh Mutlaq were out of the way. A year later, the Malikiyoun were labeling Issawi the recalcitrant Sunni who had to go, an attitude that might lead other Sunnis to conclude the Malikiyoun would be inclined to purge Iraq's top Sunni leader, whoever he might be, ad infinitum.

The purging of Hashemi had sparked some angry protests in Sunni cities, but they had stopped short of violence, partly because Sunni leaders had appealed for calm and because Hashemi had no tribal constituency. The response to the Issawi purge was a different matter. The finance minister was a popular figure, an Anbari surgeon who had worked in Fallujah's hospital during the American campaign in the city in 2004. Within days of the December 19 raids, large protest camps had formed in Iraq's major Sunni cities, especially in Anbar, where members of the Issawi tribe and its allies could take the attack against the finance minister as a tribal affront. Their attitude toward the Maliki government was clear. Though he was a wanted man in Baghdad, Issawi appeared openly at a large rally just sixty-five miles away in

Ramadi on December 26, where an enthusiastic crowd held him aloft. He gave a speech condemning the government for blockading Baghdad's Sunni neighborhoods and turning them into "huge prisons surrounded by concrete blocks." Some in the crowd held signs reading, "We Are Not a Minority."

The protests against the Issawi purge quickly grew into something larger. Crowds numbering in the tens of thousands marched through the Sunni provincial capitals, with local Sunni leaders consciously organizing an opposition movement against the Maliki government. By the first days of January 2013, the central squares of Mosul, Fallujah, Ramadi, Tikrit, and Hawijah—all former Sunni insurgent strongholds—hosted "Occupy"-style encampments and near-daily rallies at which Sunni clerics, local tribal leaders, and even mainstream national Sunni politicians gave speeches denouncing Maliki and exhorting various degrees of resistance against his government.

Video of the protest sites testified to the regional dynamics at play, for demonstrations in the Iraqi cities were replete with the flags of the Free Syrian Army. More worryingly, television viewers could also see flags of the Islamic State of Iraq and hear radical clerics occasionally urge Sunni listeners to take up arms against the Shia "infidels" who had seized power in Baghdad. The protests demonstrated a new Sunni solidarity throughout Iraq but also gave airing to Iraq's most odious Sunni bigots, a fact that kept the protest movement from spreading to Shia cities where Maliki's rule might be just as unpopular, but where no Shia leader could afford to be associated with the Sunni chauvinists the country could see on television.

Within weeks, the Sunni rage on display in the protest camps, now featuring near-constant chants of the familiar Arab Spring refrain, "the people want to topple the regime," had become a challenge Maliki and his allies could not ignore. In the restive

Sunni cities nearest Baghdad, Maliki deployed troops that surrounded the protest camps from a distance, leaving Iraqi soldiers
and Sunni protesters to keep a menacing watch across a small no-
man's land much as Israelis and Palestinians might. To forestall
large-scale violence, Maliki dispatched his Sunni deputy prime
minister, Saleh Mutlaq, to calm the Anbari protesters, but angry
crowds attacked Mutlaq and his entourage in a clash caught on
video and televised to Mutlaq's embarrassment. Under these circumstances violence was inevitable, and it came in Fallujah on
January 25, when government troops shot nine stone-throwing
protesters to death. Hours later, gunmen murdered two government soldiers at a nearby checkpoint.

The Fallujah killings sent Sunni anger to a fever pitch across the
country. Observers noted that armed militants had begun to appear
in the protest camps, foreshadowing even larger clashes. Alarmed,
the Maliki government decided the security situation in Anbar
and Ninewa would not allow for the provincial elections scheduled
for April 20; the rest of the country would vote as planned, but the
most rebellious provinces would not.

THE HAWIJAH MASSACRE

The expected clashes came in the last week of April, when several
areas in northern Iraq exploded in violence just three days after
largely peaceful local government elections. The carnage began in
the course of what was either a botched arrest attempt or a brutal
crackdown by government troops. In the early hours of April 23,
Iraqi forces who were reportedly under the command of the prime
minister's office raided a Sunni protest campsite in Hawijah, a former insurgent town near Kirkuk, ostensibly seeking suspects in
the murder of an Iraqi soldier a few days before. Which side shot

first was unclear, but when the gunfire stopped, about twenty protesters and three Iraqi soldiers were dead, with more than a hundred
people wounded. Within hours, fighting rippled across northern
Iraq. Sunni gunmen overran police and army outposts in neighboring towns, cutting the main Kirkuk-Baghdad highway after all-
day gun battles that left more than fifty dead on both sides. Within
forty-eight hours the fighting spread to Mosul, where Sunni gunmen engaged Iraqi troops in another battle that left three dozen
dead. The Iraqi Army assaulted the rebellious towns near Hawijah
with helicopter gunships, killing an unknown number of militants
on the same day the prime minister gave a nationally televised
speech warning that continued "sedition" against the government
would lead to a full-scale sectarian war. Despite Maliki's warning, or perhaps because of it, on April 26 the violence spread to
Baghdad, where four Sunni mosques were bombed following
noon prayers. On that same day, tens of thousands of antigovernment protesters took to the streets of Ramadi and Fallujah, and in
the latter, militiamen pulled five Iraqi government intelligence
officers from a car and executed them. The bloodshed culminated
on April 29 with Al Qaeda–style bombings that killed or wounded
ninety-five in Shia cities south of Baghdad, raising the month's
death toll past seven hundred, the highest since the dark days of
summer 2008.

THE REVERSAL OF THE AWAKENING

A series of high-level meetings appeared to calm the situation
after the week of violence the Hawijah raid had sparked, but the
ingredients for large-scale violence remained. The Hawijah incident had been merely a proximate cause; other, longer-term factors ensured that such clashes would continue to take place, each

of them carrying the risk of escalating to full-scale war. The political crises of 2013 showed that the Iraq conflict's fundamental causes had never been resolved: Sunni political groups continued to reject their relegation to second-class citizenship and exclusion from power, while Shia political groups remained determined never to let the Baath and Sunni tribes emerge as powers again. Alongside the unresolved Sunni-Shia question, the Kurdish question also played a part in the violence of 2013: Hawijah and the other northern towns where clashes were most intense all lay on the disputed dividing line between Arab and Kurdish Iraq.

The situation had not been helped by Maliki's continued attacks not just against Al Qaeda and other Sunni extremists, but against the Sunni center represented by Hashemi, Issawi, and others. Maliki's pressure on the most popular Sunni leaders had pushed the Sunni community from participation in the political process toward rejection of it or even armed resistance against it. Indeed, the violence of 2013 was shaping up to be not a simple matter of the government against Al Qaeda and other terrorists, but of the government against mainstream Sunni leaders and their constituents.

The most serious political consequence of this dynamic was the reversal of the Awakening, the Sunni tribal movement that helped to change the course of the Iraq war in 2007. The towns that were the setting for the violence of mid-2013 were all former insurgent strongholds that had switched sides to fight against Al Qaeda alongside U.S. and Iraqi troops. But the Awakening movement of more than eighty thousand Sunni fighters was never really embraced by a skeptical Maliki government, and as U.S. troops drew down, the Awakening came under pressure from the government on one side and Sunni insurgents on the other. In the Sunni protest movement of 2013, some Awakening leaders seemed on the verge of returning to outright resistance against the government.

THE RETURN OF THE CIVIL WAR

In the three months following the Hawijah outbreak in late April, nearly three thousand Iraqis were reported killed in insurgent and terrorist violence, the highest death toll since 2007, though some experts believed even that number to be an underreporting of the country's actual violence. In the same period, Iraqis witnessed Al Qaeda in Iraq return to a tempo of terrorist activity and geographic reach matching the height of its power in 2006–07, with the group's signature suicide bombers and car bombs devastating Shia neighborhoods as far south as Basra.

With its capacity already growing, Al Qaeda managed to dramatically swell its own ranks in an enormous jailbreak at Abu Ghraib on July 21, when scores of militants attacked the prison and freed more than five hundred inmates. The well-coordinated operation (dubbed "Breaking the Walls" by Al Qaeda's leaders) stunned the country and embarrassed the prime minister, who had long used security exigencies to justify his consolidation of power. It also prompted Muqtada Sadr and Ammar Hakim, among others, to call for Maliki's resignation on grounds of incompetence. Iraqis everywhere braced for a further spike in violence, since many of the liberated prisoners were hardened Sunni insurgents who had been captured by U.S. troops years before. In the three months following the jailbreak, another three thousand Iraqi civilians met violent deaths, including more than twelve hundred in September alone.

Throughout the summer, the grim reality was evident in the streets of Baghdad, where formerly busy shopping districts began to shut down due to the threat of car bombs from Sunni terrorists on one hand and the intimidation of puritanical Shia militiamen on the other. "People in Baghdad are terrified, just like they were in 2006 and 2007," one Sunni Baghdadi related. "Every family is stocking up on food and supplies, because they expect to be trapped in their homes again." The famous Baghdad social scene and night life, whose resurgence had signaled the slackening of civil strife in 2008, began to peter out as well, as cafés and soccer matches became favorite targets of terrorist attackers.

Shia militant groups, meanwhile, seemed to sense the right moment to restart their campaign to purify Iraqi society: in May alone, Shia militiamen executed twelve Baghdad liquor salesmen to enforce the religious prohibition against alcohol. Prime Minister Maliki made a televised pledge to rein in such serial killings, but since the worst-offending militia was Maliki's ally, Asa'ib Ahl al-Haq, Baghdadis had few expectations that their government would stop the reign of terror. "Everyone knows the Asa'ib is Maliki's right arm," said one Shia Baghdadi politician. "The fact is that we are in an undeclared civil war, just like 2006; but this time it will be worse, because the government itself is sponsoring the worst militias."

"What happened in Hawijah . . . and other places, is a point in which we should stop and think because it might lead to sectarian strife," Nuri Maliki told Iraqis a few days after the massacre that his own troops had carried out in the small northern town. "Everyone would lose. Whether he is in the north, the south, east, or west of Iraq, if the fire of sectarianism starts, everyone's fingers will be burned by it." But by the time the prime minister delivered this prediction, it had already come true: by any reasonable standard, Iraq in 2013 had reentered a state of civil war.

CHAPTER NINE

The Enduring Dilemmas of Iraq

"THE TWO MOST IMPORTANT THINGS America gave
the new Iraq were the sharing of power among the political parties and a system of checks and balances to keep
anyone from dominating the whole country the way Saddam did,"
a senior Iraqi official observed in 2011. "But now you Americans
have stood by and watched while both of those things have been
swept aside." It was a damning judgment. The nascent pluralistic
political system that the United States created for post-Saddam
Iraq has not been strong enough to withstand the powerful authoritarian, sectarian, and "resistance" factions who have had something
very different than sharing and balance in mind.

AUTHORITARIANISM

First and foremost, Iraq's parliamentary democracy has evolved
into an authoritarian regime, whose control over state institutions
has grown as time has passed. The Iraqi state that the United States
and its allies worked hard to decentralize and democratize after
2003 has reverted under Nuri al-Maliki to its old form: an Arab oil
power ruled by one sect, one party, one man. Under Maliki, the
military and security apparatus that was supposed to be profession-
alized and depoliticized has become dominated by the Malikiyoun,

with the most capable forces turned into a Shia praetorian guard loyal to Maliki and his family. The independent institutions designed to prevent the consolidation of power have been brought to heel under Maliki's executive authority, as have the other, nominally coequal branches of government, the judiciary and the parliament.

The provincial elections of April 2013 resulted in a mild setback to Maliki and his party, partly because of popular anger at the Maliki government's ineffective response to damaging floods that ravaged Iraq just weeks before the vote. Maliki's State of Law coalition lost dozens of local seats to the Sadrists and a somewhat resurgent ISCI, leading some enthusiastic critics of the prime minister to predict that he might be unseated in the parliamentary elections of April 2014. But such hopes are somewhat beside the point. Whether Maliki were to stay or go in 2014, he and the Malikiyoun have already damaged Iraq's democratic system, probably beyond repair, and the damage is certain to outlast him. The checks on the Iraqi prime minister's power that still exist lie completely outside the constitutional system: the street power of the Sadrists or the Sunni protest movement, the wealth and military strength of the Kurds, and the veto power of the Iranian regime. And there is the anger of the vast majority of the population, constantly threatening to boil over into an Arab Spring–type uprising against a government that millions of Iraqis believe has failed to live up to its end of the social bargain. These constraints are inherently destabilizing, as is the Maliki regime per se: as the Malikiyoun have consolidated control of the state and pushed their rivals out of power, they have driven the constituencies of those whom they exclude—especially Sunni Arabs and Kurds—toward political extremism. As a result, Maliki and his allies now generally hold sway in Baghdad, but whole swaths of the rest of Iraq are beyond their control: the tighter the Malikiyoun have grasped the state, the more the country has slipped through their fingers.

SECTARIANISM

Meanwhile, as Maliki and his fellow travelers have built their authoritarian regime, sectarian and ethnic identities have become hardwired into the Iraqi political culture. The Shia supremacists, Sunni chauvinists, and Kurdish maximalists who arrived or emerged in Iraq after April 2003 carried with them sectarian agendas that had been decades in the making, and they took advantage of the political vacuum to put their divisive ideas into practice. These groups have had independent but complementary interests in polarizing the country along ethnic and sectarian lines, turning a previously mixed-sect, multiethnic country into one distinguished by homogeneous political constituencies, and leading the country into a devastating sectarian civil war in the process. The end result has been an Iraq more thoroughly sorted by sect and ethnicity than ever before, ruled by community leaders so sharply at odds with one another that a return to full-scale war among them could take place at any moment.

The truth is that Iraq is already divided into at least two countries, an Arab Iraq and a Kurdish Iraq, and someday could be divided further still. And with the ongoing fragmentation of Syria, a Greater Kurdistan is emerging, one that will be beyond Baghdad's means to control. One of the dominant questions of the coming decade will be whether this enlarged Kurdistan remains within an Iraqi confederation or departs from Iraq altogether, either to become a satellite of Turkey or to become an irredentist Serbia to Turkey's Austria-Hungary. Also at issue is whether a full-scale Arab-Kurd war will ensue in either case. With these fundamental Arab-Kurd issues unresolved, Kurds will have little interest in seeing Sunni and Shia Arabs cease fighting between themselves, since Iraqi history shows that unified Iraqi Arabs invariably join forces to curb Kurdish ambitions.

Today, the Iraqi state itself has already returned to full-scale war with the resurgent Al Qaeda and Sunni resistance, and the state is losing. With each passing month, Al Qaeda has demonstrated its growing capacity to do damage inside Iraq, while the Maliki government has seemed nearly powerless to stop it. Al Qaeda has shown the Malikiyoun to be a party with ever-greater control over an increasingly ineffective state.

Perhaps the most disturbing feature of Iraq's new political scene is that the ethno-sectarian leaders who began by dragging their people toward sectarianism now often race to keep up with them. Iraqi leaders today, including Maliki, are never more popular than when they are most narrowly sectarian. Opinion polls and elections tell us that the harsher their rhetoric and the more provocative the deployment of their forces, the more their political support grows, while those Iraqi leaders who reach out to other sects or quarrel in public with others of their sect or ethnicity tend to pay a political price for doing so. After a decade of sectarians in power, the sectarians' project is threatening to take permanent root in Iraqi society.

RESISTANCE

Among the sectarians, it is perhaps the Shia Islamist "resistance" that can claim to have gained the most ground and enjoy the best future prospects after a decade of insurgency and civil war. Muhammad Sadiq al-Sadr's heirs control both Iraq's largest political movement and its closest parallel to Lebanese Hezbollah, and enjoy the bountiful patronage of the Iranian regime.

The strength of the Shia resistance bodes ill for the Shia politicians who have dominated the post-Saddam Iraqi governments, portending an eventual and probably violent struggle between Shia elites and lower-class Shia radicals of which the intra-Shia war of 2007–08 was a preview. If history is a guide, the Shia elite are likely to attempt in the meantime to co-opt and distract the Shia underclasses by channeling their energies deeper into sectarian pursuits against the region's Sunnis or against Kurdish nationalism. In that case, Shia leaders would see little reason to prevent the militias from taking their places alongside Lebanese Hezbollah in the Iranian regime's regional resistance front and in the regional sectarian struggle raging in Syria, Bahrain, Lebanon, Yemen, and Iraq itself.

As Asa'ib Ahl al-Haqq's October 2011 gathering in Beirut signified, the Iraqi Shia militants will pursue these expanded aims while enjoying resources, open political support, and freedom of movement that Sunni groups like Al Qaeda cannot replicate. Given their youthfulness, the Iraqi Shia resistance groups could visit violence on their enemies, real and imagined, for at least a generation to come, making the wave of anger created by their beloved Sadiq Sadr reverberate through the region decades after his death.

THE TEARING OF THE IRAQI SOCIAL FABRIC

The Iraqi civil war has been many things: a struggle between terrorists and the state; between religious extremes; between the Malikiyoun and their rivals; between regional proxies; between sects and ethnicities that have not relearned how to coexist. But it is most essentially a war on Iraqi society itself, a slow draining of the lifeblood of the world's oldest country, which after five millenia of history has begun to disintegrate before our eyes.

Iraq's people know they live in a country at civil war: it is impossible to understand them or predict what they will do without recognizing that they make decisions, conduct their daily lives, and behave toward one another according to that simple reality. Few of

them can afford to do otherwise for very long without risking their
own survival, as the numbers of the killed and wounded, the suicide
bombs, the kidnappings, and the shootings attest, week in and
week out, month after month, year after year.

As horrible as the casualty figures are, they do not tell the full
story of what has happened to Iraqi society. Throughout Iraq's
modern history, Iraqis who migrated into the country's urban areas
worked, studied, and lived alongside other sects and ethnicities.
Several million Iraqis live in families created by intermarriage,
especially those in the greater Baghdad region where young Shia
and Sunni men and women for many decades have been able to
meet each other in universities and government workplaces. The
idea of partitioning the country into sectarian cantons would leave
these families with no clear place to go, precipitating a vast human
tragedy. Even so, this conundrum may someday be a thing of the
past: the Baghdadis of 2014 report that the separation of the sects
has extended into Iraq's schools, markets, and offices, with the
result that intermarriage has virtually ceased. For Sunnis and Shia,
sect is hardening into a new ethnicity.

The aggregate casualty figures also do not tell us who exactly is
being killed, and there, too, is an untold story. The UK-based *Iraq-
bodycount.org* maintains a database of every reported violent death
in Iraq, with the victims' names and occupations recorded whenever possible. The listed livelihoods of those murdered in just the
month or so following the April 2013 Hawijah massacre instruct
us about the war's true toll:

Judge; Awakening council member; Imam; election candidate; Sunni tribal leader; demonstration organizer; police
lieutenant; lawyer; university professor; politician; election
official; political party official; citizenship department head;
money exchange shop owner; provincial council member;

council member; civil defense worker; car salesman; provincial ministry employee; Sunni cleric; police captain; mayor; soccer player; tribal leader.

These are the pillars of the community, and across Iraq they are falling.

Reflections on a Mandate

These outcomes—after a decade of such heavy American investment in the Iraq project—will be disappointing to many. They are doubly disappointing when we think of the opportunities that were lost as a result of American mistakes or flawed assumptions—most significant of which was the American failure to fully appreciate the political nature of the conflict in which the United States was engaged. The United States did not understand the extreme and divisive political objectives that the sectarian and authoritarian factions brought with them in 2003, or that they would take such extensive advantage of the process of building the new Iraqi state to push their schemes forward. The United States generally built state institutions as though they were not subject to politics, only to find later that such institutions had become tools for warring parties to use against each other. The United States also failed to understand the local roots of conflict, such as territorial encroachment or demographic alterations, so that it was sometimes manipulated by one side or other into becoming an inadvertent party to longstanding local disputes.

Nor did Americans fully appreciate the direct links between local and national politics. The U.S. military presence conveyed overwhelming local power in most of Iraq, but because the United States so seldom understood the relationship between local actors and national-level politicians and parties, and therefore the local dynamics that for good or ill drove national-level political behavior, it often had undiscovered leverage that could have been aggregated for a strategic effect, but was not.

Finally, throughout the campaign in Iraq, the United States interjected itself in Iraqi politics inconsistently, applying and then relieving incentives and disincentives mainly without a larger plan. The United States exerted great power when it chose to do so, as just a few examples suffice to show: in 2003, when the United States selected the entire Iraqi Interim Governing Council; in 2004–05, when the United States set the parameters for the Iraqi constitution; in 2006, when the United States blocked the return of Ibrahim Jaafari as prime minister and promoted Nuri Maliki as premier instead; or 2007, when U.S. officials shut down the Kurds' push for a Kirkuk referendum that could have sparked a full-scale Arab-Kurd war. But the United States exerted influence like this only episodically, while U.S. adversaries fought constantly to shape the new Iraq: an around-the-clock, calculated effort to undermine or reverse what the United States was trying to achieve.

Nevertheless, it was far from inevitable that the American project in Iraq should end in a state of affairs so far from its original objectives. The sectarians, would-be authoritarians, and Iranian regime proxies who hold sway now had to work exceedingly hard toward their goals, not all of which have been attained even now, and as recently as 2010 it appeared they might be thwarted by the popular backlash from Iraqis who blamed them for causing the ruinous civil war and who were ready to throw them over in favor of the kind of pluralistic democracy the United States had hoped Iraq would become. These same factions were also no match for American political influence when it was intelligently applied and backed up with overwhelming military power, as it was in the "surge" period of 2007–09. It is no accident that the "surge" period, when U.S. military commanders and Coalition diplomats worked most closely together to accomplish joint objectives, culminated with the 2009 provincial elections that dealt such a blow to sectarian Islamist parties across the country, one they struggled to overcome in the national elections of 2010—though they eventually succeeded when U.S. political objectives and military presence were decoupled in that same year. The outcome in Iraq should not be an argument for refusing to become involved in foreign politics, but rather a warning that the United States should be better equipped when it inevitably happens, as well as a lesson that when the instruments of national power are aligned and informed by a full understanding of the local political context, the United States can have a powerful impact.

Beyond consideration of Iraq as a case study, there remains the strategic problem of what to do about Iraq going forward. For quite some time, the prevailing view in the United States was that the U.S. military withdrawal would be a positive development for both the United States and Iraq; that Iraq in the absence of the United States would be an increasingly stable democracy with an increasingly capable state; and that Iraq would be a strategic partner sharing core common interests with the United States. But each of these claims is now suspect. The actions that the Malikiyoun have taken and must continue to take to stay in power have weakened Iraq's democratic institutions and destabilized the country. The actions the sectarians have had to take to pursue their narrow agendas have done the same. And the actions both the Malikiyoun and the sectarians are driven to take to further their respective interests lead them down paths that diverge from the United States, so that the United States is increasingly at odds with them on the strategic questions that dominate the Middle East, such as Bahrain, Syria, the Iranian nuclear program, and even how best to defeat Al Qaeda.

The disparity between U.S. and Iraqi sectarian interests on these questions and many more is not just a matter of tactical disagreements between strategic partners. They are strategic disagreements between occasionally tactical partners. If the Iraqi government were today what the United States intended it to be, a pluralistic parliamentary democracy at peace with its neighbors, the United States would indeed share basic interests with it. But the United States shares practically no fundamental interests with the government that has evolved: authoritarian, sectarian, tolerant of Shia militancy, and leading the country toward fragmentation as it intervenes in regional crises on the side of the Iranian regime.

*   *   *

Iraq's prospects are dim. The country's politics lie in disarray, and there is no clear route back to stability. The Iraqi political environment that has resulted from the three dominant forces of sectarianism, authoritarianism, and "resistance" is a truly zero-sum game in which each party appears to seek the complete exclusion of its rivals from the political system and the state. There seems to be in the post-Saddam Iraqi political class no sense of limits on what the various parties may do to one another and to one another's constituencies. Perhaps this is because one must look so far into the past, before the regicidal revolution of 1958, to find Iraq's last real plural political culture. Gone are the days when an Iraqi leader could lose power and yet live on in Baghdad undisturbed, or even join the loyal opposition and wait for his turn to rule again, as the thirteen-time Iraqi Prime Minister Nuri al-Said was once able to do.

Today, the principle goes even beyond individual leaders. Eight years into their rough rule and consolidation of power, what member of the Malikiyoun could trust that the Maliki party could hand power to a successor party and be left to live in peace, or peaceful opposition? Similarly, after a decade of attempting to push the Green Line far into Sunni Arab territory, what Kurdish leader believes that Sunni Arabs, if ever back in power, would not immediately attempt to push the Kurds back into the mountains and try to crush Kurdish nationalism? And after a decade of attempting to make Sunnis a permanent minority underclass, what Shia supremacist does not fear what the Sunnis would do if ever they regained control of Baghdad? The fundamental questions that have dogged Iraq and led to near-constant conflict since its creation—the relationship between Shia and Sunni Arabs; the relationship between the people and the state; the relationship between Kurdistan and the rest of the Iraq; the relationship between Iraq and its neighbors—remain unsettled, and as long as it is Iraq's strongmen, sectarians, and "resistance" that control the way toward resolving them, further conflict among the Iraqi communities is assured. "Many Americans seem to think this means the end of the power struggle in Iraq," an Iraqi politician said in the last days of 2011, commenting on the impending departure of U.S. troops from his country. "It does not. Now that the Americans are going, we will see the real start of the struggle for power in Iraq, not the end." The war that began in 2003 and seemed to have ended for a time in 2008–09, is far from over.

The tragedy of post-Saddam Iraq is that it need not have turned out this way, and it still need not continue this way in the future. There is a popular trope among western academics that since Iraq's borders are an artificiality created by European diplomats, it must follow that Iraq itself is an artificiality, and that there is no genuine Iraqi national identity. But this is not borne out among Iraqis inside Iraq—at least not for the present. For all the fractures that run through Iraqi society and that divisive politicians and militants have exploited so well, there seems to remain a silent majority of Iraqis of all kinds who would greatly prefer to live together as one people, in one country. They consider themselves heirs to a common ancient Iraqi heritage, a people sharing the country where civilization was born. The popular antisectarian backlash of 2007–08 and the nationalist politics of 2009 showed that even in the darkest days of their civil war, common Iraqis thirsted for opportunities to assert a common Iraqi identity. If ever a political movement could harness the cross-sectarian spirit of 2008–09, it might just captivate a large following and perhaps break Iraqi politics out of its zero-sum game. But such a movement would have to arise from the connections that bind Iraq's institutions, professions, civil society groups, tribes, and local communities together—the very ties that sectarians and others are working so hard to sever. The longer the strongmen, sectarians, and "resistance" hold sway in Iraq, the further they will lead their followers down a maximalist path to ruin, and the smaller will be the chance that Iraq will hold together. It is not yet too late for Iraq, but someday not far distant, it will be.

O N APRIL 30, 2014, as this book was being printed, Iraqis went to the polls to elect the country's fourth new parliamentary government in the post-Saddam era, the first to be elected in the absence of American troops. As in previous elections, the major parties had organized themselves into electoral coalitions mainly based on sect and ethnicity. Among the Shia parties, the preliminary results showed Prime Minister Nuri Maliki and his State of Law coalition with ninety-four seats, slightly above their 2010 total, while Moqtada Sadr won thirty-one and Ammar Hakim's Islamic Supreme Council of Iraq (ISCI) won thirty. The major Kurdish parties secured fifty-five seats, twenty-five of them for the Kurdistan Democratic Party (KDP) of Massoud Barzani and twenty-one for the Patriotic Union of Kurdistan (PUK) of the comatose Jalal Talabani. Finally, the Sunni-majority parties that had combined to win a plurality of ninety-one seats in 2010 fragmented in 2014, with Osama Nujaifi winning twenty-eight seats, Ayad Allawi winning twenty-one, and Saleh Mutlaq winning eleven, meaning that Sunnis and Allawi loyalists would have a much smaller share of the new parliament. As in the three previous elections, no single party dominated the vote, meaning that the new government would be the result of extended bargaining to produce a broad governing coalition.

THE WAR AGAINST "DASH" AND THE SUNNIS

One reason for the Sunnis' diminished performance in the 2014 elections was that sectarian violence had intensified in the months preceding the April polling, depressing the vote in large swathes of the Sunni provinces. In late 2013, what had begun as a political standoff between the Maliki government and its Sunni opponents in Anbar and the north had deteriorated into open warfare. For the third December in a row, Maliki's forces had raided one of Iraq's top Sunni politicians, this time arresting parliamentarian Ahmed al-Alwani in Ramadi. In the following weeks a near-exact rerun of 2004 had unfolded, as eastern Anbar became an epicenter of insurgency just as it had been a decade before. Led by commanders fresh from the Syrian front, the militants of the Islamic State of Iraq and the Levant—Al Qaeda in Iraq's new incarnation, best known by its Arabic acronym of DASH—moved openly through Fallujah's streets and launched waves of sectarian attacks against Baghdad thirty miles away. DASH even seized control of the Fallujah Dam and flooded the local Euphrates valley, thereby lowering the water supply for the southern Shia provinces downstream. Days ahead of the voting, DASH fighters advanced to Abu Ghraib and clashed with government troops sixteen miles from the Green Zone housing the Iraqi government. Nor was the opposition to the Maliki government limited to DASH: in the months preceding the elections, Iraqi troops in Anbar found themselves clashing frequently with Sunni tribal militias that had once formed the core of the Awakening, the anti-Al Qaeda movement that had helped turn the tide of the war in 2007.

Other regions around the capital began to resemble themselves during the height of the sectarian killing of 2006. Sunni militants gradually returned to the "belts" around Baghdad and in Diyala, attacking government troops and Shia populations in the same mixed-sect areas that had been violently contested in 2005–07. As the Sunni militant threat grew in these areas, Shia militant groups such as Asa'ib Ahl al Haqq (AAH) responded as they had in 2006, roaming through mixed-sect towns and terrorizing Sunnis into leaving. In 2007 and 2008, the Maliki government had eventually cooperated with coalition troops to put a stop to such sectarian cleansing, but with Asa'ib Ahl al Haqq having won a parliamentary seat in the April 30 elections as allies of Maliki, few Iraqis would expect Maliki to restrain AAH similarly in 2014.

The government response to the DASH offensive, held in abeyance in the weeks ahead of the election, resumed in full ten days after the voting. Maliki's troops launched assaults against the region around Fallujah, encountering stiff DASH resistance. The fighting drove thousands of families from their homes, adding to the estimated 420,000 Anbaris already displaced by the war in 2014. A week later, the United States and Iraq announced a deal for $1 billion in American military hardware and training, signifying that the Maliki government now found it expedient to accept the American military assistance it had spurned in 2011.

THE FUTURE STRUGGLE FOR POWER

The mounting sectarian violence had not harmed Maliki and his party in the parliamentary poll. As the Sunni militant threat gathered in Anbar and the Baghdad region, Maliki had campaigned as a defender of the Shia population, appealing to Shia voters as a strongman who would crack down harshly on DASH and its supporters. The appeal seems to have worked: Maliki was by far the most popular individual candidate in the elections, garnering more than 720,000 votes himself in Baghdad, with his two sons-in-law tallying another 100,000 between them in Karbala. Even so, the other major Shia parties began in the election season to combine against Maliki to try to deny him a third term, mainly out of concern that Maliki might be heading toward a permanent premiership. "If we have a third [Maliki] term," ISCI's Adel Abd al-Mahdi warned western reporters, "then we will have a fourth, fifth, and sixth term." In a turnabout from their intra-Shia war of 2006–08, Hakim and Sadr had joined forces against Maliki, aiming to force him back into a broad Shia bloc within which he could be outvoted in favor of alternatives such as ISCI's Bayan Jabr, the man who had overseen the infiltration of the Interior Ministry by Shia militants in 2005–06. For his part, Maliki spoke of forming a "majority government" with his ninety-four members of Parliament and a few other parties rather than reprise the unity governments in which all major parties had participated since 2005, but this idea was set back by Kurdistan President Massoud Barzani's declaration that if Maliki were to return as premier, the Kurdish parties might boycott the Iraqi government altogether and accelerate their move toward independence.

The opening post-election moves from indicated that Maliki's opposition was potentially formidable. Sadr and Hakim, the Sunnis and Allawi, and the Kurds, respectively, constituted three blocs with about sixty MPs each, and all were vocally opposed to a third Maliki term. To return to the premiership Maliki would have to prevent these three rival blocs from forming a government without him, and then fracture each of them in turn to form his own. But having far outpolled their main Shia rivals, winning more than a million votes in Baghdad alone, Maliki and State of Law seemed well-positioned to repeat their successful 2010 strategy of using the power of their incumbency to assert control of the government formation process and wait for the other parties to grudgingly accept Maliki's return as premier, with Iran's endorsement.

Ironically, Maliki had pledged repeatedly before 2014 not to seek a third term, but as the election approached, the State of Law coalition had subtly papered over the pledge, and Maliki himself had behaved increasingly like a man who intended never to give up power at all. One sign was the empowerment of his son, Ahmed, whom Iraqis began privately describing as a new Uday Saddam Hussein, entrusted with his father's security and rumored to hold vast wealth garnered through corrupt government contracts. Having quietly taken charge of much of the Green Zone and its security forces, Ahmed Maliki came into prominent view in 2013 when he led government security forces on a raid against an Iraqi businessman accused of corruption. Asked about Ahmed's unusual role in the operation, Prime Minister Maliki explained to an Iraqi TV interviewer that he had been forced to rely on his son because "When an arrest warrant was issued, everyone was afraid to go near [the businessman] . . . . But Ahmed said, 'Give me the arrest warrant and I will bring him in.' . . . Ahmed is tough." Speaking privately, however, some Iraqis observed not a tough public servant, but a young man being groomed to succeed his father as leader of a new dynasty.

The Malikis are not the only budding dynasty in the post-Saddam political class, of course. Instances abound of the children of ministers and politicians readying themselves to exert their fathers' power. The most egregious case came in March 2014, when Mahdi al Ameri, son of Transportation Minister—and former Badr Corps commander—Hadi al Ameri, missed his Middle East Airlines flight home from Beirut but then forced the aircraft to turn around in mid-flight by having Baghdad airport officials deny it permission to land without him.

If Maliki were to return for a third term, there would be no real obstacle to his remaining as prime minister for life—or until choosing to retire in favor of a designated successor such as his son. Whether he returns to the premiership or not, however, the effects of the Maliki era of government are probably already permanent. The Iraqi state now belongs to its political class, which divides most of the country's more than $100 billion in annual oil revenues among its members and treats public assets as private property. Ahmed Maliki's activities and the Beirut airport incident were just two of many indications of the extent to which Iraq's state institutions have become fiefdoms, with families and cronies of senior officials often living beyond the rule of law.

Beyond the halls of power, however, the country continues to unravel. There is no end in sight to the sectarian civil war in the Sunni provinces and on the outskirts of Baghdad. Iraqis quietly report Sunni militants in de facto control of the streets in Mosul and Tikrit, with the Iraqi security forces (ISF) too weak or unwilling to dislodge them. With large portions of northern and eastern Syria already in Sunni militant hands, a new Sunni militant region is emerging from Raqqa to Mosul and Deir ez Zour to Fallujah, with Sunni factions competing for power. This is the domain the Islamic State of Iraq and the Levant hopes to carve into a *takfiri* caliphate, and with ineffective states in Damascus and Baghdad, there is little reason to think they cannot accomplish their goal.

The Shia parties of Iraq, meanwhile, seem ready to insulate Baghdad and the Iraqi south from this potential Sunni Islamic State by adopting Syria's "Shabiha Solution": they are likely to allow Shia militants to form into auxiliaries of Iraqi government security forces and evict Sunnis from the region around Baghdad, all in the name of counterterrorism and with the advice and assistance of the Iranian regime and Lebanese Hezbollah.

IMPLICATIONS FOR THE UNITED STATES

Iraq's political, military, and social environments are extraordinarily complex, making it difficult to gauge in the present the consequences of US policies toward the country and its leaders and factions. But extrapolating those policies into the future can bring some clarity to the questions that seem near-unsolvable now.

Nuri Maliki has long presented himself as an indispensable partner against Al Qaeda-type terrorism in Iraq and Syria, and it is the United States' willingness to entertain such a partnership that has underpinned its security relationship with Iraq. But the Iraqi government weapons and troops that the United States wishes to see Maliki deploy effectively against DASH and its ilk often have been turned against Maliki's mainstream Sunni political rivals as well, sending some of them into alignment with DASH. The simple truth is that the Iraqi government's "counterterrorism" activities are part of a broad regional Sunni-Shia conflict in which Maliki's forces are aligned with those of the Iranian regime. If the United States maintains its security relationship with an Iraqi government that is at war with Sunni tribes and the United States' former "Awakening" allies, then will Iraqi Sunnis a few years hence view the United States in the same way that Syrian Sunnis view Russia: an enemy power supplying a Shia-dominated government with weapons to make war on its Sunni population?

The United States has long accepted the idea that Maliki—or any Iraqi Shia leader—must balance relations with Iran and the United States, and Maliki has occasionally offered his government as a go-between with Tehran. But in the past few years the balance has seemed to swing increasingly in Tehran's direction: at the same time that Maliki seeks counterterrorism assistance from the United States, he has formed partnerships with the Iranian-sponsored terrorist groups Asa'ib Ahl al Haqq and Kata'ib Hizballah, two anti-American militant groups that fought US troops in Iraq directly until 2011 and now send Shia fighters to Syria to fight for the Assad regime. The leaders of both groups live near Maliki in Baghdad's Green Zone, the enclave policed by Maliki's son. If relations between the United States and Iran deteriorate further in the coming years, or come to war, it is likely these and other Iranian-sponsored Iraqi militant groups will resume their attacks against the United States and its allies. Could the United States someday find itself at war with these political partners of Nuri Maliki, while Maliki shelters them for his own reasons in the Iraqi parliament and the Green Zone, in a case similar to the United States, Bin Laden, and the Taliban in 2001?

In the tense relationship between the Iraqi government and Kurdistan, meanwhile, the United States has long maintained a policy of encouraging Iraqi national integrity over Kurdish separatism, looking unfavorably on matters such as the Kurdistan Regional Government's (KRG) new oil pipeline to Turkey. But if the sectarian conflict in Iraq continues to worsen, and Nuri Maliki returns as premier, then the balance between Kurds who favor remaining in Iraq and those who favor independence is likely to shift for good in favor of the separatists. If the United States continues to encourage Iraqi integrity in that case, then will the Kurds spurn US partnership in favor of others—Turkey, Iran, Russia—who may be more willing to accommodate them?

To a great degree, military ties have dominated the US-Iraq relationship, and the United States has explicitly sought to maintain a deep relationship with the Iraqi Security Forces. But the voting of April 2014 showed that the million-strong ISF has become one of Nuri Maliki's biggest constituencies, able to exercise a sort of "swing vote" in the parliamentary tally. Whether Maliki goes or stays, has a large portion of the ISF become an extension of the ruler's political coalition? If so, then Iraqi history may be on the verge of repeating itself, so that any ruler or would-be ruler need only gain the support of the ISF to hold power. Could the United States thus eventually find itself with deep ties to a militarized state in which political front men rule through committees of generals? This would be a familiar sight indeed in the Arab world.

The United States has developed extensive ties with the men who lead Iraq's parties and government ministries. But Iraq's most powerful politicians have become a fabulously wealthy, permanent elite that is able to draw upon large portions of Iraq's more than $100 billion in annual oil revenues for its own use, with no accountability to the public—the exact dynamics that led to the 2010–12 revolutions in six Arab countries. Common Iraqis are increasingly alienated from their government and the political process, and it is not implausible to imagine their anger boiling over in the next few years. As the United States maintains ties with the Iraqi political elite, will common Iraqis come to view America as an enemy–the friend of Iraq's hated kleptocrats?

Finally, the United States has since 2003 sided with the Iraqi government against the Sadr movement, and still appears to view the Maliki government today as a necessary bulwark against Sadrist power. If the Sadrists and the Maliki government eventually fight one another for supremacy, as seems likely, the United States seems poised to support Maliki in that showdown. But with a base of millions of supporters among the Iraqi Shia and dozens of members of parliament, neither Moqtada Sadr nor the political movement his father created will be easily swept aside. They are more likely to be a force in Iraqi politics and society for decades to come. Is it in the United States' interest to keep the Sadrists as permanent enemies?

These are difficult questions, and the future that they describe would be a difficult one indeed. To avoid this outcome, the United

States must help Iraqis return to the constructive ideas that achieved a dramatic reduction in sectarian violence and a broad political accommodation among Iraqi communities in 2007–09. Many of the policies that enabled progress during that period unfortunately have been undone, most notably by the Iraqi government's failure to continue its support for reconciliation with Sunni Arabs and for the programs designed to make that reconciliation endure. If the United States cannot find ways to reverse these trends once again, as it did in 2007, the outcome is likely to be a war-torn region and a bloodily fragmenting Iraq in which America has no friends.

M
UCH OF THE MATERIAL in this book was drawn from interviews and discussions with scholars, analysts, and officials in America, Britain, and the Middle East, and particularly from discussions with numerous Iraqis since 2006. Most of the Iraqis will remain unnamed, as I have mentioned in the Acknowledgments to this book. The same is true for other sources from Syria, Lebanon, Iran, and elsewhere who shared views and information freely. Many of those mentioned in the Acknowledgments were also occasional sources for this book, as were Sheikh Shammar al-Yawar, Dr. (Lieutenant Colonel) Ahmed Hashim, Lieutenant Colonel Jason Awadi, Jim Sindle, Colonel Marty Stanton, Lieutenant General Jim Dubik, Colonel Jim Coffman, and Colonel J. B. Burton.

These source notes omit significant dates and events documented in multiple wire service reports, such as terror attacks or press statements, though I should acknowledge that Niqash, Aswat al-Iraq, *Al-Jazeera*, Reuters, McClatchy, and CNN were particularly useful in reviewing the daily documentary record.

I. THE ROOTS OF THE DAWA STATE

For further reading on the origins of the Dawa Party, see the Iraqi scholar Faleh Jabar's *The Shiite Movement in Iraq*, London, Saqi Books, 2003. In his seminal book, *The Old Social Classes and the Revolutionary Movements of Iraq*, London, Saqi Books, 1978, Hanna

Batatu describes the struggle between the Shia Islamists and the Iraqi Communists.

Baqir al-Sadr's son Jaafar spoke of his family history in a 2010 interview with *Al Sharq al-Awsat*. The best account of Musa Sadr's role is Fouad Ajami's *The Vanished Imam: Musa al Sadr and the Shia of Lebanon*, Ithaca, New York, Cornell University Press, 1986. More recent was Nicholas Blanford's "As Gaddafi Teeters, Will the Mystery of Lebanon's Missing Imam Be Solved?," *Time*, February 25, 2011.

For the Dawa-Baath confrontation, I drew from Charles Tripp, *A History of Iraq*, 3rd ed., New York, Cambridge University Press, 2007. Anthony Shadid recounts Baqir Sadr's murder in *Night Draws Near: Iraq's People in the Shadow of America's War*, New York, Henry Holt, 2005.

The pressures upon Dawa in Iran are described in Rodger Shanahan, "Shi'a Political Development in Iraq: The Case of the Islamic Da'wa Party," *Third World Quarterly* 104, 2004. Joseph Felter and Brian Fishman discuss SCIRI/Badr's early relationship with the Iranian regime in *Iranian Strategy in Iraq: Politics and "Other Means,"* West Point, Combating Terrorism Center, 2008.

The rivalry between the Syrian Baath and Iraqi Baath is described in Eberhard Kienle, *Ba'th Versus Ba'th: The Conflict between Syria and Iraq*, London, I. B. Tauris, 1990. Dawa activities and connections with its Lebanese counterparts are covered in Jamal Sankari's *Fadlallah, The Making of a Radical Shi'ite Leader*, London, Saqi Books, 2005.

2. The Dawa's Road to Nuri Maliki

For more on Maliki's personal history, see Juan Cole, "Saving Iraq: Mission Impossible," *Salon*, 11 May 2006. The Syrian regime's regional strategy is described in Marius Deeb, *Syria's Terrorist War on Lebanon and the Peace Process*, New York, Palgrave Macmillan, 2004. Dexter Filkins reported upon the Shia social aspects of the power struggle in "Boys of Baghdad College Vie for Prime Minister," *New York Times*, December 12, 2005.

Stephen Hadley's memo on Maliki was leaked to the *New York Times* two weeks after it was written and published on November 29, 2006.

For the parliamentary maneuvers to unseat Maliki in late 2007 to early 2009, and perhaps the best published account of the Basra campaign, see Michael Gordon's *The Endgame*, New York, Pantheon Books, 2012.

Joshua Partlow and Sudarsan Raghavan reported the Karbala shootout in "Sadr's Militia Blamed for Deadly Shiite-on-Shiite Melee," *Washington Post*, October 7, 2007. I also drew from "Maliki Sacks Karbala Police Chief, Runs Operations by Himself," Kuwait News Agency, August 29, 2007, and Stephen Farrell, "Sadr Suspends His Militia's Military Operations," *New York Times*, August 30, 2007. The Sadr-Hakim struggle can be seen in "Provincial Governor Is Assassinated; Second in Two Weeks," Iraq-Nam, August 20, 2007; "Sadr, Hakim Forge Deal to End Rivalry," Agence France Press, October 6, 2007; and Patrick Gaughen, "The Fight for Diwaniyah: The Sadrist Trend and ISCI Struggle for Supremacy," Institute for the Study of War, December 2007. Mona Mahmoud et al. described the situation in Basra in late 2007 in "UK Has Left Behind Murder and Chaos, Says Basra Police Chief," *Guardian* (London), December 16, 2007.

Marisa Cochrane's "The Battle for Basra," Institute for the Study of War, May 2008, is also thorough and useful. The description of Ibrahim Jaafari's political problems and his relations with the Sadrists comes from Edward Wong and Joel Brinkley, "Iraq's Premier Is Asked to Quit as Shiites Split," *New York Times*, April 3, 2006;

David Enders, "Letter from Baghdad: The Growing Sectarian Divide," *The Nation*, April 8, 2006. The defeat of the Sadrists in Sadr City comes from Michael Gordon, "U.S. Begins Erecting Wall in Sadr City," *New York Times*, April 18, 2008, and Michael Gordon and Stephen Farrell, "Iraqi Troops Take Charge of Sadr City in Swift Push," *New York Times*, May 21.

3. THE NEW AUTHORITARIAN REGIME OF NURI MALIKI

See Bill Roggio, "Iraqi Forces Detain Sadrist Leaders, Uncover Special Groups Headquarters in Amarah," *Long War Journal*, July 2, 2008. Michael Gordon recounts Maliki's opposition to the extension of the Awakening in *The Endgame*.

The polling of 2009 was reported by Stephen Farrell and Alissa J. Rubin in "Under Tight Security, Iraqis Vote on Almost Violence-Free Election Day," *New York Times*, January 31, 2009.

For Sistani's reluctance to endorse parties in 2009, as seen in Steven Lee Myers, "Iraq's Top Cleric Refuses to Influence Elections," *New York Times*, March 2, 2010.

Johan Spanner reported on Maliki's new political grouping in "Iraqi Leader Creates Broad Coalition," *New York Times*, October 1, 2009. The speeches from Maliki and Ali Adeeb are covered in Steven Lee Myers and Marc Santora, "Premier Casting U.S. Withdrawal as Iraq Victory," *New York Times*, June 26, 2009.

For more on Maliki's "Politburo," see Joyce Wiley, *The Islamic Movement of Iraqi Shi'as*; Nibras Kazimi, "Daggers Drawn in Maliki's Office," *Talisman Gate blog*, August 26, 2008; and Nibras Kazimi, *Imara wa al-Tijara blog* (in Arabic), December 2011. Nimrod Raphaeli, "Iraqi Prime Minister Nouri Kamal al-Maliki, Critical of Consensus Democracy, Calls for a Presidential System," Middle East

Media Research Institute, Inquiry & Analysis Series Report No. 530, July 1, 2009.

Maliki's use of the Iraqi Special Operations Forces is addressed in "Police: Iraqi Troops Raid Diyala Governor's Office," *USA Today*, August 19, 2008; "Iraqi Anti-terror Force Does Not Legally Exist: Chief," Agence France Presse, June 19, 2009; and D. J. Elliott, "Iraqi Security Forces Order of Battle Update: February 2009," *Long War Journal*, February 5, 2009.

The confrontation between Saddam and his generals in 1986 is described in Charles Tripp, *A History of Iraq*, 3rd edition.

4. THE SHIA SUPREMACISTS

An example of the numerous reports of the Supreme Council for Islamic Revolution in Iraq (SCIRI) and Badr reshaping the sectarian map of Baghdad can be seen in Sabrina Tavernise, "District by District, Shiites Make Baghdad Their Own," *New York Times*, December 23, 2006.

"Bush Meets Iraqi Shia Leader," *al-Jazeera*, December 5, 2006. SCIRI's ongoing relationship with the Quds Force was detailed in Michael Gordon, *The Endgame*, and in James Glanz, "U.S. Says Arms Link Iranians to Iraqi Shiites," *New York Times*, February 12, 2007.

Engineer Ahmed's secret prisons are described in a PBS Frontline interview with Brigadier General Karl Horst (the U.S. official who uncovered them), posted at *PBS.org* on April 17, 2007. General Mehdi Gharrawi's role is described by Linda Robinson in *Tell Me How This Ends*, New York, Perseus Books, 2008.

The acceleration of sectarian cleansing after the Sammara mosque bombing is covered in "Baghdad's New Owners," *Newsweek*, September 9, 2007. Claudio Guler depicted the new sectarian balance of the city in "Baghdad Divided," *ISN Security Watch*, November 9, 2009. For a snapshot of Baghdad's sectarian "shibboleths," see "Amid Violence, Iraqis Turn to Fake IDs," NBC News, July 10, 2006.

Shada Hussein's "Star Academy" win was reported in Karin Brulliard, "Iraqis Unite behind Their Heroine on Arab 'Idol,'" *Washington Post*, March 31, 2007. The Iraqi soccer victory was described in "Iraq Celebrates Football Victory," BBC News, July 29, 2007.

Examples of those wrongly crediting the completion of sectarian cleansing for the drop in violence in 2007–08 include Juan Cole, "Forget the Surge—Violence Is Down in Iraq Because Ethnic Cleansing Was Brutally Effective," AlterNet, July 28, 2008; Judah Grunstein, "The Limits of the Surge: An Interview with Gian Gentile," World Politics Review Briefing, April 11, 2008; Tom Friedman, "Syria is Iraq," *New York Times*, July 25, 2012; and UCLA Professor John Agnew and Claudio Guler in "False Advertising about the Iraq Surge," *Truthout.org*, June 13, 2010.

5. THE SUNNI CHAUVINISTS

Amatzia Baram describes Saddam's turn to Islamism in "From Militant Secularism to Islamism: The Iraqi Ba'th Regime 1968–2003," Wilson Center History and Public Policy Program Occasional Paper, October 2011.

Baram's article also quotes Barzan al-Tikriti's journal entry, October 21, 2000, though the original entry is in the National Defense University Conflict Records Research Center, SH-MISC-D-000-950. Dhari's grandfather's role was described in Lieutenant General Sir Aylmer Haldane, *The Insurrection in Mesopotamia*, London, Blackwood and Sons, 1922. Haldane was commander of the

British forces that put down the Iraqi insurgency of 1920 in central-southern Iraq and some areas of the north.

The Saddam regime's contingency orders are found in the Conflict Records Resource Center, document SH-PDWN-D-000-012: Contingency instructions for Iraqi government personnel in case of regime defeat (January 23, 2003.)

The general struggle between the two regimes is recounted in Eberhard Kienle, *Ba'th versus Ba'th: The Conflict between Syria and Iraq.*

The best early account of the motives and aims of the Sunni insurgent groups is Ahmed Hashim's *Insurgency and Counterinsurgency in Iraq*, Ithaca, New York, Cornell University Press, 2006. I also benefited from many discussions with Ahmed Hashim when we served together in Baghdad in 2007. For the Sunni insurgency's rejection of the political process, see Roel Meijer, "Muslim Politics under Occupation: The Association of Muslim Scholars and the Politics of Resistance in Iraq," *Arab Studies Journal*, Fall 2005. The Sunnis' realization that their boycott was a mistake is described in Ali Allawi, *The Occupation of Iraq.*

Zarqawi's role is covered in Nimrod Raphaeli, "'The Sheikh of the Slaughterers': Abu Mus'ab al-Zarqawi and the al-Qa'ida Connection," Middle East Media Research Institute Inquiry and Analysis no. 231 (2005). Zarqawi's intercepted letter is quoted in Anthony H. Cordesman and Emma R. Davies, *Iraq's Insurgency and the Road to Civil Conflict*, Westport, Connecticut, Praeger Security International, 2008.

The mujahideen's ease of movement through Syria was described in Joseph Felter and Brian Fishman's report, *Al Qaeda's Foreign Fighters in Iraq: A First Look at the Sinjar Records*, U.S. Military Academy Combating Terrorism Center, January 2008. Michael Gordon and Wesley Morgan also covered the Syrian factor in "The General's Gambit," *ForeignPolicy.com*, October 1, 2012.

Al Qaeda in Iraq's activities beyond Iraq can be seen in Brian Fishman, "After Zarqawi: The Dilemmas and Future of Al Qaeda in Iraq," *Washington Quarterly*, October 2006; Murad Batal al-Shishani, "Jordanian Poll Indicates Erosion of Public Support for al-Qaeda," *Jamestown Terrorism Focus*, February 2006; Thair Abbas, "Worrying Signs about the Growth of Al Qaeda in Lebanon," *Al Sharq al Awsat*, March 18, 2006.

Zawahiri's reply to Zarqawi is quoted in "Zawahiri's Letter to Zaraqawi (English Translation)," U.S. Military Academy Combating Terrorism Center. Zarqawi's warning to Iraqis not to vote is covered in the International Crisis Group's *In Their Own Words: Reading the Iraqi Insurgency*, Middle East Report no. 50, 2006. Sunni turnout in the December 2005 election comes from Ellen Knickmeyer and Jonathan Finer, "Iraqi Vote Draws Big Turnout of Sunnis," *Washington Post*, December 16, 2005.

For the Islamic State of Iraq and its partition plans, see Brian Fishman, "Al-Qa'ida Secedes from Iraq: Implications for Bleedout and U.S. Policy," U.S. Military Academy Combating Terrorism Center, November 2008. For a summary of Salafi criticism of the Islamic State of Iraq, see "Al-Qaeda Declares Islamic Iraqi State," *Abu Aardvark blog*, 2006.

David Kilcullen describes the overreach of Al Qaeda in Anbar in "Anatomy of a Tribal Revolt," *Small Wars Journal*, August 29, 2007. Kathleen Ridolfo reported Iraqi insurgents' appeal to bin Laden to control AQI in "Iraq: Al-Qaeda Tactics Lead to Splits among Insurgents," Radio Free Europe/Radio Liberty, April 17, 2007. Harith al-Dhari's quotes come from "Top Cleric Asks Iraqis Not to Join Anti-Qaeda Fight," Reuters, October 5, 2007.

The Awakening's new political role in Anbar was reported in Liz Sly, "In Iraq's Anbar Province, the Awakening Grapples with a New Role," *Los Angeles Times*, May 4, 2009. For the changed situation beyond Anbar, see Suadad al-Salhy, "Analysis: Provincial Elections Outcome," *New York Times*, March 2, 2009. For the

2009 election's impact in Ninewa, see the International Crisis Group's "Iraq's New Battlefront: The Struggle over Ninewa," Middle East Report No. 90, September 28, 2009.

The Naqshbandis' new role was covered in Quil Lawrence, "U.S. Sees New Threat in Iraq from Sufi Sect," National Public Radio, June 17, 2009.

Heather Sharp described the displacement of Iraq's Marsh Arabs in "Iraq's 'Devastated' Marsh Arabs," BBC News, March 3, 2003. Interim Iraqi President Ghazi al-Yawar made the implausible claim in a BBC interview in December 2004 that the Iranian regime had sent one million people into Iraq to vote in the impending Iraqi elections of January 2005 (quoted in John Burns and Robert Wo, "Iraqi Shiite with Ties to Iran Gains Top Billing," *World Security Network*, December 16, 2004).

Elie Kedourie is quoted from "The Kingdom of Iraq: A Retrospect," in *The Chatham House Version and Other Middle Eastern Studies*, New York, Praeger, 1970. The Sunni saying "For us, political power" comes from Fouad Ajami's remarks in "The Emerging Shi'a Crescent," a Council on Foreign Relations symposium held on June 5, 2006.

6. The Kurdish Maximalists

Jalal Talabani is quoted in Metin Turcan, "Confrontation or Conciliation? Kirkuk Question as the Tightest Knot in Iraq and Iraqi Kurdish Politics to Resolve It through Compromise," *Perceptions*, Autumn–Winter 2009. Barham Salih is quoted in Aram Rafaat, "Kirkuk: The Central Issue of Kurdish Politics and Iraq's Knotty Problem," *Journal of Muslim Minority Affairs* no. 28, 2008.

For *The War of Demographics*, I drew upon Liam Anderson and Gareth Stansfield, *Crisis in Kirkuk: The Ethnopolitics of Conflict and Compromise*, University of Pennsylvania Press, 2009; Aram Rafaat,

"Kirkuk: The Central Issue of Kurdish Politics and Iraq's Knotty Problem"; and Shak Hanish, "The Kirkuk Problem and Article 140 of the Iraqi Constitution," *DOMES: Digest of Middle East Studies* no. 19, 2010.

For *The Kurdish Expansion*, I drew from Major Isaac Peltier, "Surrogate Warfare: The Role of U.S. Army Special Forces," Leavenworth, School for Advanced Military Studies, 2005; Master Sergeant (Retired) Mike McElmeel, "Kirkuk," *Real Combat Life*, May 22, 2010.

Kirkuk's population growth to 2011 was reported in "Iraq," *City Population*, http://www.citypopulation.de/Iraq.html. The divisive effect of the Article 140 referendum was reported in "Kirkuk Tensions Rise as Fateful Ballot Nears," Institute for War and Peace Reporting, August 15, 2007. For this section, I also drew upon Shak Hanish, "The Kirkuk Problem and Article 140 of the Iraqi Constitution."

The Arab protest organizer is quoted in Anderson and Stansfield, *Crisis in Kirkuk*. Abdul Rahman al-Obeidi is quoted in Michael Howard, "Iraq: As Violence Grows, Oil-Rich Kirkuk Could Hold Key to Iraq's Future: Tribal Chiefs Call for Return of Saddam While Kurds Eye a New Federal State," *Guardian* (UK), October 27, 2006. The Turcoman Democratic Movement is covered in Tanya Goudsouzian, "We Cannot Stand against the Kurds," Soma, July 22, 2006.

For the specific attacks and statistics, I drew from *Iraqbodycount. org*. The extortion of the northern oil industry was reported by Richard Oppel in "Iraq's Insurgency Runs on Stolen Oil Profits," *New York Times*, March 16, 2008.

For the Kirkuk referendum's impact on local government and security, see James Brandon, "Kirkuk's Referendum Revives Fears of Ethnic Violence," *Jamestown Terrorism Focus*, February 14, 2007. Massoud Barzani's warning of civil war was quoted in Hamza

Hendawi, "Kurdish Leader Warns of Iraqi Civil War," Associated Press, July 31, 2007. Nechirvan Barzani's denunciation of the PKK is quoted in "PM Barzani on the PKK and Turkey," *Kurdish Globe* (Irbil), March 4, 2008. The Turkish general staff's use of U.S. intelligence was reported in Burak Bekdil, "Smoother Times Ahead for Troubled Allies U.S. and Turkey," *Eurasia Daily Monitor*, December 19, 2007.

The Kirkuk dispute's impact on the Iraqi parliament's actions can be seen in "Iraqi Factions Join Against Kurd Oil Deals," UPI, January 15, 2008, and Erica Goode, "Iraq Passes Election Law, Setting Aside Kirkuk Status," *New York Times*, September 25, 2008.

The Lloyd George-Clemenceau agreement on Mosul is described in David Fromkin, *A Peace to End All Peace*, London, Avon Books, 1990.

Many of the ethnic tensions in Ninewa province are described in the Human Rights Watch report "On Vulnerable Ground," November 2009. The Mark Sykes quote comes from Sykes's "Journeys in North Mesopotamia," *Geographical Journal*, September 1907.

A profile of Misha'an Jabouri can be found in the Jamestown Foundation's "Broadcasting Qaddafi: A View of Iraq's Mishan al-Juburi," October 2011. A large number of Misha'an's bizarre pro-insurgent media appearances can be found on the Middle East Media Research Institute website, such as "Former Iraqi MP and Owner of the Syrian-Based Arrai TV Channel Mish'an Jabouri Admits Financing Terror Attacks against U.S. Forces in Iraq," September 20, 2009.

Tel Afar's seizure by Sunni militants in 2004 was recounted by Scott Taylor in "Hostage in Iraq: Five Days in Hell," *Esprit de Corps*, September 7, 2004. For 2005 election results, see Joel Wing, "Comparing the January 2009 to January 2005 Provincial Elections," *Musings on Iraq*, February 1, 2009.

The Ninewa tribes' discontent in 2005 was reported by Ann Scott Tyson in "Vying for a Voice, Tribe in N. Iraq Feels Let Down," *Washington Post*, December 27, 2005.

The massacre of Sunnis by Tel Afari policemen was reported in "Gunmen Kill Dozens in Iraqi Town," BBC News, March 28, 2007. Estimates of damage to Ninewa's Christian community come from two Human Rights Watch reports, "Iraq: Protect Christians from Violence," February 23, 2010, and "On Vulnerable Ground," November 10, 2009, as does the discussion of a Christian "region" in Ninewa. Al Qaeda's war against the Yezidis was reported in Michael Howard, "'They Won't Stop Until We Are All Wiped Out,' Among the Yezidi, A People in Mourning," *Guardian* (UK), August 17, 2007, and in Campbell Robertson, "Qahtaniyah Journal," *New York Times*, October 14, 2008.

The Kurdish parties' determination to stall the Sunnis' recovery of power in Ninewa was reported in the International Crisis Group report "Iraq's New Battlefront," September 13, 2009.

7. THE IRAQI "RESISTANCE"

The Tamar Rotana conference was reported on the Iraqi *Iraq al-Muqawamah* in Arabic, November 1, 2011, copied from the official Lebanese Government National News Agency (NNA) website, dated October 31, 2011.

Ali Allawi retells the story of Sadiq Sadr's tensions with Saddam and rivalry with the Iranians in *The Occupation of Iraq*. The unrest that followed Sadiq Sadr's murder was reported in Philip Sherwell, "Saddam City, Iraq, 28 February 1999," *Daily Telegraph* (London), February 28, 1999; Ian Black, "Mass Execution Claim after Iraq Revolt," (UK), September 27, 1999; and Douglas Jehl, "Assassination of Shiite Cleric Threatens Further Unrest," *New York Times*,

February 22, 1999. The crackdown on Sadr followers was reported by the United States Bureau of Citizenship and Immigration Services, *Iraq: Information on followers of Ayatollah Mohammad Sadeq al-Sadr*, May 23, 2002. Patrick Coburn recounted the Sadiq Sadr-Hakim rivalry and the murder of Abd al-Majid al-Khoei in *Moqtada*.

The finest accounts of the 2004 Sadrist uprisings are Mark Etherington's *Revolt on the Tigris*, Cornell University Press, 2005, and Michael Gordon's *The Endgame*.

For the Sadrist Resistance and Iran, I drew from Alex Berenson and John Burns, "8-Day Battle for Najaf: From Attack to Stalemate," *New York Times*, August 18, 2004, and Marisa C. Sullivan, "The Fragmentation of the Sadr Movement," Institute for the Study of War, 2009.

For the section on "Hajji Qassem" I drew from Joseph Felter and Brian Fishman, "Iranian Strategy in Iraq: Politics and 'Other Means,'" Combating Terrorism Center, West Point, October 2008; Ali Alfoneh, "Brigadier General Qassem Suleimani: A Biography," American Enterprise Institute Middle East Outlook, January 24, 2011; "Shiite Politics in Iraq: The Role of the Supreme Council," International Crisis Group, November 15, 2007; Martin Chulov, "Qassem Suleimani: The Iranian General 'Secretly Running' Iraq," *Guardian* (UK), July 28, 2011; Elie Chalhoub, "Imad Mughniyah in Iran: The Stuff of Legends," *Al Akhbar* (English), February 14, 2012. See also Dexter Filkins, "The Shadow Commander," *New Yorker*, September 30, 2013.

For the Quds Force's presence in Iraq, I drew from Felter and Fishman, "Iranian Strategy in Iraq," and Bill Roggio, "General Petraeus: Iran's Ambassador to Iraq 'Is a Quds Force Member,'" *Long War Journal*, October 7, 2007. John Burns and Michael Gordon, "U.S. Says Iran Helped Kill Five G.I.s," *New York Times*, July 3, 2007. For Abu Mahdi's role, I drew from Michael

Ware, "U.S. Military: Iraq Lawmaker Is U.S. Embassy Bomber," CNN, February 22, 2007; Thomas Strouse, "Kata'ib Hezbollah and the Intricate Web of Iranian Involvement in Iraq," Jamestown Foundation *Terrorism Monitor*, March 4, 2010.

Also see "Southern Iraq Backgrounder," Institute for the Study of War, undated.

For the Sadrists' enforcement of their interpretation of Islamic standards, see Ellen Knickmeyer, "Sadr's Militia and the Slaughter in the Streets," *Washington Post* Foreign Service, August 25, 2006. For details on the Promised Day Brigade, see Babak Rahimi, "The Future of Moqtada al-Sadr's New Jaysh al-Mahdi," Combating Terrorism Center *Sentinel*, January 15, 2009.

On the role of Sistani and the *hawza* and their relationship with the broader Shia community and Iran, I drew from Mehdi Khalaji's *The Last Marja: Sistani and the End of Traditional Religious Authority in Shiism*, Washington Institute for Near East Policy, 2006.

For the pressuring of Sistani and his representatives, I drew from many media reports from 2005 to 2007. See, for example, Hamza Hendawi, "Two More Al-Sistani Aides Killed," Associated Press, September 21, 2007.

Negotiations between Sadrists and Maliki were extensively covered by Iraqi media, as in "Maliki, Sadr Bloc in Reconciliation Meeting," Al Sumaria TV, January 22, 2009. Stephen Farrell reported on Sadrist opposition to the U.S.-Iraq military agreement in "Protests in Baghdad on U.S. Pact," *New York Times*, November 21, 2008. For analysis of the Sadrists' fortunes in the 2009 and 2013 provincial elections, see Ahmed Ali, "Iraq's Provincial Elections and Their National Implications," Institute for the Study of War, April 19, 2013.

For details on Asa'ib Ahl al-Haqq, I drew upon Michael Knights, "The Evolution of Iran's Special Groups in Iraq," Combating Terrorism Center *Sentinel*, November 1, 2010. For the group's role in abducting five Britons, I drew from Elie Chalhoub, "Qais al-Khazali: In the Shadows of Resistance," *Al Akhbar* (English), January 21, 2012; "Revealed: Evidence of Iran's Involvement in the Kidnapping of the Five Britons in Baghdad," Guardian Films, December 30, 2009; and Rafid Fadhil Ali, "The People of Righteousness: Iraq's Shia Insurgents Issue Demands for Hostages," Jamestown Foundation *Terrorism Monitor*, February 12, 2010.

For the collapse of reconciliation talks with the group, I drew from Jane Arraf, "Kidnapping of American in Iraq Sparked by Faltering Reconciliation Talks," *Christian Science Monitor*, February 11, 2010.

Michael Ware described Abu Mahdi's role in 1980s terrorism in "U.S. Military: Iraq Lawmaker Is U.S. Embassy Bomber," CNN, February 22, 2007. The Kata'ib Hezbollah targeting of the Mujahideen-e Khalq was described in Qassim Abdul-Zahra and Adam Schreck, "Shiite Militant Threatens Iranian Exiles Inside Iraq," Associated Press, February 26, 2013.

Ted Koppel reported the attacks against the Basra consulate in "No Exit: Iraq's Oil and Iran's Influence," Rock Center (NBC), broadcast December 12, 2011. The abduction of Randy Hulz was covered by Chelsea Carter and Mohammed Tawfeeq in "More Questions Than Answers in Account of American's Abduction in Iraq," CNN, March 18, 2012.

Asa'ib Ahl al-Haqq's entry into politics in 2012 was covered by Jack Healy and Michael Schmidt, "Political Role for Militants Worsens Fault Lines in Iraq," *New York Times*, January 5, 2012, and by Marisa C. Sullivan, "The Resurgence of Asa'ib Ahl al-Haq," Institute for the Study of War, 2012. The Shia militants' serial killings of liquor store owners was reported by Mohammed Tawfeeq and Chelsea Carter in "Iraq Liquor Store Owners Fear for Their Lives amid Attacks," CNN, June 7, 2013. The Shia militants' murder of dozens (or more) Emo youths was reported in Rami Ruhayem, "Iraq's Emo Killings: A Horror Story Out of Control?," BBC News, March 20, 2012, and Seth Abramovitch, "Truth Check: Is Iraq Killing Hundreds of Emo Teens?," *Atlantic Wire*, March 10, 2012.

8. The Interregnum, Crackdown, and Spillover

The best summary of the long government formation stalemate is in Stephen Wicken, "Iraq's Sunnis in Crisis," Institute for the Study of War, May 2013. For the post-election recount and de-Baathification maneuvers, I drew from Ned Park and Caeser Ahmed, "Maliki Seeks Recount in Iraq Elections," *Los Angeles Times*, March 22, 2010; Anthony Shadid, "Recount in Iraq Preserves Victory for Maliki Rival," *New York Times*, May 16, 2010; Martin Chulov, "Iraq Election Challenged Over 'Banned' Candidates," *Guardian* (UK), March 29, 2010; and Michael Gordon, *The Endgame*.

Rod Nordland reported Talabani's trip to Tehran to preempt government formation in "Iran Plays Host to Delegations after Iraq Election," *New York Times*, April 1, 2010. Nibras Kazimi reported on the Sadrist "referendum" for prime minister in "Sadrist Referendum Results," Talisman Gate, April 7, 2010. The alleged quid pro quo between Maliki and the Sadrists was covered in "Sources Say State of Law to Give Up Governor Posts in Favor of Sadrists," Aswat al-Iraq (Irbil), November 16, 2010. Jalal Talabani referred to Kurdish redlines for the apportionment of ministries in an interview with Al-Sharq al-Awsat on November 18, 2010. The political aftermath of Maliki's return as premier was covered in Marina Ottaway and Daniel Anas Kaysi, "Iraq: Protest, Democracy, and Autocracy," Carnegie Endowment for International

Peace, March 28, 2011, and in Marisa Sullivan, "Maliki's Authoritarian Regime," Institute for the Study of War, April 2013.

Portions of "2011: Year of the Crackdown" first appeared in
print in the author's article "Rise of the Maliki Regime," in the
Journal of International Security Affairs, Spring/Summer 2012. The
excerpted portions of that article appear here by permission of the
Journal of International Security Affairs.

The estimated Iraqi housing shortfall comes from "Iraq to
Finance New Housing to Ease Shortage," Radio Free Europe/
Radio Liberty, October 6, 2011. Tim Arango reported on the
"Days of Rage" in "Iraqi Youths' Political Rise is Stunted by
Elites," *New York Times*, April 13, 2011. The killing and beating
of protesters was covered in Andrew Raine, "Iraq Authorities
'Using Violence and Bribes' to Curb Dissent," *National* (Abu
Dhabi), March 2, 2011, in the Human Rights Watch report, "Iraq:
Attacks by Government-Backed Thugs Chill Protests," June 30,
2011, and in Stephanie McCrummen, "Iraq 'Day of Rage' Protests
Followed by Detentions, Beatings," *Washington Post*, February 26,
2011. Hadi al-Mahdi's murder was reported in the Committee to
Protect Journalists, "Iraqi Journalist Shot Dead in Baghdad," Sep-
tember 9, 2011, and Annie Gowen and Aziz Alwan, "Hadi al-
Mahdi, Slain Iraqi Journalist, Had Warned of Threats,"
Washington Post, September 9, 2011.

The team of Jack Healy, Tim Arango, and Michael S. Schmidt
reported on the crackdown against the Baath in "Premier's
Actions in Iraq Raise U.S. Concerns," *New York Times*, December 12, 2011. The consequent move toward federalism was covered in Nasrawi, Salah, "Break-Up of Iraq," *Al Ahram Weekly*
(Cairo), November 17–23, 2011. Joel Wing analyzed Maliki's
response to these moves in "Iraq's Prime Minister Flexes His
Muscles in Diyala Province Again," AK News, January 26, 2012,

as did Reidar Visser in "Welcome to Malikistan," *Gulf Analysis blog*, October 29, 2011.

The best summary of the December 2011 crisis is Ramzy Mardini's "Iraq's Post-Withdrawal Crisis, Update 1, December 15–19, 2011," Institute for the Study of War, December 19, 2011. The Iraqiyah leaders' op-ed was "How to Save Iraq from Civil War," *New York Times*, December 28, 2011. Saleh Mutlaq is quoted in Arwa Damon and Mohammed Tawfeeq, "Iraq's Leader Becoming a New 'Dictator,' Deputy Warns," CNN, December 13, 2011. The Iraqi officials who claimed Hashemi's men had been beaten by their interrogators are quoted in Gaith Abdul-Ahad, "Corruption in Iraq: 'Your Son Is Being Tortured. He Will Die If You Don't Pay,'" *Guardian* (London), January 15, 2012. An example of western media reports on Maliki's growing authoritarianism can be seen in Hannah Allam, "Iraq Unstable, Sectarian, with Signs of Authoritarian Rule," McClatchy DC, April 5, 2012.

For an example of western diplomats' enthusiasm for Iraqi "national reconciliation," see "UN Calls for National Reconciliation in Iraq," Associated Press, July 25, 2012. For the Arab states' spurning of the Baghdad Arab Summit, see Hamza Hendawi and Lara Jakes, "Arab Leaders Stay Away from Baghdad Summit," Associated Press, March 29, 2012.

Sam Wyer's "The Resurgence of Asa'ib Ahl al-Haq," Institute for the Study of War, December 2012, provides a useful treatment. Stephen Wicken documented Iraqiyah's loss of Shia members in "Iraq's Sunnis in Crisis," Institute for the Study of War, May 2013. The discussion of Misha'an Jabouri and Izzat al-Douri I took from my earlier essay, "Making the Maliki State in Iraq and the Resurgence of Izzat Ibrahim al-Douri," *Syria Comment*, April 11, 2012. Al-Douri's speech was reported in Adam Schenk, "Izzat Ibrahim al-Douri, Fugitive Saddam Hussein Deputy, Purportedly Shown in New Video," Associated Press, April 7, 2012.

Muqtada Sadr was quoted in *Azzaman*, May 31, 2012. Talabani's requirement of a petition was covered in Ahmed Hevidar, "Maliki Given Ultimatum at Leaders Meeting in Erbil," Rudaw News, April 20, 2012, and Qassim Abdul Zahra, "Iraq President: PM Critics Didn't Muster Majority," AP, June 10, 2012.

Maliki's 2009 allegations against the Assad regime were reported in Jason Keyser, "Maliki Urges UN Tribunal for Syria-Based Bomb Suspects," Associated Press, September 7, 2009. Maliki's criticism of the Syrian opposition comes from Michael S. Schmidt and Yasir Ghazi, "Iraqi Leader Backs Syria, with a Nudge from Iran," *New York Times*, August 12, 2011. Syrian and Iranian use of Iraqi currency sales was reported in Aseel Kami, "Iraq Becomes Dollar Source for Sanctions-hit Iran, Syria," Reuters, February 1, 2012. Iraqi Shia support for the Assad regime in general was covered in Joel Wing, "Are the Iraqi Government and Shiite Parties Supporting Syria's President Assad?," AK News, January 19, 2012. An example of western complaints about this support can be seen in Michael Gordon and Tim Arango, "In 'Spirited Talks,' Kerry Tells Iraq to Help Stop Arms Shipments to Syria," *New York Times*, March 24, 2013. The massacre of Syrian troops inside Iraq was covered by Bill Roggio in "Al Qaeda in Iraq Claims Ambush That Killed Syrian, Iraqi Troops," *Long War Journal*, March 11, 2013. Maliki's declaration that Assad would not fall was quoted in *Al-Arabiyah*, April 1, 2012.

The reversal of flow of support between Iraq and Syria was covered in Tim Arango and Duraid Adnan, "For Iraqis, Aid to Rebels in Syria Repays a Debt," *New York Times*, February 12, 2012, and Khalid al-Taie, "Iraqi Fighters, Arms Trickle into Syria as Violence Grows," Reuters, February 14, 2012. The switching of Al Qaeda's "tooth" and "tail" was reported in Rowan Scarborough, "Al Qaeda 'Rat Line' from Syria to Iraq Turns Back against Assad," *Washington Times*, August 19, 2013, and Martina Fuchs, "Al Qaeda Leader

Backs Syrian Revolt against Assad," Reuters, February 12, 2012. Thomas Joscelyn reported the AQI and Nusrah "merger" in "Al Qaeda in Iraq, Al Nusrah Front emerge as rebranded single entity," *Long War Journal*, April 9, 2013, though later reports in 2014 showed rifts in this united front.

Michael Knights surveyed the Iraqi Shia militants' involvement in the Syrian war in "Iran's Foreign Legion: The Role of Iraqi Shiite Militias in Syria," Washington Institute for Near East Policy, June 27, 2013. The Iranian regime's deployment of Iraqis to Syria and other sectarian battlefields was reported in "Iran Grooms Mehdi Army for Gulf Ops," UPI, June 9, 2011, and "Evidence Grows Iran Aiding Syria's Assad," UPI, June 2, 2011. Sam Dagher reported on Iraqi Shia "martyrs" in Syria in "Iranians Dial Up Presence in Syria: Shiite Militiamen from across the Arab World Train at a Base Near Tehran to Do Battle in Syria," *Wall Street Journal*, September 16, 2013.

Andrea Giloti reported the growing independence of the Syrian Kurds in "Kurdish Group Gaining Autonomy in Northern Syria," *Al-Monitor*, May 7, 2013. The PKK-KDP rapprochement can be gleaned from "Iraqi Kurdistan's Premier Played Key Role in Turkey-PKK Talks, Official Says," Rudaw News, October 4, 2013. Maliki's deployment of new Iraqi troops to Kirkuk was reported in Karim Abdul Zayer, "Maliki Deploys 'Tigris Force' to Kirkuk," *Al-Monitor*, November 13, 2012. The reduction of the Kurds' share of the Iraqi budget can be found in "Baghdad to Reduce Kurdistan Region's 2013 Budget," *eKurd.net*, November 30, 2012. Reports of the Turkey-Kurdistan pipeline have appeared in many places, including "Iraqi Kurds Announce New Oil Pipeline to Turkish Border," *Hurriyet*, June 20, 2013.

The best summary of the December 2012 raid against Issawi is in Stephen Wicken, "Weekly Iraq Update # 51: Political Update: Maliki Sends Security Forces against Sunni Rivals—Again," Insti-

tute for the Study of War, December 19, 2012. The massive pro-
tests that followed the raid are described in the International
Crisis Group report "Make or Break: Iraq's Sunnis and the State,"
August 14, 2013. Issawi's December 2012 speech is quoted in
Adam Schreck and Qassim Abdul Zahra, "Iraq: New Protests
Break Out in Sunni Stronghold," Associated Press, December 26,
2012. Colin Freeman reported the assault against Saleh Mutlaq in
"Gunfire and a Stone-Throwing Mob—A Day in the Life of an
Iraqi Politician," *Telegraph* (UK), January 2, 2013. The shootings
in Fallujah were covered in "Iraq Troops Pay Heavy Price for Fal-
lujah Protest Killings," Associated Press, January 27, 2013.

Ned Parker and Raheem Salman covered Al Qaeda's Abu
Ghraib jailbreak in "The Great Escape," *Foreign Policy*, August 5,
2013. Casualty figures for 2013 are taken from *Iraqbodycount.org*.
The targeting of public places was reported in Ahmed Rasheed,
"Cafes Shut, Sports Field Empty as War Returns to Iraq," Reuters,
August 5, 2013. The Shia militants' crackdown on liquor stores was
reported in "Gunmen Attack Baghdad Liquor Stores, 12 Killed,"
Reuters, May 12, 2013. Maliki's warning during the Hawijah cri-
sis is quoted in Tim Arango, "Iraqi Premier Urges Talks But Vows
to Battle Insurgents," *New York Times*, April 25, 2013.

EPILOGUE

For an early analysis of the preliminary election results, see Reidar
Visser, "The Iraq Election Results: Maliki's Complicated Win,"
Iraq and Gulf Analysis, May 19, 2014. The Maliki government's
raid on Ahmad al-Alwani, during which government troops killed
Alwani's brother, was reported by BBC News, December 28, 2013.
The DASH offensive in eastern Anbar was reported by Jessica
Lewis in "Warning Intelligence Update: ISIS Besieged Areas Near

Baghdad on Eve of Elections," Institute for the Study of War, April 24, 2014. David Ignatius reported the conflict between the government and the Sunni tribes in "War Returns to Iraq on the Eve of Elections," *Washington Post*, April 25, 2014. Jessica Lewis reported the worsening situation in the mixed-sect region around Baghdad in "The Islamic State of Iraq Returns to Diyala Province," Institute for the Study of War, April 2014. The estimate of 420,000 displaced from Anbar was reported by Ned Parker and Ahmed Rasheed in "Iraqis vote on Wednesday as violence grips country," Reuters, April 30, 2014. The $1 billion US-Iraq arms deal was reported by AFP and other news outlets on May 15, 2014.

Tim Arango and Michael Gordon reported Maliki's sectarian campaign platform in "Amid Iraq's Unrest, Maliki Campaigns as Strongman," *New York Times*, April 29, 2014. Adel Abd al-Mahdi was quoted in Reuters Baghdad bureau chief Ned Parker's Twitter feed on May 19, 2014. Massoud Barzani's threat to boycott the Baghdad government was reported by Ned Parker and Isabel Coles in "Kurds could opt out of next Iraqi government—president," Reuters, May 13, 2014.

Paul Crompton and Hind Mustafa reported on the new role of Ahmed al-Maliki in "Rise of 'Hamoudi': is Maliki's son the new Uday?" Al Arabiyah, April 17, 2014. Nuri Maliki's interview with Al Arabiyah TV is quoted in Dexter Filkins, "What We Left Behind," *The New Yorker*, April 28, 2014. The incident in which Hadi al-Ameri's son forced a Baghdad-bound airliner to turn back to Beirut was reported by AP and AFP on March 6, 2014.

Reidar Visser analyzed the voting of the Iraqi Security Forces in "IHEC Releases Data from the Special Vote in Iraq's General Election," Iraq and Gulf Analysis, May 23, 2014.

L IEUTENANT COLONEL JOEL RAYBURN is a U.S. Army strategic intelligence officer with twenty years' experience in national security and political-military affairs, focusing on the greater Middle East. He has served in multiple assignments in Iraq, Afghanistan, and the Persian Gulf region. He is currently a research fellow at the National Defense University in Washington, DC; a member of the Hoover Institution's Working Group on Islamism and the International Order; and an adjunct military fellow at the New America Foundation. The views he presents here are his own and do not necessarily represent those of the National Defense University and the Department of Defense.

HERBERT AND JANE DWIGHT
WORKING GROUP ON
ISLAMISM AND THE
INTERNATIONAL ORDER

THE HERBERT AND JANE DWIGHT WORKING GROUP ON ISLAMISM AND THE INTERNATIONAL ORDER seeks to engage in the task of reversing Islamic radicalism through reforming and strengthening the legitimate role of the state across the entire Muslim world. Efforts will draw on the intellectual resources of an array of scholars and practitioners from within the United States and abroad, to foster the pursuit of modernity, human flourishing, and the rule of law and reason in Islamic lands—developments that are critical to the very order of the international system.

The Working Group is cochaired by Hoover fellows Fouad Ajami and Charles Hill, with an active participation by Hoover Institution Director John Raisian. Current core membership includes Russell A. Berman, Abbas Milani, with contributions from Zeyno Baran, Marius Deeb, Reuel Marc Gerecht, Ziad Haider, R. John Hughes, Nibras Kazimi, Bernard Lewis, Habib C. Malik, Camille Pecastaing, Itamar Rabinovich, Lieutenant Colonel Joel Rayburn, Lee Smith, Samuel Tadros, Joshua Teitelbaum, and Tunku Varadarajan.

BOOKS OF RELATED INTEREST FROM THE
HERBERT AND JANE DWIGHT WORKING GROUP
ON ISLAMISM AND THE INTERNATIONAL ORDER

Freedom or Terror: Europe Faces Jihad
Russell A. Berman

The Myth of the Great Satan: A New Look at America's Relations with Iran
Abbas Milani

Torn Country: Turkey between Secularism and Islamism
Zeyno Baran

Islamic Extremism and the War of Ideas: Lessons from Indonesia
John Hughes

The End of Modern History in the Middle East
Bernard Lewis

The Wave: Man, God, and the Ballot Box in the Middle East
Reuel Marc Gerecht

Trial of a Thousand Years: World Order and Islamism
Charles Hill

Jihad in the Arabian Sea
Camille Pecastaing

The Syrian Rebellion
Fouad Ajami

Motherland Lost: The Egyptian and Coptic Quest for Modernity
Samuel Tadros

Iraq after America: Strongmen, Sectarians, Resistance
Joel Rayburn

Sunni chauvinism relating to, 149–50
Sunni-Shia war and, 158–59
Kurdistan
elections and national dispute in,
148–49
geography of, 138
Greater Kurdistan, 233–34
Green Line, Mosul, and, 152–54
oil revenues in, 144–45, 148–49
stalemate in, 165–67
Kurdistan Democratic Party (KDP)
Goran, Kesro, relating to, 156
Jazeera relating to, 152–54
Shammar tribe struggle with, 159–60
Sunni dispute with, 165–67
Kurdistan Regional Government
(KRG), 147, 152, 163, 233–34
Kurdistan Workers' Party (PKK), 145–47

Lebanon
Dawa movement in, 17–18
Hezbollah in, 197
Al Qaeda in, 117
London, 18

al-Mahdi, Hadi, 219
Mahdi Army. See Jaysh al-Mahdi
al-Mahmoud, Medhat, 63–64
Majid, Yassin, 53
Maliki, Ahmed, 57
al-Maliki, Nuri
background on, 21–22
"Charge of the Knights," and, 31–33
in Dawa movement, 21–24
Dawa movement's dispersal relating
to, 16
in elections, 2010, 209–13, 215–16
in elections, 2012, 227–28
Abd al-Mahdi-Barzani initiative and,
27
military strategies of, 29
as nonsectarian nationalist, 44–45
parliament challenges for, 26–27
as premier, 24–26
Quds Force and Sadrist defeat, 33–35
al-Sadr, Muqtada relating to, 28,
177–78

Sadrists relating to, 25, 26, 28–29,
33–35
during sectarian cleansing, 89–90, 92
Shia civil war and, 28–31
Shia politicians on, 27
Sunnis on, 26, 239
U.S. relations with, 23–24, 29
on U.S.-Iraqi operations, 33–34
Maliki government
al-Abadi during, 39
al-Adeeb during, 39
Assad regime relating to, 229–30
autumn bombings, 2009, 46–47
the Awakening, 38–39, 238–39
Baathist plot and federalist challenge,
219–21
Basra reconstruction, 38–39
crackdown, of 2011, 216–20
Dawa movement under, 48–49
elections, 2009, and Shia politics
during, 42–44
government under, 223–24
grassroots support of, 37–38
Hashemi crisis, 221–23, 235
independent institutions, 61–64
Iraqi political culture, 64–69
Iraqi Spring, 216–19
ISCI during, 40–42
Issawi crisis, 234–37
al-Khazali in, 189, 198
Maliki "politburo," 51–55
Malikiyoun, 49–50, 55–64, 190–91
partners with, 40–42
al-Rubaie during, 39
Sadrists during, 40–42
al-Shahristani during, 39–40
Shia front during, 47–49
State of Law in, 43–44, 48
Syria relating to, 228–30
U.S. during, 40, 44–46
victory for, 37–40
Maliki "politburo"
Abdullah, Tariq, in, 51, 54
al-Allaq, Ali, in, 52
al-Askari, Sami, in, 51–52
al-Dabbagh, Ali, in, 52–53, 54–55
Green Zone controlled by, 53–54
Majid, Yassin, in, 53